A GUIDE TO THE
PRACTICE OF INTERNATIONAL CONFERENCES

CARNEGIE ENDOWMENT FOR INTERNATIONAL PEACE
DIVISION OF INTERNATIONAL LAW

George A. Finch, *Director*

———

*Studies in the Administration
of International Law and Organization*

No. 1. *The International Law of the Future: Postulates, Principles,
Proposals.*

No. 2. *International Tribunals: Past and Future.* By Manley O.
Hudson.

No. 3. *The International Secretariat: A Great Experiment in International Administration.* By Egon F. Ranshofen-
Wertheimer.

No. 4. *A Guide to the Practice of International Conferences.* By
Vladimir D. Pastuhov.

A GUIDE
TO THE PRACTICE OF
INTERNATIONAL CONFERENCES

By
VLADIMIR D. PASTUHOV
Former Member, League of Nations Secretariat

WASHINGTON
CARNEGIE ENDOWMENT FOR INTERNATIONAL PEACE
700 JACKSON PLACE, N.W.
1945

PRINTED IN THE UNITED STATES OF AMERICA
AT THE RUMFORD PRESS, CONCORD, N. H.

PREFACE

Mr. Pastuhov's *Guide to the Practice of International Conferences* is a revised and enlarged edition of a monograph by the author issued last year in mimeographed form by the Division of International Law of the Endowment under the title *International Conferences and Their Technique.* This study presents the vast experience gained since the Paris Peace Conference in the technical organization of international conferences in such a manner as to serve as an interpretative account and as a reference book. The book covers the entire international conference practice, with particular emphasis upon the experience gained by the League at Geneva; it includes important material relative to procedures followed in the International Conferences of American States and experience gained in the recent United Nations Conferences. Specifically, the text deals with the planning, staffing, budgeting, organizing, directing, and actual holding of conferences and committee meetings. Special attention is devoted to the follow-up work in the light of international administrative experience. While emphasis is placed on the technical, administrative, and secretarial aspects of the subject, the training of the author as an international lawyer permits him constantly to link the technical processes with the theory and the representative literature in this field. Familiarity with half a dozen languages has enabled the author to extend his research into sources which are usually not available to students of international organization and administration.

The wide experience acquired by Mr. Pastuhov as a member of the League Secretariat, as officer attached to the International Labor Office, and as official of the United Nations Relief and Rehabilitation Administration has given him a unique insight into the inner workings of the international legislative processes and has enabled him to illustrate his text with numerous and heretofore unknown or little known examples. Hardly noticed even by experts, the practice of international conferences has undergone a considerable evolution during the last quarter of a century and this volume comes nearer to a codification of the procedure of international conferences than anything attempted hitherto.

At this moment, when the foundation for future international cooperation is being laid through the instrumentality of major multinational conferences, the publication of this authoritative handbook corresponds to a real need, and the volume should prove an invaluable aid to officers of international conferences and committees, to experts, and to persons engaged in international secretarial work, as well as to students of international organization and administration.

GEORGE A. FINCH

Director of the Division of International Law

WASHINGTON, D. C.
  March 15, 1945

FOREWORD

This handbook deals with the practice of international conferences. The main aspect studied will be the technical problems raised in the preparation for and conduct of international conferences. The historico-political aspect of diplomatic gatherings has been omitted as far as possible, and while in many instances legal problems have been discussed care has been taken not to overemphasize this phase of the subject. Such an approach has led to setting aside a plan of work which would have been more adequate for a legal treatise and wherein the developments would have been divided into two distinct parts; the first part devoted to international conferences *strictu sensu*, i.e., as they take place in the field of general international law (for instance, the Paris Peace Conference), the second part dealing with such international gatherings as take place under what may be called an international constitution. The Covenant of the League of Nations is one example of such a constitution, the United Nations Relief and Rehabilitation Agreement is another. Strictly speaking, a meeting of the Assembly or the Council or a committee of the League of Nations is not an international conference, but the meeting of an international organ. The same must be said of a meeting of the Council of the United Nations Relief and Rehabilitation Administration, which is an organ of the Administration. Such an exposition of the subject would have been more legalistic but would have been repetitious and sometimes confusing for the reader.

The purpose of the author has been to proceed pragmatically and to base the plan of his work on what all international gatherings have more or less in common, namely, the actual mechanism, interpreting the word "conferences" broadly enough to include among them the sessions of the Council and the Assembly of the League of Nations, as well as of the Council of the United Nations Relief and Rehabilitation Administration. As the handbook belongs to a series of monographs concerning the administrative experience of the Secretariat of the League of Nations, this study of international conferences will be closely related to the League of Nations; but, for the sake of comparison, reference will often be made to the Conferences of the International Labor Organization and to the Pan American and other public or semipublic conferences. Special effort has been made to bring the study up to date in integrating therein the main regulations and the first results of the practice of the United Nations Relief and Rehabilitation Administration. Even within the limitations mentioned by the author at the beginning of this Foreword the field to be explored is vast, and consequently this monograph cannot pretend to be an exhaustive study of the subject. Its aim has been confined to supplying, in the form of a handbook, information which past experience has shown to be useful for anyone who has to deal with international public conferences.

Many of the statements are personal recollections. A very important source of information has been the records of the conferences. Official publications of the League of Nations, the International Labor Organization, the Pan American Union, and the United Nations Relief and Rehabilitation Administration constitute the principal source materials used. A short bibliography of the most important secondary material has been appended.

The author takes great pleasure in acknowledging his indebtedness to the Carnegie Endowment for International Peace, which has made this study possible, and more particularly to Mr. George A. Finch, Director of the Division of International Law of the Endowment, who constantly gave his personal support. Of the many others who have given helpful assistance, particular gratitude is due to Dr. Gertrude Dixon, Dr. Joseph Nisot, and Dr. Egon Ranshofen-Wertheimer, former members of the Secretariat of the League of Nations, and Monsieur Robert Lafrance, Head of the Diplomatic Division of the International Labor Office, who read the manuscript and gave to the author the benefit of their criticism and suggestions. However, responsibility for any opinions expressed in this study is not to be ascribed either to these former colleagues or to the Division of International Law of the Carnegie Endowment for International Peace. The author wishes to express special appreciation of the excellent aid given by Mr. Irwin Dalin, who helped with the editing of the first manuscript. Acknowledgment should also be made to the editorial staff of the Carnegie Endowment, and more particularly to Miss Ruth Stanton, to Miss Rosa Gordon, who prepared the Index, and to the staffs of the libraries of the Carnegie Endowment and the University of Syracuse.

VLADIMIR D. PASTUHOV

CONTENTS

PART III

ORGANIZING – DIRECTING – COORDINATING
(*Continued*)

MEETINGS OF THE CONFERENCE AND THE COMMITTEES

PART IV

RECORDING AND REVIEWING

APPENDICES

A GUIDE TO THE
PRACTICE OF INTERNATIONAL CONFERENCES

INTRODUCTION

Is the codification of the procedure of international conferences and the procedure for the conclusion and drafting of treaties feasible, is it advisable? Strong doubts have been expressed regarding the possibility of establishing a system for these procedures owing to the many different kinds of international conferences and the endless combination of their different types.[1] The question was carefully studied in 1925–1927 by a subcommittee of the Committee of Experts for the Progressive Codification of International Law of the League of Nations. While admitting the difficulty of the problem, the *Rapporteur*, Dr. A. Mastny, of Czechoslovakia, expressed the conviction that it was possible to draw up certain rules both for the procedure and the organization of international conferences, provided that these rules were sufficiently general to allow the States and their representatives the requisite freedom in settling the details in each case according to the particular circumstances that accompany it and with due regard to the special requirements which may arise in practice.[2]

Dr. Mastny and his colleague on the subcommittee, Dr. S. Rundstein, of Poland, attached to their report a list of subjects related to the procedure of international conferences and to the conclusion and drafting of treaties which in their opinion were susceptible of regulation.

The report of the Committee of Experts, with the list drawn up by Dr. Mastny and Dr. Rundstein, was referred by the Secretary General of the League to the governments for their observations.

Twenty-eight replies were received. Fourteen of these twenty-eight replies were in the affirmative. In its reply the French Government expressed the opinion that it was desirable and practicable to draw up a body of rules for the use of international conferences and pointed out that it would be necessary to prepare a preliminary draft containing provisions drawn up with some degree of precision. Six states, while expressing a favorable opinion, made certain reservations relative to the handling of a number of problems not suitable for regulation by convention; at the same time these states desired to put forward spe-

[1] Ludwig Bittner, *Die Lehre von den völkerrechtlichen Vertragsurkunden* (Stuttgart: Deutsche Verlagsanstalt, 1924), p. 104.

[2] Report by Dr. A. Mastny and Dr. S. Rundstein to the Committee of Experts for the Progressive Codification of International Law of the League of Nations in L.N. Document C.196.M.70.1927.V., p. 106. A condensed version of this report has been appended to this handbook as Appendix I, *infra*.

cial amendments whenever an international conference was to be convened. The Italian Government, which was among these six states, expressed the view that the matter did not require urgent action. The countries which had submitted affirmative replies accepted the Committee's opinion that any rules which would be formulated could only be a *jus dispositivum*, which would not restrict the independence of the States. The fate of the proposals of the Committee was, however, decided by the eight negative replies. Among them were the replies of four big powers: the British Empire, Germany, Japan, and the United States of America. Germany believed that it would be difficult to regulate the matters in question by means of collective agreements. Difficulties might arise owing to the differences in the constitutions of the contracting parties. Moreover, such regulations would appear to be premature as certain questions of international law would first have to be settled. The German Government therefore suggested that treatment of the questions referred to in the report of the Committee of Experts should be postponed for the time being. The British Empire, with whose views the Governments of India and New Zealand associated themselves, did not consider the question to be a subject of international law the codification of which was deemed desirable and feasible, especially as the Committee itself had pointed out that there could be no question of a body of rules which would be binding and obligatory. The Government of the United States of America expressed a similar view. It considered that the determination of the procedure of international conferences and the concluding of treaties might well be left to the parties themselves and to the discretion of the delegates representing the respective governments. The dissent of the Japanese Government was expressed in a less definite form. It held that these questions were not yet ripe for the conclusion of an international convention but suggested that it would be desirable for representatives of the various countries to examine the proposals with a view to preparing an agreement, which should contain nothing more than recommendations.[3]

The Committee was compelled to yield. At its third session, held in April, 1927, it adopted the following report to the Council:

In its general report on the question of procedure, the Committee emphasised the necessity of taking certain preparatory measures with a view to facilitating and shortening the work of any conferences that may be held.

This necessity appears particularly great as regards the question of conferences, since the report approved by the Committee is accompanied neither by a

[3] L.N. Document C.196.M.70.1927.V., pp. 271-73.

draft nor by a questionnaire in the proper sense of the term, and since the matter in question is, in a certain sense, highly technical.

The Committee would recommend to the Council that the subject should first be examined by a small Committee of Experts. Such a preliminary measure may, it is true, seem costly, unless the Committee could be composed of Secretariat officials already possessing wide experience of conferences and the conclusion of treaties. The Committee would venture to point out, however, that the results of the work of the Conference of Experts would in any case be of great value. Even if the drafts framed by it were not accepted by a conference of all the States, they would be most valuable as models. It would be possible, at the beginning of a conference or of negotiations in respect of any treaty, to adopt en bloc the rules contained in such drafts; this would prevent the loss of time entailed by detailed discussions concerning the procedure to be followed.

The Committee would point out in this connection that even drafts accepted on this subject by a conference of all the States would simply be in the nature of *droit dispositif*, that is, of rules which would leave the parties concerned quite free to come to some different arrangement.[4]

The Secretariat never formally reported on the subject, but the problem was considered again from another angle when the Assembly in 1930 and 1931 discussed and adopted certain regulations concerning the preparatory procedure for general conventions negotiated under the auspices of the League of Nations.[5] The adoption of these regulations constituted real progress in the unification of methods of preparation of *ad hoc* conferences held under the auspices of the League and was a first step in the codification of the procedure for the conclusion of treaties. The next step was the setting up by the Secretariat of model *clauses protocolaires* for conventions concluded under the auspices of the League. The Secretariat did not seek a formal approval of these model clauses by the Assembly of the League, but the head of the Treaty Registration Branch of the Legal Section of the Secretariat took special care in giving the greatest possible uniformity to the *clauses protocolaires* in the conventions concluded under the auspices of the League in

[4] L.N. Document C.198.M.72.1927.V.

[5] See *infra*, pp. 22–23, for the text of the resolution adopted by the Assembly on September 25, 1931. This resolution had its origin in a joint proposal submitted by the British and Danish delegations to the 1930 Assembly. Chapter IV of this proposal dealt with the adequate preparation for the international conferences to be convened in the future.

It will be remembered that in 1926 the conservative British Government voiced its opposition to an attempt at codification of the procedure of international conferences. In 1930, however, the representative of the British Government, this time a member of the Labor Party, Mr. Noel Baker, said in recommending the British-Danish proposal: "We think it would be of immense value to have a regular procedure which, unless there was some overwhelming reason against it, should be followed. We think such a *code of procedure* providing the best possible method of preparation is laid down in chapter IV." L.N., *Official Journal*, Special Supplement No. 85, p. 73. (Italics by the author.)

the thirties. Similarly the International Labor Organization developed a uniform procedure for the conventions drawn up under its auspices.[6] The Seventh and Eighth International Conferences of American States also paid special attention to the question of the preparation and drafting of the treaties and agreements framed under the auspices of the Pan American Union. The handbook prepared for the delegates at the Eighth International Conference of American States, held at Lima in December, 1938, contained a detailed summary of the practice followed in this field by the League of Nations and the International Labor Organization. The regulations adopted by the Conference of Lima were very similar to those of the League, and thus a further step was taken in the direction of an eventual codification of the procedure for the conclusion and drafting of treaties.

The progress toward a codification of rules for the procedure and the organization of international conferences has been less noticeable. But a series of techniques in planning, budgeting, staffing, organizing, directing, coordinating, recording, and reviewing their meetings has been developed by the League of Nations and the International Labor Organization. It is the gist of this experience which this study attempts to describe and evaluate. The trend of the League of Nations in this field has been constantly towards simplification. The rules of procedure drawn up for the conferences held under the auspices of the League in the thirties are shorter and clearer than those framed in the twenties. The formalities accompanying the opening of the sessions of the Assembly or the first meetings of *ad hoc* conferences, such as verification of credentials, election of officers, setting-up of committees, and formal speeches, were curtailed as much as was feasible, and the language of the reports and resolutions was simplified as far as possible. Long preambles with numerous "whereas" clauses were avoided in the resolutions. Florid compliments and expressions of thanks at the end of sessions were summarized or suppressed in the minutes. A similar trend existed and has been maintained in the International Labor Organiza-

---

[6] In a remarkable article, Mr. C. Wilfred Jenks, Legal Adviser of the International Labor Office, proposes the establishment of an International Legislative Drafting Bureau. This Bureau, without in any manner interfering with the autonomy regarding questions of policy of the institutions or conferences using its services, would act as a coordinating agency for specialized international drafting services. Mr. Jenks' plan makes the Bureau (1) responsible for preparing and keeping up to date the reference material; (2) a cooperating agency in the preparation of the drafts of multipartite instruments; (3) an office entrusted with the authority to formulate proposals for the improvement of international legislative technique in general as well as in the specific cases of instruments in course of preparation. C. Wilfred Jenks, "The Need for an International Legislative Drafting Bureau," *American Journal of International Law*, Vol. 39 (1945), pp. 163–79.

tion. References made in this handbook to the procedure of the International Conferences of American States and to the recent experience of the United Nations Relief and Rehabilitation Administration prove that many techniques employed by the League of Nations and the International Labor Organizations have served as prototypes to these two agencies. Just as the rules of procedure of the Assembly of the League and the Standing Orders of the International Labor Conferences are a compilation of various systems used in different parliaments, the Rules of Procedure of the Council of the United Nations Relief and Rehabilitation Administration are influenced by the rules of procedure of the League, the International Labor Organization, and the International Conferences of American States.

The standardization of techniques in preparing, organizing, and conducting conferences attained by the League, the International Labor Organization, and the Pan American Union, the influence of the procedure adopted by these organizations, the similarity of the methods employed during recent United Nations and international conferences at Hot Springs, Bretton Woods, and Chicago — all favor a renewal of the effort that was made in the middle twenties by the Committee of Experts for the Progressive Codification of International Law.

It will be the task of the new Organization of the United Nations, the foundation of which was laid at Dumbarton Oaks, to decide if a further and more conclusive effort should be made towards a codification of certain rules for the organization and procedure of conferences. The future international meetings to be held under its auspices would benefit from such an effort.

PART I

CLASSIFYING – PLANNING – STAFFING – BUDGETING

International conferences are generally divided into three main categories: intergovernmental or public conferences, semipublic conferences, and private conferences. This handbook is essentially devoted to the first category mentioned above.

1. INTERGOVERNMENTAL OR PUBLIC CONFERENCES

To the first category belong the conferences composed of representatives of governments who are generally provided with full powers. These conferences are convened and supported by governments or by an official international organization like the League of Nations. The results of such public conferences are usually embodied in formal instruments, such as treaties, conventions, or protocols, or in a final act. In this category are obviously included the numerous conferences convened by the League in order to discuss and adopt an international convention. To the same category belong also the peace congresses and such political conferences as the Conference of Genoa in 1922 or the Conference of Locarno in 1925. The Food and Agriculture Conference of the United Nations held at Hot Springs, Virginia, in May–June, 1943, is of the same type, although the aim of the conference was primarily technical and not political.

Indeed, public conferences may be convened to deal not only with political problems, but with such highly technical questions as the unification of road signals, or the unification of laws on bills of exchange, promissory notes and cheques, etc. The name of "International Committee" or "International Commission" will, however, be given to a gathering of representatives of governments (provided with full powers or not) if they are assembled mainly for the purpose of exchanging information or in order to adjust different national policies and if no conclusion of a formal international compact is aimed at. The fact that the subject under discussion may be highly political is irrelevant in this respect. An example of such a gathering was the Non-intervention Committee during the Spanish Civil War and many of the committees of the League of Nations. In general, however, all such meetings as the

8

Assembly of the League, the International Labor Conferences, the Council of the League, most of the committees of the League or of the International Labor Organization — in which delegates may or may not be provided with full powers — must for the purpose of this handbook be classified as international public conferences. The same is obviously true of all *ad hoc* international conferences and committees composed of representatives of governments.[1]

2. CONGRESSES AND CONFERENCES [2]

In the past century several authors in the field of international law made a distinction between congresses and conferences,[3] but the word "congress" as the designation of an assembly of plenipotentiaries has today become more or less obsolete. Sir Ernest Satow, in his treatise on international congresses, states that "There is no essential difference between a Congress and a Conference, but the former term is more frequently applied to assemblies of plenipotentiaries for the purpose of concluding peace, and is regarded as implying a specially important occasion. But the gathering at Bucarest in the autumn of 1913 to conclude peace between Bulgaria on the one hand, and Greece, Montenegro, Rumania, and Serbia on the other, was termed a Conference. Other distinctions sometimes made are that at a Congress a larger

[1] The *Rapporteur* of the "Sub-Committee to examine the possibility of formulating rules to be recommended for the procedure of international conferences and the conclusion and drafting of treaties," appointed on April 8, 1925, by the Committee of Experts for the Progressive Codification of International Law, suggested, in his report to the Committee, the following classification of international conferences for the purpose of the codification of the rules which govern the procedure of international intergovernmental conferences:
"In the first place a distinction might be made between conferences planned and organized by the League of Nations and held under its auspices, and all conferences unconnected with the League. A further distinction should be made between political conferences and non-political conferences (administrative, economic, social, etc.). From the legal point of view, a distinction should be made between conferences on international conventional law (codification conferences) and special conferences (conferences settling particular relations between the contracting states). Lastly, according to the character of the representatives, a distinction should be made between diplomatic conferences (diplomatic agents) and technical conferences (experts)." See L.N. Document C.196M.70.1927.V., p. 108. A summary of this report is annexed to this handbook as Appendix I. For a discussion of the above classification, see Raoul Genet, *Traité de diplomatie et de droit diplomatique* (Paris: A. Pedone, 1931), Vol. 3, pp. 33–35.
[2] For information concerning the more important congresses from the middle of the seventeenth century onwards and the principal international conferences held during the nineteenth and twentieth centuries prior to 1921, see Sir Ernest Satow, *A Guide to Diplomatic Practice*, 2d and revised edition (London, etc.: Longmans, Green and Co., 1922, 2 vols.).
[3] See, *inter alia*, F. de Martens, *Traité de droit international*, traduit du russe par Alfred Léo (Paris: Chevalier-Maresq et Cie, 1883–1887, 3 vols.), Vol. I, pp. 298–99.

number of Powers takes part than at a Conference; or that at a Congress (e.g., at those of Vienna, Paris, and Berlin) the representatives of the Powers are men of unusual political importance in their own countries, whereas at a Conference (e.g., those on Greece, 1827–32, and Belgium, 1830–33) some at least of the plenipotentiaries are the resident diplomatic representatives of their respective countries. The Congress of Paris, 1856, was at first designated a Conference, but subsequently, during the course of the negotiations, came, by an unperceived transition, to be styled Congress." [4]

The gathering of plenipotentiaries which led to the conclusion of the Peace Treaties after the first World War is known as the Paris Conference. In recent years no diplomatic gatherings have been labeled congresses, and the word "congress" has been used largely in connection with semipublic conferences, such as the Pan American Scientific Congress, the "Congrès International des Sciences Historiques," and private conferences, such as the International Congress of Students, etc.

As early as 1899, Pradier-Fodéré, after examining a series of definitions of the words congress and conference, came to the conclusion that "These distinctions, one must recognize, are arbitrary, very controversial, and do not give an equal satisfaction to the mind." [5] Planas Suárez says that since "in the current language of diplomacy and international law there is no difference at all between congresses and conferences and there is also no difference at all between congresses and conferences from the legal point of view, we can consider these terms as synonymous." [6] Oppenheim says that "Several writers allege that there are characteristic differences between a congress and a conference. But all such differences vanish in face of the fact that the Powers when summoning a meeting of representatives, use the terms 'congress' and 'conference' indiscriminately." [7] Such is also the opinion of Axel Möller, who writes that "These terms are really used indiscriminately of the official meetings at which delegates from several states discuss international affairs." [8] Finally, Antonio Sánchez de Bustamante states that "In America, the word congress seems to have been practically

[4] Sir Ernest Satow, *International Congresses* (London: Published by H. M. Stationery Office, 1920), p. 1.

[5] P. Pradier-Fodéré, *Cours de droit diplomatique* (Paris: A. Pedone, 1899), Vol. II, p. 342.

[6] Simón Planas Suárez, *Tratado de derecho internacional público* (Madrid: Hijos de Reus, Editors, 1916), Vol. I, p. 419.

[7] L. Oppenheim, *International Law*, 5th edition (London, etc.: Longmans, Green & Co., 1937), Vol. I, p. 686.

[8] Axel Möller, *International Law in Peace and War*, translated by H. M. Pratt (London: Stevens and Sons, Limited, 1931–1935, 2 vols.), Part I, p. 187.

abandoned in the case of official gatherings and to have been replaced
by the word conference which can be expected to gain an absolute pre-
ponderance. This word is to a certain extent more democratic and the
practical results are equal." [9] On the other hand, however, a French
jurist, Sibert, as late as 1934 still differentiated between congresses
and conferences. The first are, in his opinion, the heirs of the ancient
assemblies in which sovereigns took part and are aimed to end struggles
between nations or to give a clearer direction to general policies,
whereas conferences are essentially legislative gatherings.[10] But Sibert
seems to be an exception among the modern jurists.

The Division of International Law of the Carnegie Endowment for
International Peace suggested in 1943 "that the meetings of plenipotentiaries of states be called Conferences and that the use of the
word Congress to designate such meetings be discontinued." [11] The
acceptance of this suggestion would simply sanction an already existing practice.

3. SEMIPUBLIC CONFERENCES

Governments or public international bodies are involved to a lesser
extent in the organization or conduct of semipublic conferences. The
rôle of a government or of an official international body may be limited
to issuing invitations, assuming all or part of the expenses or providing
housing facilities, etc. Obviously the composition of such a gathering
will not consist of plenipotentiaries of governments, although official
representatives of governments may take part in the discussions. The
results of such conferences will not be embodied in a formal instrument.
No conventions or protocols having a binding force will be drawn up,
but resolutions or recommendations of a merely advisory character
will generally be adopted. If resolutions or recommendations are not
adopted, the ideas exchanged will simply be recorded or embodied in
one or several reports. The semipublic conferences have been a common feature in the annals of the Pan American Union. The League of
Nations, however, only occasionally sponsored such gatherings. Some
meetings concerning refugees held under the auspices of the League of
Nations are samples of conferences of this kind.

[9] Antonio Sánchez de Bustamante y Sirvén, *Droit international public*, traduction
par Paul Goulé (Paris: Librairie du Recueil Sirey, 1934–1939), Vol. I, p. 543.
[10] Marcel Sibert, "Quelques aspects de l'organisation et de la technique des conférences internationales," in Académie de Droit International, *Recueil des Cours*,
Vol. 48, pp. 395 ff.
[11] *Definitions and Use of Certain Terms; A Memorandum Prepared in the Division
of International Law of the Carnegie Endowment for International Peace* (Washington,
1943), p. 54.

4. PRIVATE CONFERENCES

When no close relationship exists between governmental agencies and the international gathering, or when such relationship is so loose that it is difficult to discern it, the conference is said to be an international private conference. There are those who hold that such gatherings properly belong to the field of cosmopolitanism rather than to that of internationalism. Indeed, members of such meetings often endeavor to cooperate on the basis of moral, professional, or other interests apart from nationality.[12] It is impossible to list all the subjects treated in conferences of this type. They range from religious or philosophical problems to jurisprudence, administration and finance. Some of these conferences are periodical; others are held only occasionally. Some are composed of members of national academic associations or national professional or commercial organizations; others attract prominent personalities of different countries engaged in an analogous type of activity. And still others welcome any individual interested in the subject treated at the conference sessions, provided he pays a fee for his participation. No precise rules govern the composition, the procedure and the functions of this type of conference.[13]

5. INTERRELATIONSHIP BETWEEN THE DIFFERENT TYPES OF CONFERENCES

It is impossible to differentiate rigidly between the three types of conferences or congresses as above classified. Indeed, very often overlappings occur, especially as far as their composition is concerned. An intergovernmental conference may include representatives of semi-public or private international organizations. At many intergovernmental conferences convoked under the auspices of the League of Nations, representatives of bodies like the International Chamber of Commerce were invited, although in an advisory capacity.

Article 3 of the Constitution of the International Labor Organization provides that the General Conference of the Organization "shall be composed of four Representatives of each of the Members,[14] of whom two shall be Government Delegates and the two others shall be Delegates representing respectively the employers and the workpeople of

---

[12] Norman L. Hill, *The Public International Conference; Its Function, Organization and Procedure* (Stanford University, California: Stanford University Press, 1929), p. 165.

[13] For a study of international private conferences, see R. Doré, *Essai d'une Bibliographie des congrès internationaux* (Paris: E. Champion, 1923). See also L. N., *Handbook of International Organizations* (Geneva, 1938).

[14] The members of the Organization are states.

each of the Members." Thus the general conferences of the International Labor Organization which evidently belong to the category of Public Conferences are not purely intergovernmental in their composition. Nevertheless, the delegates representing the employers and the employees are entitled to voting privileges just as are the government delegates.

With a few exceptions, the standing committees of the League were composed of members appointed in their personal capacity. But inasmuch as they reported to the Council or the Assembly of the League, they should rightfully be classified as public rather than semipublic conferences.

A Conference of Press Experts convoked by the League in 1927 is perhaps one of the best examples of a combination of three types of conferences—public, semipublic, and private. It was composed of national members appointed by the Council in their personal capacity, of representatives of the Association of Journalists accredited to the League of Nations, of representatives of the International Federation of Journalists, of representatives of the International Union of Press Associations, and of representatives of governmental press bureaus. Thus governmental, semipublic, and private interests were represented. The composition of the conference, therefore, cannot be an absolute criterion for assigning it to one of the three categories of public, semipublic, or private conferences.

On the other hand, governmental international conferences may be preceded by one or by a series of semipublic or even private international gatherings which prepare the work for such conferences; or, conversely, decisions taken by an intergovernmental conference might lead to semipublic or private conferences. Finally, powers of delegates or the adoption of a formal instrument embodying the result of the conference are not indispensable characteristics of a public conference.

6. OBJECTIVE OF THE CONFERENCE

International intergovernmental conferences need careful planning and preparation. Whether the purpose of the conference is the conclusion of peace or the signing of an agreement concerning a political or a technical matter or simply the discussion of a subject of international interest, a program of the matters to be considered is needed. The objective of the conference should therefore be defined as precisely and as early as possible.

In wartime the calling of international conferences is generally necessitated by the development of military events. The conferences have as their objective the consideration of a common policy or strategy towards a changing military situation. Also, conferences held under such circumstances may be summoned with a more remote objective, namely, for planning and preparing a basis for eventual peace settlement. A very good example is the series of conferences held during the first World War which led to the conclusion of the so-called "secret treaties." Wartime conferences may even have an objective which is beyond the peace settlement proper; an example is the United Nations Conference on Food and Agriculture held at Hot Springs, Virginia, in May, 1943. The invitations addressed by the United States Government to the governments concerned described the purpose of the Conference as the beginning of "joint consideration of the basic economic problems with which they and the world will be confronted after complete military victory shall have been attained."

The prime objective of international conferences in time of peace is the settlement of questions which are considered ripe for international discussion and decision. Verbal or written information may be exchanged between governments for the purpose of ascertaining whether or not a given subject has actually reached that stage and whether an international conference convoked to deal with it would have fair chances of success. Several experts on international cooperation even recommend a method whereby policies of national ministries would be coordinated as completely as possible before any international conference is summoned or any negotiations between foreign offices are undertaken. In advocating the principle of coordination of national policies in the formative stages they point out that a genuine international policy cannot be evolved by each nation first formulating a national policy and then presenting it as an accomplished fact to confront the policies of other nations, for, they say, a completed joint policy can be achieved only by bargaining and compromise. To obtain integration the interpenetration of policies must begin before they are completed, in the formative stage.[15] If this method of coordination in "early stages" were widely adopted, international conferences would be mainly convoked with a view to giving merely a legal blessing to agreements al-

---

[15] See Sir J. Arthur Salter, *Allied Shipping Control; An Experiment in International Administration* (Oxford: The Clarendon Press, 1921); and "The Process of Control" by Mary Parker Follett, in *Papers on the Science of Administration*, edited by Luther Gulick and Lyndall Urwick (New York: Institute of Public Administration, Columbia University, 1937).

ready reached between national administrations. The main function of the conferences would then be to embody such agreements in written conventions or protocols.

In that case the objective of the conference would be very exactly defined beforehand. But international cooperation has not yet reached this advanced stage, and at least for some time to come international conferences will conform to the pattern set up before the outbreak of World War II.[16] Hence a preliminary clarification of the aims of the planned conference will be indispensable.

Frequently in the history of the League of Nations the idea of holding a particular international conference first arose during private exchanges of views among delegates to the Assembly or to the Council, or between members of committees of the League or between them and members of the Secretariat. If the idea was successfully developed in these conversations, the next step was to find a member of the League willing to promote the idea of convoking an international conference on the selected subject, or to secure the adoption of a resolution or a decision by the Assembly, the Council, or a standing committee leading to the summoning of the projected conference.

It may happen that, for reasons of national or international policy, a government will take the initiative in proposing the summoning of an international conference without any previous consultation with other governments (or with very little consultation). In such a case the objective of the conference may or may not be very precisely defined.

As for the sessions of the Assembly and the Council of the League of Nations, no previous definition of the aims of those gatherings was necessary, and any item might be included on their agenda. Indeed, Article 3, paragraph 3, of the Covenant states that "The Assembly may deal at its meetings with any matter within the sphere of action of the League or affecting the peace of the world." A corresponding provision of Article 4 of the Covenant defines the general competence of the Council in identical terms.

---

[16] The successive steps which led to the convocation of an international conference and the main phases of it are well illustrated by Pradier-Fodéré, who quotes the correspondence between the French Minister for Foreign Affairs and the French Ambassador at Madrid relative to the conference held in Madrid in 1880 concerning the diplomatic and consular protection of foreigners in Morocco. One can observe from it how the idea of the conference originates, the acceptance of the project by the governments, the definition of the character of the conference, the determination of the date of the conference, the notification of the names of the plenipotentiaries, the instructions given to them, the list of representatives, the communication of credentials, the minutes of the first and the last meetings, the details concerning the exchange of ratifications, etc. Pradier-Fodéré, op. cit., Vol. II, pp. 413–35.

7. INITIATIVE IN CONVOKING AN INTERNATIONAL CONFERENCE

Once the objective of the contemplated conference has been outlined in a more or less precise manner, someone must take the initiative in calling the international gathering. Opportunity is lacking here to describe in detail the preliminaries leading in wartime to the convocation of a peace conference. Suffice it to say that the summoning of a peace conference is generally preceded by the conclusion of an armistice. Ordinarily the armistice is asked either by the military command or the government of the losing side, sometimes directly and sometimes through a neutral power. It may be concluded by the high command of each side or by their diplomatic representatives [17] or by delegations including both diplomatic and military representatives.

The peace conference may also be preceded by the conclusion of preliminaries of peace. In such a case the parties agree to hold, in a more or less remote future, a peace conference or congress for the final settlement of the conflict.[18]

Sometimes the preliminaries of peace are agreed upon, either in a general or partial form, at the time the armistice is concluded.[19] The initiative for peace parleys may take the form of "peace feelers"; a good example of such "peace feelers" is to be seen in the conversations conducted during World War I by the Princes of Bourbon Parma between the Court of Austria and the Allied Governments. Peace parleys may also result from the initiative taken by a third party in requesting the belligerents to meet in a peace conference. Such action by a third party is sometimes accompanied by an offer of good offices or mediation. An example of parleys thus initiated is the Portsmouth Conference of 1905, which marked the end of the Russo-Japanese War, and in which President Theodore Roosevelt played an important part:

On May 31 the Japanese government privately asked Roosevelt "directly and entirely of his own motion and initiative to invite the two belligerents to come together for the purpose of direct negotiation." On June 6 Ambassador Meyer had an audience with the Czar in order to convey a personal message from Roosevelt. The President felt that the interests of all parties required peace and he was pre-

[17] Satow, *International Congresses, op. cit.*, pp. 10–11.
[18] It will be recalled that the Congress of Vienna met in pursuance of Article 32 of the second Treaty of Paris, which provided that "All the Powers engaged on either side in the present war, shall, within the space of 2 months, send plenipotentiaries to Vienna, for the purpose of regulating, in General Congress, the arrangements which are to complete the present Treaty."
[19] Satow, *ibid.*, p. 12.

pared on his own initiative to ask both powers to meet in a conference. If the Russians would approve, the President would endeavor to secure the assent of the Japanese, without informing them of the Russian acceptance. After some delay the Czar acquiesced and on June 8 Roosevelt sent a message to each government, proposing negotiations. Late in July the Russian and Japanese commissioners arrived in the United States and on August 5, Roosevelt received them formally aboard the *Mayflower* at Oyster Bay. On August 8 the conference began work in Portsmouth, New Hampshire.[20]

At the beginning of the present war the Queen of the Netherlands and the King of Belgium offered their good offices for a peaceful settlement which, if accepted, would have led to a peace conference.

Finally, as has been pointed out above with regard to the United Nations Conference on Food and Agriculture, a government may, even in wartime, take the initiative in convoking an international conference, whose objective is not to further the progress of the war but to make plans for dealing with problems arising after the war.[21]

With respect to peacetime international conferences a distinction must be made between periodical conferences and occasional gatherings. Paragraph 2 of Article 3 of the Covenant provides that "The Assembly shall meet at stated intervals and from time to time as occasion may require." Similarly paragraph 3 of Article 4 states that "the Council shall meet from time to time as occasion may require." Paragraph 1 of Article 3 of the Constitution of the International Labor Organization states that "The meetings of the General Conference of Representatives of the Members shall be held from time to time as occasion may require, and at least once in every year." In these examples no initiative is necessary for calling the international meetings; they are summoned in accordance with definite modes of procedure adopted with respect to each of the bodies mentioned.

The initiative for calling an occasional international conference may take various forms. Without attempting to cover all cases, some possibilities will be listed below:

1. A nation or a group of nations may assume the leadership in proposing an international meeting because of a special interest in the solution of an international problem for reasons of national or international policy. The Lausanne Conference on Reparations held in the summer of 1932 under the presidency of the Right Honorable Ramsay

[20] Quoted, with the permission of Henry Holt and Company, from *The Growth of the United States* by Ralph Volney Harlow (New York, 1943, 2 vols.), Vol. II, p. 276.
[21] The United Nations Monetary and Financial Conference held at Bretton Woods during the summer of 1944, and the International Civil Aviation Conference held in Chicago in November–December, 1944, were of the same type.

MacDonald, Prime Minister of the United Kingdom, was summoned
on the invitation of the Belgian, British, French, German, Italian, and
Japanese Governments. Its purpose was defined in the following terms,
in a declaration issued by the inviting Powers at Geneva on February
13, 1932:

. . . to agree to a lasting settlement of the questions raised in the Report of the
Basle Experts and on the measures necessary to solve the other economic and
financial difficulties which are responsible for, and may prolong, the present world
crisis.
This decision has been reached by the above Governments in the hope that it
will ease the international situation.

For a person unfamiliar with the question the aims of the conference
might appear somewhat cryptic. In fact, the main result of the conference was a final settlement of reparations which enabled preparation for a World Monetary and Economic Conference to be inaugurated.

2. A nation or a group of nations may foster an international gathering without selfish motives. The reason for taking the initiative may
be to promote moral and humanitarian ideas in the international field.
In the sixties and seventies of the past century Russia took the initiative in calling several conferences related to the humanization of war.
The United States took the lead in summoning the Shanghai International Committee in 1909 and the Hague Conference in 1912 for the
purpose of dealing with the international drug traffic. Russia and the
United States were respectively responsible for the First and Second
Hague Peace Conferences.

3. A nation or a group of nations may take the initiative during
a regular session of an international permanent organization in proposing the summoning of an international conference on a particular
subject. Thus the Conference of Press Experts held in 1927 under the
auspices of the League of Nations was initiated by a proposal made
by the delegate of Chile at the sixth ordinary session of the Assembly
of the League.

4. A public international conference may decide to request the summoning of another public international conference. In a final resolution the Lausanne Conference, above referred to, decided "to invite
the League of Nations to convoke at a convenient date and at a place
to be fixed (not necessarily Geneva) a Conference on Monetary and
Economic Questions."

5. The work done by a semipublic or a private organization, na-

tional or international, may lead to the summoning of an international intergovernmental conference. The classical example is the Geneva Conference of 1864 for the purpose of drafting rules for the protection of the sick and wounded in land warfare, convoked by Switzerland after long and eventually successful efforts of the Société Genevoise d'Utilité Publique and the unwearying activity of Henri Dunant.[22]

8. Preliminary Negotiations and Correspondence

The initiative for convoking the conference having been taken, the preparatory work to be accomplished before the first meeting of the conference must start immediately. The work of planning includes a great number of items, which will be considered in later pages and of which the most important are the drafting of a provisional agenda of the conference and the issuing of invitations. But before this stage of preparatory work is reached, a series of questions must be settled which necessitate a preliminary exchange of official or semiofficial correspondence. Many conversations will take place among the members of the proposed conference and among those who are to serve on its secretariat. This sounding of views may take the form of a questionnaire issued by the government which has taken the initiative in proposing the conference or by the secretariat of an official international organization under whose auspices the conference will be held. If necessary, semipublic or private organizations may also be consulted, as

[22] The story of the convocation of the Geneva Conference of 1864 may be briefly summarized as follows:

Henri Dunant published at Geneva in 1862 a booklet entitled *Un Souvenir de Solferino* which gave a shocking account of the distress of the wounded left to perish on the battlefield for lack of medical assistance. He suggested as a remedy that "the leaders of the military art of different nationalities agree upon some sacred international principle, sanctioned by convention, which, once signed and ratified, would serve as the basis for the creation of societies for the aid of the wounded in the different European countries." At the request of Gustave Moynier, president of the Société Genevoise d'Utilité Publique, Henri Dunant explained his views before the Society. The Society appointed a committee to study Henri Dunant's suggestions. The committee, which was destined to become the Comité International de la Croix Rouge, comprised among other members, all of Swiss nationality, General Dufour, Commander in Chief of the Swiss Army. The committee drafted the project of an agreement providing for the formation of national committees whose purpose was to assist army medical services by creating voluntary aid corps. An international meeting was then summoned at Geneva in October, 1863. Thirty-six experts and government representatives were present at the meeting, which laid down the fundamental principles of the Red Cross. The next task was to secure an international status for the scheme worked out at this semipublic conference. The International Committee succeeded in obtaining the support of Napoleon III in behalf of the project, and finally, on August 8, 1864, the Swiss Government convoked in Geneva a diplomatic conference at which twenty-six governments were represented.

well as governments. A good example of such preliminary negotiations is the preparation for the Monetary and Economic Conference held in London in 1933.

The Lausanne Conference on Reparations, it will be remembered, invited the League of Nations to convoke a Conference on Monetary and Economic Questions. At the same time it listed a number of objectives to which the future conference should pay particular attention. The Lausanne Conference also decided that the preliminary examination of the problems submitted to the proposed conference should be entrusted to a committee of experts. The Belgian, British, French, German, Italian, and Japanese governments were consequently invited to nominate two experts each, one to be an authority on economic questions, the other on financial matters. They were to sit on a Preparatory Commission which was to be divided into economic and financial subcommittees. The Conference also invited the United States of America to be similarly represented on the Preparatory Commission, and asked the Council of the League to appoint three financial authorities and three economic authorities to the Commission; the Bank of International Settlements was asked to appoint two financial experts.

Shortly after the Lausanne Conference, the Council of the League accepted the invitation to summon the conference and a Council Committee was appointed to organize it. The committee was composed of the representatives of the United Kingdom, France, Germany, Italy, Japan, and Norway, and it co-opted the representatives of Belgium and the United States of America. Sir John Simon, British Foreign Secretary, who was the British representative on the Council, became chairman of the Organizing Committee.

The Council, again acting on the proposals of the Lausanne Conference, took steps to set up the Commission of Experts which was to prepare the agenda of the Conference. The services of the Economic and Financial Organizations of the League were put at the disposal of this Preparatory Commission, and the International Labor Office and the International Institute of Agriculture were invited to give the Commission the benefit of their technical assistance. Thus two preliminary bodies were created — the Organizing Committee of the Council, and the Preparatory Commission of Experts.

One can imagine the amount of official and semiofficial negotiations necessary for setting up the machinery described above. And all these steps were preliminary to the starting of the planning work as such.

9. PREPARATORY PROCEDURE FOR INTERNATIONAL CONFERENCES OF AMERICAN STATES

The Seventh International Conference of American States, held at Montevideo in 1933, recognizing the importance of the preparatory work of the Conferences of American States, adopted the following resolution:

The Seventh International Conference of American States, Resolves: To request the Pan American Union to take the necessary measures to secure the preparation of projects on topics included in the programs of International Conferences. These projects will be sent in due course to the governments, members of the Union.

Pursuant to this resolution the Governing Board of the Pan American Union at its session of May 2, 1934, approved the following procedure for the execution of the preparatory work of the conferences:

1. The preparation of the program of each Conference shall begin immediately after the close of the previous one and shall be carried out gradually in the interval between the two Conferences.

2. After the close of a Conference, the Governing Board shall name a permanent program committee which shall direct the preparatory work.

3. A list of subjects shall be prepared which the Governing Board may consider suitable for consideration as possible topics of the program.

4. The Pan American Union shall gather the fundamental information for the study of the subjects included in the list referred to in the preceding paragraph and shall request from the Pan American Committees and Offices the report indicated in the resolutions of the International Conferences of American States which created and defined the functions of these committees.

5. Once a draft program is formulated it shall be submitted to the Governments, members of the Union, and they shall be requested to express, as soon as possible, their opinion on the proposed topics and indicate the new topics that they desire to have included in the program, so that the definitive program may be completed a year before the date fixed for the meeting of the Conference.

6. The Pan American Union shall request of the technical organizations whose collaboration may be deemed desirable by the Governing Board, as well as from the Pan American Committees, the formulation of projects on the topics included in the draft program.

7. Once the definitive program has been approved it shall be transmitted to the Governments, members of the Union, together with the projects on the topics of the program which the Governing Board may deem desirable to submit to their consideration.

8. A similar procedure shall be observed with respect to any special Pan American conferences meeting in the interval between two International Conferences of American States, the time limits being reduced as, in the opinion of the Governing Board, circumstances may require.

This procedure, with certain modifications, was followed in connection with the program of the Eighth International Conference of American States, held at Lima in December, 1938. The modifications were these: (1) at the suggestion of the Subcommittee on Program, the Governing Board adopted the rule that the governments proposing topics for the agenda of a conference be requested, whenever feasible, to present the respective project of treaty or resolution for submission to the governments before the Conference; (2) at the suggestion of the Government of Chile, the Board also approved a procedure whereby, after the approval of the definitive program of a conference, the topics for which another procedure had not been devised were to be assigned, prior to consultation, to individual governments for the preparation of the respective projects.

10. Preparatory Procedure for General Conventions Negotiated Under the Auspices of the League of Nations or Drawn up by the International Labor Organization

The League of Nations prescribed a special procedure to be followed in the preparation of an international convention for those instances in which it was proposed that a conference should end with the signing of such an instrument.

In 1931, the Assembly of the League had adopted the following resolution concerning conventions to be negotiated under the auspices of the League:

That, in the case of all general conventions to be negotiated under the auspices of the League of Nations, the following preparatory procedure should, in principle, be followed, except in the cases where previous conventions or arrangements have established a special procedure or where, owing to the nature of the questions to be treated or to special circumstances, the Assembly or the Council consider other methods to be more appropriate:

1. Where an organ of the League of Nations recommends the conclusion of a general convention on any matter, it shall prepare a memorandum explaining the objects which it is desired to achieve by the conclusion of the convention and the benefits which result therefrom. Such memorandum shall be submitted to the Council of the League of Nations.

2. If the Council approves the proposal in principle, a first draft convention shall be prepared and communicated, together with the explanatory memorandum, to Governments, with the request that, if they feel that the draft should be taken into consideration, they shall inform the Secretary-General of their views, both with regard to the main objects or the suggested means of attaining them, and also with regard to the draft convention. In some cases, it may be desirable to annex a specific questionnaire.

3. The draft convention and the observations of Governments (together with

the answers to the questionnaire, if any) shall be communicated to the Assembly, and the Assembly shall then decide whether the subject appears *prima facie* suitable for the conclusion of a convention.

4. If the Assembly considers the subject *prima facie* suitable for the conclusion of a convention, the Council shall arrange for the preparation of a draft convention in the light of the replies received from Governments, and the new draft convention (together with the replies of other Governments) shall be transmitted to each Government with a request for their opinion on the provisions of the draft and any observations on the above-mentioned replies of the other Governments.

5. In the light of the results of this second consultation of the Governments, the Assembly shall decide whether a convention should be concluded and, if so, whether the draft should be submitted to a conference, the date of which it will request the Council to fix.

6. The Council, in fixing the date for the convocation of a conference, shall endeavour, as far as possible, to avoid two League of Nations conferences being held simultaneously, and to ensure the lapse of a reasonable interval between two conferences.

7. The procedure set out in the preceding paragraphs will be followed, as far as possible, in the case of draft conventions the desirability of which is recognised by a decision of the Assembly either on its own initiative or as the result of a proposal by a Government. In these cases, the Council will instruct either the Secretariat or some other organ of the League or specially selected experts to prepare the above-mentioned report, which shall subsequently be submitted to the Council.

The procedure described above may appear long and complicated. Indeed, according to the rules thus set up by the Assembly, about two years were required for completing the necessary consultations with the governments and for securing the final authorization of the Assembly to complete the negotiating of the convention.

On the whole the procedure adopted by the Assembly operated smoothly. The precautions taken were wise and justified, since it is useless to adopt and sign hastily and badly drafted conventions which may never be ratified. Moreover, it may be pointed out by way of comparison that in many countries with efficient administrative and legislative bodies, the preparation and the adoption of national laws — which often are easier to draw up than international conventions — take a much longer time.

The preparatory procedure followed by the International Labor Organization for drawing up its conventions is perhaps even more complicated than that of the League. It should be noted, however, that draft conventions framed by the International Labor Organization are not signed at the end of the conferences.[23] They are adopted

[23] For a discussion of the practice of the International Labor Organization abolishing the signature of international conventions, see Frederick Sherwood Dunn, *The Practice and Procedure of International Conferences* (Baltimore: The Johns Hopkins Press, 1929), pp. 169–80.

by a qualified majority, and for this reason more caution is perhaps necessary than for League conventions. Indeed, the representative of a government may be tempted to join the majority in a vote which is not binding on his government, but he will hesitate to sign a convention which may not be acceptable to his government and for which he may be blamed later.[24]

Two procedures have been evolved by the International Labor Organization.

(a) *The Single Discussion Procedure.*

1. The International Labor Office circulates to governments a summary report upon the questions which are to come up for consideration before the international conference. This report contains a statement of the law and practice in the different countries. It is accompanied by a questionnaire drawn up with a view to the preparation of draft conventions or recommendations. Governments are allowed three months to prepare their reasoned replies. These replies must reach the Office promptly, and not later than six months prior to the opening of the conference.

2. On the basis of the replies of the governments, the Office draws up a final report, which may contain one or more draft conventions or recommendations. This report is communicated by the Office to the governments as soon as possible. Every effort is made to insure that the report reaches them not later than four months before the opening of the conference.

3. When the conference convenes, it decides whether it will take as the basis of discussion the draft conventions or recommendations prepared by the Office, and whether these drafts shall be considered in

[24] Discussing the question of the importance of the signature affixed to international compacts, Francis O. Wilcox says: "If the form alone were to be considered, the signature given by a plenipotentiary possessing full-powers from most governments might seem to carry with it the solemn promise of the state to accept the arrangements agreed to. Furthermore, the fact that signatures are not always freely given to international instruments indicates that the act is not completely devoid of significance. At times, when delegates have not been given the power to sign by their governments or when they have felt that the agreement must be subject to further study, they have refused to approve the results of the conference which they attended. The United States delegate to the Conference on Counterfeiting Currency (April 1929) stated that it was necessary for his government to 'see the texts of the documents before pronouncing any definite opinion upon them.' He was therefore unable to sign the agreements drawn up. At the same Conference the delegations of Sweden, Turkey, Yugoslavia, Denmark, Finland, and China announced that they could not officially sign the results of the deliberations, either because they did not possess the necessary full-powers or because they were awaiting instructions from their governments. The Nicaraguan delegate thought that he had sufficient power to sign, but 'in order to meet his conscientious scruples, he preferred to await a telegraphic reply' telling him what to do." *The Ratification of International Conventions* (London: George Allen & Unwin, Ltd., 1935), pp. 24–25.

full conference or referred to a committee for report. These decisions may be preceded by a debate in full conference on the general principles of the suggested drafts.

4. Further detailed rules determine the procedure to be followed by the conference for the discussion of the draft conventions and recommendations.

(b) *The Procedure of Double Discussion.*

1. Under this procedure the first step is the preparation by the International Labor Office of a preliminary report setting forth the law and practice in the different countries with regard to the question at issue; other useful information as well as a questionnaire are generally included. These documents are sent at the earliest possible date to governments, so as to reach them at least six months before the opening of the conference.

2. The Office subsequently submits to the conference the preliminary report referred to above, together with a further report. The latter is drawn up on the basis of the replies from the governments and indicates the principal questions requiring consideration by the conference. These reports are submitted for discussion. If the conference decides that the subject is a suitable one for a draft convention or for a recommendation, it adopts such conclusions as it sees fit. It may choose between two alternatives. It may: (*a*) decide to include the question on the agenda at the subsequent session, or (*b*) ask the Governing Body of the Office to place the question on the agenda of a later session.

3. On the basis of the replies from governments to the questionnaire referred to above under (1) and on the basis of the first discussion by the conference, the Office prepares one or more draft conventions or recommendations. It transmits these to the governments with the request that they submit amendments or comments within four months.

4. On the basis of the replies from governments, the Office draws up a final report which contains the text of draft conventions or recommendations, together with any amendments which may have been proposed. The report must reach the governments not later than three months before the opening of the conference.

5. Further discussions of these texts by the conference are governed by the same rules as in the single discussion procedure.

II. PREPARATORY COMMITTEES AND COMMISSIONS AND THEIR WORK

The drawing up of the draft convention is sometimes done through a standing committee of the international organization. In the practice of the League of Nations this task was more often entrusted to an *ad hoc* committee appointed by the Council. The two procedures were frequently combined. Thus a preparatory committee was set up by altering slightly the composition of the standing committee or by interlocking it with the work of the *ad hoc* committee.[25]

The preparatory work for a projected "Conference to consider the possibility of limiting and controlling the cultivation of the opium poppy and the production of raw opium and controlling other raw materials for the manufacture of opium alkaloids"[26] was entrusted to the Advisory Committee on Traffic in Opium and Other Dangerous Drugs.

The best example of an *ad hoc* body is the Preparatory Commission for the Disarmament Conference. In September, 1925, the Assembly requested the Council to make a preparatory study for a prospective Conference on the Reduction and Limitation of Armaments. In giving effect to this request, the Council, on September 12, 1925, set up the Preparatory Commission for the Disarmament Conference consisting of representatives of a certain number of states comprising both members and non-members of the League. The Preparatory Commission held six sessions: in May and September, 1926; in March, April, November, and December, 1927; in March, 1928; in April–May, 1929 (first part) and November–December, 1930 (second part). The Commission finally was dissolved on December 9, 1930, after preparing a

[25] For instance, the Economic Committee of the League of Nations, with the assistance of the Secretariat of the League of Nations, prepared draft conventions or assisted in the preparation of international agreements or conferences on the following subjects:
International Convention relating to the Simplification of Customs Formalities, 1923; Protocol of 1923 and Convention of 1927 on Arbitration Clauses and the Execution of Foreign Arbitral Awards; Conference for the Revision of International Conventions on the Protection of Industrial Property, The Hague, 1925 (Unfair Competition); preparation of the World Economic Conference, 1927; Convention for the Abolition of Import and Export Prohibitions and Restrictions, 1927–1928; draft International Convention on the Treatment of Foreigners and Foreign Undertakings; Conference with a View to Concerted Economic Action and Commercial Convention, 1930; Conventions on the Unification of Laws on Bills of Exchange, Promissory Notes and Cheques, 1930 and 1931; International Convention on the Regulation of Whale-Fishing, 1931; Procedure for the Friendly Settlement of Economic Disputes between States, 1932; draft Conventions on Commercial Propaganda and the Unification of the Conception of Weight and the Regime of Packing in Customs Matters, 1934; Conventions on Veterinary Questions; draft Convention on the Trade in Meat and Meat Preparations, 1935. *Essential Facts about the League of Nations*, Tenth Edition, revised (Geneva, 1939), p. 229.
[26] It is generally agreed that as far as possible long and complicated names should be avoided at international conferences. Besides the waste of time and space when referring to an unusual and elaborate name in the documentation prepared for the conference, most people connected with international conferences will agree that the continuous repetition of an interminable title has a depressing psychological effect.

draft Convention on the Reduction and Limitation of Armaments and a Final Report. In addition, the Preparatory Commission made a series of studies, and the bulky documentation relating to its work fills several volumes.

Indeed, preceding, paralleling, or following the drawing up of the draft convention, a considerable amount of documentation must be prepared in order to facilitate the work of the future conference.

The rôle of the Secretariat of the League in the preparatory work of international conferences held under its auspices was considerable. The same is true for the International Labor Office. The Secretariat gathered, classified, and compared data supplied by governments or semiofficial or private organizations, made technical and legal studies, wrote monographs and memoranda. In drawing up draft conventions, the preparatory bodies of the League or of the International Labor Organization had at their disposal the permanent machinery of the Secretariat of the League or of the International Labor Office. This facilitated their work considerably.

In the early days of the League, the representatives of governments and the members of the standing committee had been somewhat skeptical regarding the ability of the Secretariat to draw up draft conventions. Because of the complicated and technical nature of such conventions and because of the legal points involved, they were inclined to entrust the work to experts in the field. In time, however, the skill and precision of the work of the Secretariat received more and more recognition. For instance, in 1938, the Advisory Committee on Traffic in Opium asked the Secretariat to prepare a draft of the principal articles which might appear in a future convention for controlling the cultivation of opium. This work was done by the Opium Section of the Secretariat in collaboration with the Legal Section. Sitting as a Preparatory Committee of the planned conference, the Advisory Committee made very few changes in the project of the Secretariat.

The same procedure in preparing documentation was used also when no signing of a convention was contemplated as a result of the conference. Preparations for the Economic and Monetary Conference, held in 1933, in London, were made jointly by an Organizing Committee of the Council, by a Preparatory Commission of Experts, and by the Secretariat of the League. A series of monographs, memoranda, etc., was prepared and distributed before the conference. An analogous procedure had been used for the preparation of the Economic Conference held in Geneva in 1927. A Preparatory Committee appointed by the

Council issued a huge quantity of preparatory documentation,[27] with the collaboration of the Secretariat of the League and various individual experts.

Regular gatherings of permanent international organizations like the sessions of the Assembly and the Council of the League or the sessions of the General Labor Conferences and of the Governing Body of the International Labor Office were all prepared for in a similar manner. Standing or *ad hoc* committees, with the help of the Secretariat of the League or of the International Labor Office, drafted reports and proposals which were subsequently submitted to the main bodies.

As already stated, much of the work of preparation for all meetings held under the auspices of the League and the International Labor Organization was facilitated by the existence of permanent secretarial bodies.

12. Preparation of a Conference by a Nation or a Group of Nations

The situation is different when an individual state takes the initiative of summoning an international conference and is the inviting power. In such a case the responsibility for making the preparations needed for the forthcoming conference rests upon the inviting power, which is obliged either to gather by itself the necessary material and to draw up the required instruments, or to improvise a method of collaboration, with all or some of the members of the proposed conference. The same is true when a conference is sponsored by a group of nations.

[27] For the International Economic Conference of 1927, the preparatory documentation was so voluminous that it was necessary to issue a *Guide to the Documents of the Conference*, L.N. Document C.E.I.40(1), Geneva, 1927. Sir Arthur Salter, who was the Director of the Economic and Financial Section of the Secretariat of the League, wrote in Preliminary Remarks concerning the documentation that "A documentation so wide alike in its scope and in its authorship is necessarily very voluminous. There is obviously a danger that, on this account, it may defeat its own purpose. The object of documentation is to summarise, simplify and explain the multitudinous detail of the actual economic life of the world. But documents so numerous and so detailed themselves need summary, simplification and explanation. It is the object of the present pamphlet to provide a few threads which may assist the reader to penetrate the labyrinth without losing his way. I say 'threads' rather than 'thread,' for few, if any, will wish to cover the whole ground equally and impartially; most will doubtless wish to obtain a general conspectus and then to specialise in a particular part of the field." *Ibid.*, p. 2.

The "Guide" reviewed forty-three "Conference Documents" which, as the author explained, carried more than an individual authority because they had all been authorized for issuance as Conference Documents by the Preparatory Committee, and thirteen monographs (selected among approximately one hundred documents of the same kind) which had been written by individual experts and which carried the individual authority of the names they bore. *Ibid.*, p. 3.

The beginning of the twentieth century marked a noteworthy progress in the preparatory work of this type of conference. The London Naval Conference of 1908–9 served as a model for future conferences of this kind.[27a]

A separate study would be necessary to go into details of the diplomatic negotiations, preparation of the subject, preliminary meetings, form of invitation, and drafting of provisional agenda of such conferences, convoked after World War I. Examples are the Conference on Limitation of Armaments held in Washington in 1921–22, the Locarno Conference, 1925, the London Naval Conference, 1930, and the series of United Nations Conferences following the outbreak of World War II, such as the United Nations Food and Agriculture Conference held at Hot Springs in 1943, the United Nations Monetary and Financial Conference held at Bretton Woods in 1944, and the United Nations Conference on International Organization summoned at San Francisco in the spring of 1945.

Lately a new development has taken place. The first meeting of the Council of the United Nations Relief and Rehabilitation Administration, held in November, 1943, at Atlantic City, was prepared in a quite exceptional manner. Probably for the first time in history an international organization was set up without being preceded by an international conference. The League of Nations and the International Labor Organization, to give only these examples, were created by the Paris Peace Conference; the UNRRA Agreement, however, was negotiated through foreign offices and diplomatic missions rather than at a conference. The negotiations began as early as the summer of 1942, with the United States taking the initiative. In a further stage China, the Soviet Union, and the United Kingdom shared in the leadership. When these four governments had agreed upon a text, it was communicated to the other United Nations and to the associated nations, and released to the public. Modifications were made to meet the views of other governments and members of the United States Senate and House of Representatives. When general agreement appeared to have been reached through this process of multiple individual negotiation, all of the governments involved were invited to send representatives to sign the Agreement. The ceremony of signature took place in the White House on November 9, 1943. The United Nations Relief and Rehabili-

---

[27a] For the preparatory procedure of the London Naval Conference of 1908–9, see Great Britain, Foreign Office, *Miscellaneous Series*, Nos. 4–5 (1909); see also M. de Taube, *La politique russe d'avant-guerre et la fin de l'Empire des Tsars (1904–1917)* (Paris: Librairie Ernest-Leroux, 1928), pp. 202–31.

tation Administration was thereby brought into existence and the
Council of the Administration met in its first session on the following
day, November 10, at Atlantic City.[28]

13. The Draft Agenda

Among the preparatory documents for an international meeting, the
draft agenda is of outstanding importance. The scope and the program
of the future gathering necessarily remain vague until this document
has been framed. This is true for the meetings of permanent international bodies possessing broad powers like the Assembly and the Council of the League, or for permanent bodies with more limited powers
like the International Labor Conference, the Governing Body of the
Labor Office, or for the standing committees of both institutions. It is
also true for *ad hoc* international conferences. For this last category
the preliminary negotiations conducted for their summoning and the
preparatory documentation drawn up will, of course, result in some
clarification of the purpose and the work of the conferences, especially
in the case where a draft convention has been framed. Nevertheless,
not until a draft agenda has been formulated is it possible to have a
sufficient knowledge of the scope and character of the forthcoming
conference.[29]

DRAFT AGENDA FOR THE MEETINGS OF THE ASSEMBLY AND THE COUNCIL OF THE LEAGUE

The preparation of the draft agenda for the regular sessions is regulated by Rule 4 of the Rules of Procedure of the Assembly, which states
that:

1. The agenda shall be drawn up by the Secretary-General with the approval
of the President of the Council. The complete agenda shall be circulated as nearly
as possible four months before the date fixed for the opening of the session.
2. The agenda of a general session shall include:
(a) A report on the work of the Council since the last session of the Assembly,
   on the work of the Secretariat, and on the measures taken to execute the
   decisions of the Assembly;
(b) All items whose inclusion has been ordered by the Assembly at a previous
   session;
(c) All items proposed by the Council;

[28] Philip C. Jessup, "The First Session of the Council of UNRRA," *American
Journal of International Law*, Vol. 38 (1944), pp. 102–3.
[29] For a brief but interesting discussion of different problems in relation to the
agenda of conferences, see Dunn, *op. cit.*, pp. 201–5.

(*d*) All items proposed by a Member of the League; and

(*e*) The Budget for the next fiscal period, and the report on the accounts of the last fiscal period.

3. Any Member of the League may, at least one month before the date fixed for the opening of the session, request the inclusion of additional items in the agenda. Such items shall be placed on a supplementary list, which shall be circulated to the Members of the League at least three weeks before the date fixed for the opening of the session. The Assembly shall decide whether items on the supplementary list shall be included in the agenda of the session.

Thus the primary responsibility for drawing up the draft agenda of the Assembly sessions lies with the Secretary General. For this reason the internal procedure followed by the Secretariat for framing this document may be of some interest.

Approximately four and a half months before the opening of the session of the Assembly (i.e., at the beginning of May) the Central Section of the Secretariat sent to all the other sections a note asking them to supply the Central Section within the next few days with any item in their province which in their opinion should be included in the draft agenda. The sections were also asked to supply at the same time a brief note explaining, *inter alia*, why the item should be included in the draft agenda, with a very brief description of the question to be considered by the Assembly. A note of this type would, for example, read as follows:

Nationality of Women.

This question was brought before the Assembly at its session of 1931, in accordance with the Council's resolution of January 24th, 1931, by a report from the Secretary-General, to which were annexed proposals by a Committee of Representatives of various Women's International Organisations. The Assembly decided to consider the question further at its ordinary session of 1932. The Governments had been invited to submit their observations, including their views regarding the Convention on Nationality concluded at the Hague Conference of 1930. Such further observations as the Committee of Representatives of the Women's International Organisations may desire to present will also be laid before the Assembly.[30]

On the basis of the answers from the sections, the Central Section framed a provisional draft agenda and distributed it to the Directors and Heads of Sections of the Secretariat; and this draft was discussed at a Directors' meeting. Under the first Secretary General, the discussion of the provisional draft agenda included questions of general policy connected with the forthcoming Assembly meeting. Under the

[30] *Agenda of the Thirteenth Ordinary Session of the Assembly*, L.N. Document A.2. 1932., p. 2.

second Secretary General, the meetings of the Secretariat at which the provisional draft agenda were discussed bore the name of "Section Meetings." They were seldom presided over by the Secretary General himself. All that was generally discussed was the order in which the items were to be classified in the draft agenda. As soon as the draft was agreed upon in the Secretariat, the Secretary General got in touch with the acting President of the Council in order to get his approval.

Once the President's approval was obtained, the draft agenda was printed and circulated to the members of the League. Early in August a second edition of the draft agenda was framed by the Central Section. The revised edition contained the additional items covered by the provisions of the third paragraph of Rule 4 of the Rules of Procedure. This second edition was distributed to the members of the League on or about August 15, i.e., approximately one month before the beginning of the session of the Assembly, which was bound to meet, in accordance with the Rules of Procedure, on the Monday which fell in the period between September 10 and September 16 of each year.

The drawing up of the provisional agenda of the Council of the League is regulated by Article III of the Rules of Procedure which reads:

1. A provisional agenda shall be drawn up by the Secretary-General and approved by the President of the Council. It shall in all cases include any questions which a Member of the League has asked the Council to consider.

. . . . . .

2. The provisional agenda shall be sent to the Members of the Council not less than three weeks before the opening of the session, except in the case of the fourth ordinary session of the year or of a session the date of which is such as to make it impossible to maintain this interval.

3. Any subsequent modification of the provisional agenda shall be communicated to the Members of the Council.

The internal arrangements within the Secretariat for drawing up the provisional agenda of the sessions of the Council, were the same, *mutatis mutandis*, as for the Assembly agenda.

A request by League members for the inclusion of an item in the provisional agenda of the Assembly or the Council was subject only to the time-limit set in the Rules of Procedure. Even reference to a specific article of the Covenant was not necessary. Indeed, the provisions of Articles 3 and 4 of the Covenant allowed the Assembly and Council to deal with any matter within the sphere of action of the League or affecting the peace of the world. The Secretary General had no legal power for refusing to a member of the League the inclusion of an item on the agenda of either of the two bodies. It happened at times that a government, before asking the inclusion of an item on the agenda, made a semiofficial enquiry as to what prospects of success its initiative would have. In several cases the Secretary General either *proprio motu*, or after consulting privately with the more influential members of the Council and the League, advised a government not to insist on the inclusion of a proposed item in the provisional agenda. Sometimes the interested government, of its own accord, made such an enquiry among other members of the League. If it gained the impression that the chances for success were slight, the matter was usually dropped.

The fact that no limitation concerning the inclusion of an item on the agenda was imposed upon governments, had a direct influence on the length of the sessions of the Council and the Assembly. This is an aspect of the question, however, which will be dealt with in a later section.[30a]

AGENDA OF THE INTERNATIONAL LABOR CONFERENCES

The system of the International Labor Organization in dealing with the agenda is somewhat different from that of the League.

The relevant articles of the Constitution read as follows:

ARTICLE 14. The agenda for all meetings of the Conference will be settled by the Governing Body, who shall consider any suggestion as to the agenda that may be made by the Government of any of the Members or by any representative organisation recognised for the purpose of Article 3.

ARTICLE 15. The Director shall act as the Secretary of the Conference, and shall transmit the agenda so as to reach the Members four months before the meeting of the Conference, and, through them, the non-Government Delegates when appointed.

ARTICLE 16. — 1. Any of the Governments of the Members may formally object to the inclusion of any item or items in the agenda. The grounds for such objection shall be set forth in a reasoned statement addressed to the Director, who shall circulate it to all the Members of the Permanent Organisation.

Thus a procedure has been created for avoiding both the overloading of the agenda and the inclusion of items objectionable to governments.

The drawing up of the agenda is a function, not of the head of the Secretariat of the Organization, as in the case of the League of Nations, but of the Governing Body which has the power to act upon the proposals under consideration. It may either accept or reject the proposals.

[30a] See section 27 of this handbook, page 116, *infra*.

The Governing Body set up a special method for framing the draft agenda. It consists: (1) in a preliminary discussion of the proposals made; (2) in the decision whether or not all the items proposed shall be included in the draft agenda. If it is decided to include only a part of the items originally proposed, the Governing Body takes a series of eliminatory votes until the final result is obtained.[31]

AGENDA OF THE STANDING COMMITTEES OF THE LEAGUE

The method of drafting the provisional agenda of the standing committees of the League differed widely according to the character of work, the rules of procedure, and the customs of each committee. Sometimes the draft agenda was framed by the Secretariat and the chair; sometimes a special subcommittee of the body drew up the agenda. This was the case with the Advisory Committee on Traffic in Opium. The contents of the agenda depended upon the duties of the committee and the needs of the moment. The following, for instance, is the agenda of the twenty-fifth session of the Advisory Committee on Traffic in Opium held in May, 1940 (the subheadings have been eliminated):

  I. Elections and Appointments.
 II. Adoption of Agenda.
III. Influence of War Conditions on the Work of the Advisory Committee.
 IV. Consideration of the Secretary's Progress Report.
  V. Consideration of Annual Reports of Traffic in Opium and other Dangerous Drugs and of Synoptical Statistical Tables prepared by the Secretariat.
 VI. Illicit Traffic.
VII. Situation in the Far East.
VIII. Budget.
 IX. Other Questions.

AGENDA OF THE INTERNATIONAL CONFERENCES OF AMERICAN STATES

The agenda of the International Conferences of American States are prepared by the Governing Board of the Pan American Union which appoints for this purpose before each conference a special Committee on Program and Regulations. The full membership of this committee consists of all the members of the Board. At the same time a subcommittee of five members is designated to undertake the preparatory

[31] For details concerning this procedure, see William O'Davoren, *Post-War Reconstruction Conferences* (Geneva: Alexandre Julien, 1942), pp. 24–25.

work. The subcommittee submits to the Governing Board a preliminary report to which is attached a list of topics for possible inclusion in the agenda. After discussion by the Governing Board this list is forwarded to the governments members of the Union with the request that their observations and comments thereon be transmitted to the Pan American Union by a fixed date. On the basis of the replies received from governments the subcommittee on Program prepares and submits to the Governing Board a revised draft program which is again submitted to the governments with the request that they transmit their observations at a given date. After this second consultation the agenda is passed and definitively approved by the Governing Board.

AGENDA OF THE COUNCIL OF THE UNITED NATIONS RELIEF AND REHABILITATION ADMINISTRATION

Article VIII of the Rules of Procedure of the Council of the United Nations Relief and Rehabilitation Administration provides that:

1. The provisional agenda of each session of the Council shall be prepared by the Director General, and shall include
  (a) all items proposed by the Council at any previous session;
  (b) all items proposed by the Central Committee;
  (c) all items proposed by any member of the Council and transmitted to the Director General at least ten days in advance of the session; and
  (d) any item which the Director General desires to put before the Council.
2. The provisional agenda shall be communicated to member governments as far as possible in advance of and not less than three weeks before the opening day of the session. Items transmitted to the Director General too late for inclusion will be at once communicated to member governments.
3. The provisional agenda so communicated shall be passed upon by the General Committee and submitted to the Council for approval as soon as convenient after the opening of any session.
4. The Council may later revise or add to the agenda.

AGENDA OF "AD HOC" CONFERENCES

(a) *Conferences Convoked under the Auspices of a Standing International Organization.*

The drafting of the agenda of such conferences is generally entrusted to a preparatory committee. It has already been noted that the preparatory committee might be a standing committee of the organization or a special committee. The procedure followed for drawing up the draft agenda of the London Economic Conference of 1933 may serve as an example: The Preparatory Commission of Experts, whose task was to prepare an annotated agenda for the Conference, was composed of some thirty members. The Commission met for the first time in November, 1932, appointed its Chairman, and separated into two subcommittees, the first dealing with monetary questions, and the second with economic questions. The Commission then reviewed the questions which in its opinion should be dealt with by the Conference. The results of this preliminary discussion were incorporated in a number of memoranda, and the Commission decided to hold a second session after its members had obtained the views of their governments and of economic and financial circles in their respective countries on the various proposals. The second session of the Preparatory Commission, held in January, 1933, drafted an annotated agenda, which served as the basis for the work of the Conference.

The agenda of *ad hoc* conferences differ widely according to the task entrusted to each conference. If an international convention is to be signed, and if a draft convention has been prepared beforehand for consideration by the conference, the draft agenda of the conference may be very simple. It may indeed be reduced to a single important item, "Consideration of the Draft Convention," the other items being related to mere questions of procedure. If the preparation of the conference has not resulted in the framing of a draft convention, however, the draft agenda is generally very detailed and indicates clearly the scope of the conference.

The provisional agenda of the International Economic Conference of London, for instance, contained the following items:

1. Monetary and Credit Policy
2. Prices
3. Resumption of the Movement of Capital
4. Restrictions on International Trade
5. Tariff and Treaty Policy
6. Organization of Production and Trade

The list of subjects was preceded by an introduction outlining the general program of the conference and followed by "annotations to the agenda" containing the observations of the Preparatory Commission on the various problems raised by the main questions in the agenda. Thus, the draft agenda was a rather bulky document covering several printed pages.

(b) *Conferences Convoked by a Single Country or a Group of Countries.*

If a conference is convoked by a single country or a group of countries, this power or group of powers will frame a draft agenda for the conference. If a single power summons a conference, it generally consults, through the ordinary diplomatic channels, some of the most important members of the proposed conference on the draft agenda. If a group of states takes the initiative, those states usually convene for a preliminary exchange of views among themselves during which the draft agenda will be framed. The draft agenda in this case is generally detailed, for it is necessary to make the purpose which induced the inviting country or the group of countries to convoke the conference as clear as possible.[32]

14. SELECTION OF THE PLACE AND THE DATE OF A CONFERENCE

The next preparatory step after drafting the provisional agenda consists in the selection of the place of the conference and its date.

PLACE OF THE CONFERENCE

(a) *Periodical Meetings of Standing Bodies of International Organizations.*

The plenary periodical meetings of a standing international organization are generally held at the headquarters of the organization. Often a provision to that effect is included in the constitution of the organization or in the rules of procedure. Thus, the Rules of Procedure of the Assembly state that "the sessions of the Assembly shall be held at the seat of the League, or, in exceptional circumstances, at such other place as is designated by the Assembly or by a majority of the Council, or approved by a majority of the Members of the League." The Constitution of the International Labor Organization (Article 5) provides that "The meetings of the Conference shall be held at the seat of the League of Nations, or at such other place as may be decided by the Conference at a previous meeting by two-thirds of the votes cast by the Delegates present." All the Assemblies of the League were held at Geneva, but the first meeting of the International Labor Conference was held in Washington, the second in Genoa, and its last two in New York in 1941 and in Philadelphia in 1944.

Occasionally, the meetings of the Council of the League [33] or of the

[32] As an example, the draft agenda of the recent United Nations Conference on Food and Agriculture has been reproduced as Appendix II, *infra*.

[33] Article II of the Council's Rules of Procedure reads: "The sessions of the Council shall be held at the seat of the League of Nations, except in cases where the majority of the Members of the Council consider that the Council should meet elsewhere." In point of fact, the Council's sessions have generally been held at Geneva. Of the one hundred and seven sessions, twenty-two have been held at places other than Geneva, and these occurred more particularly in the early years of the League.

Governing Body of the International Labor Office were held outside Geneva. The reasons for holding the meetings of the Council outside Geneva were generally connected with the international situation existing at the moment. For instance, it was difficult for the British or French Ministers for Foreign Affairs to come to Geneva during an international crisis. Certain meetings of the Council were also held outside Geneva because some power wished to extend an invitation for reasons of international courtesy. But this laudable gesture often hid more selfish motives, such as the desire to take advantage of an important international gathering within the boundaries of the country, to increase the national prestige or to alleviate a difficult internal situation. The meetings of the standing committees of the League were generally held at Geneva. The reasons for this practice were, of course, chiefly of an administrative and financial nature. It is to be regretted that such committee meetings were not held more often outside Geneva as meetings held elsewhere helped to make the League more widely known.[34]

The Pan American Conferences are held by rotation in the capitals of one of the affiliated countries, the seat of the next conference being fixed by a resolution of the conference in session.[35]

(b) *"Ad hoc" Conferences Held under the Auspices of an International Organization.*

Conferences concerning a special matter are often convoked at the seat of a standing international organization, especially if these conferences are sponsored by that organization.[36] When a conference was

[34] F. P. Walters, former Director of the Political Section and Under Secretary General of the League of Nations, discussing the question of holding League meetings away from Geneva, points out that: "This was discouraged both on financial grounds and because the limited staff of the Secretariat made it very difficult to spare the extra time for travelling. Governments were more than ready to issue invitations and provide facilities, but under the League's financial regulations the inviting Government was called upon to pay the whole extra cost involved by holding the meeting outside Geneva. The result was, of course, that outside meetings were rare: yet when they took place their educative value was evident, alike for the inviting country, the other Delegates, and the Secretariat." *Administrative Problems of International Organization*, Barnett House Papers, No. 24 (London: Oxford University Press, 1941), p. 13.

[35] The Eighth International Conference of American States, held in Lima in December, 1938, adopted the following resolution (Resolution CVIII):

"1. That the City of Bogotá be the seat of the Ninth International Conference of American States.

"2. That the date of the Conference and other preparations for its meeting be determined jointly by the Government of Colombia and the Governing Board of the Pan American Union."

[36] Numerous private or semipublic international conferences were held at Geneva during the period 1920–1939 without being sponsored by the League of Nations. Geneva was, however, a convenient place for such international gatherings because the League had its seat at Geneva. Some fifty or sixty international organizations maintained standing secretariats at Geneva.

held under the auspices of the League the Council decided most frequently upon the place of the conference. Just as in the case of meetings of standing committees, there was a tendency to convoke at Geneva all international conferences held under the auspices of the League. In these cases financial and administrative considerations played a preponderant rôle in decisions as to the place of meeting. But there was no absolute rule. It occurred frequently that international conferences sponsored by the League or by the Labor Organization, were held outside Geneva; and a similar situation obtained as regards the holding of Council sessions elsewhere. Sometimes supplementary reasons contributed to the choice of a place, i.e., a country appeared as best suited for the meeting because it had a wider experience with the subject-matter, or because traditionally conferences of a certain kind were held at a certain place. Thus, the Conference for the Unification of International Law, held under the auspices of the League in 1930, was convoked at The Hague.

The standing committee, or the special body to which had been entrusted the preparation of a conference, often made proposals to the Council concerning the place of a projected conference. This procedure was not adopted by the Preparatory Commission of the Disarmament Conference. It was the Council itself that designated Geneva as the seat of the Conference.[37] In this instance the Council made its decision contingent upon replies to an enquiry by the Secretary General of the League relative to the desirability of Geneva as the most suitable place for the Conference. As a result of his enquiry, the Secretary General received a flow of proposals emanating from governments and municipalities offering accommodations for the Conference. Geneva was finally selected as the place of the Conference.

(c) *"Ad hoc" Conferences Summoned by a Single Government or a Group of Governments.*

In the case of conferences sponsored by a single government or by a group of governments, the territory of the country which takes the initiative in convoking the conference, or the territory of one of the countries belonging to the group of states which participates in this initiative, is as a rule selected as the place of the conference. Thus, Hot Springs, Virginia, was selected as the place for the United Nations Conference on Food and Agriculture sponsored by the United States Government. Similarly the first session of the United Nations Relief and Rehabilitation Administration was held at Atlantic City, New

[37] Resolution of January 24, 1931.

Jersey, the United Nations Monetary and Financial Conference at Bretton Woods, New Hampshire, and the International Conference on Civil Aviation at Chicago.

Sometimes a place situated outside the country or the countries which have taken the initiative in calling the conference is suggested. Manifold reasons may motivate such suggestions. By common agreement Swiss towns were often designated as seats of international conferences either because of Switzerland's neutrality (Conference of Locarno) or because it was thought convenient to hold the conference in the vicinity of Geneva (Conferences of Montreux concerning the suppression of capitulations in Egypt and concerning the Turkish Straits, Conference of Nyon concerning the Security in the Mediterranean, etc.).

(d) *Considerations to be Taken into Account in Fixing the Place of a Conference.*

A favorable atmosphere for an international conference depends, to a certain extent, on the place selected as seat of the meeting. The greatest care should therefore be taken in weighing the pros and cons before a decision is taken. Climatic conditions, the existence of proper communications by sea, air, rail, or road, as well as radio, telegraphic, and telephone facilities, must all be taken into account. The place chosen must also provide accommodation for the meetings themselves and for sheltering the delegates; and it must possess sufficient resources in hotels, boarding houses, and restaurants. The national political situation must also be taken into account; the country which is to be the host must fulfil the necessary prerequisites of public order and tranquillity. The deliberations must not be hampered by the existence of censorship or by abusive police regulations. Preliminary attention should also be paid to the language spoken in the country. The delegates should be able to make themselves understood in hotels, shops, etc., and it may be necessary to arrange in advance for a sufficient number of interpreters. Local customs or habits must not interfere with the work of the conference (for instance, such traditions as the "siesta" or religious holidays).

As a general rule the government of the country selected as the place of the conference and the local authorities are only too willing to cooperate in settling the material arrangements. They are eager to provide customs facilities, and to see that passport and visa formalities for the delegates, their families, and their staff are greatly simplified. Similar facilities are extended to the personnel of the secretariat of the conference,[38] and very often to journalists. Sometimes free passes or fare reductions on railways are granted (the Netherlands Indies authorities, for instance, provided special identity cards to the delegates and the members of the Secretariat of the Conference on Traffic in Women and Children held at Bandoeng, Java, in 1937, entitling them to reduced fares on trains and planes). In order to facilitate the task of the local authorities, the members of the secretariat of the conference are usually provided with special *lettres de mission* to prove their identity.

(e) *Premises.*

Suitable premises for the meetings of the conference must be provided. Permanent international organizations usually have their own buildings fully equipped with the necessary accommodations for the holding of important assemblies. As a rule special rooms and offices are set aside for the members of the conference and its secretariat. On the other hand, certain periodical international gatherings, like the Pan American Conferences, do not possess a permanent meeting place. In that event they are often convoked in rotation, in the capitals of the different members of the organization.

The government of the country in which the conference is held assumes responsibility for the accommodations of the conference. Similarly, when a general meeting of a standing organization or an *ad hoc* conference, convoked under the auspices of the organization, is held elsewhere than at the seat of the organization, the government of the country extending its hospitality to the conference is responsible jointly with the secretariat of the organization for providing the necessary accommodations. In case of a single government taking the initiative of convoking a special conference on the national soil, this government assumes as a rule the entire responsibility for all the material arrangements.

In the early days of the League, the Assemblies of the League and the Labor Conferences met in halls which had not been specially built for the purpose. The sessions of the Assembly were held in the Salle de la Reformation and later in the Bâtiment Electoral, the Labor Conferences in the Kursal de Genève. In spite of the efforts of the local Swiss authorities, of the Secretariat of the League, and of the International Labor Office to make the best of such accommodations, these three halls were far from offering adequate facilities for the work of the con-

---

[38] The Swiss Government granted special facilities to delegations participating in the Disarmament Conference of 1932, in such matters as: (1) imports of furniture, (2) admission of motor cars, (3) telephonic and telegraphic communications.

ferences. While plenary meetings were held in the above-mentioned halls the meetings of the committees took place in the buildings of the Secretariat proper and the Labor Office where all the offices were located. This illustration is sufficient to indicate the complexity of the problems which had to be solved each year by the responsible services of the League. The difficulties encountered at Geneva during this period had, however, one good result: they prepared the ground for the planning of a very good permanent assembly hall in the new building of the League and they served as excellent training for the staffs of the Secretariat and the Labor Office which enabled them to solve the problems of needed accommodations for conferences outside Geneva. Rather than give a detailed description of the Assembly Hall at Geneva, some of the more important factors to bear in mind when organizing a conference might be pointed out. They are as follows:

1. Hall for plenary meetings.

The hall for plenary meetings must be large enough for seating not only the members of the conference, but also the necessary staff. In case of public meetings it must also offer sufficient accommodation for journalists and the public admitted to the meetings. Attention must be paid to the acoustics of the hall and to the light (both natural and artificial). The presence of precautionary measures against fire, as well as ventilation and heating facilities, must be checked carefully. Outside noise must not disturb meetings. The necessary furniture must be secured; delegates must have comfortable seats and desks on which to write. The comfort of delegates is, indeed, an important element in the success of a conference, for if the delegates are irritated by discomforts the work of the conference is bound to suffer. For large conferences a platform for the chairman and a rostrum for the speakers must be provided. A sufficient number of seats must be reserved for the experts and the secretaries accompanying the delegates and for the staff of the conference. As far as possible seats must be provided for journalists and the public, not in the hall itself but in galleries. Delegates, journalists, and public must be accommodated in such a way that all may be able to see and hear what transpires in the assembly hall. To improve the acoustics, a large hall must be equipped with devices for the amplification of sound.

2. Committee Rooms.

What has been said concerning the main hall, applies generally to committee rooms. There must be a sufficient number of them to accommodate several committees meeting simultaneously. They must be equipped with the necessary furniture, tables, chairs, rugs that will stifle noise, etc. As the members of the conference will spend long hours in these rooms, conditions must be provided that will be conducive to informal exchanges of thought and discussion. Smoking is always allowed in committee rooms (although often prohibited in the main hall); for this reason special attention must be paid to a good ventilation system. Doors must open and shut easily, for nothing disturbs a committee meeting more than the noise caused by the opening and shutting of doors by members of the staff who, owing to their secretarial duties, must enter or leave the committee room.

3. Offices.

The main hall, the committee rooms, and the offices provided for the chairman of the conference and the secretaries, must be close together. All the essential machinery of the conference should be housed under the same roof. Besides offices for the high officials of the secretariat, rooms must be provided for the interpreters, translators, stenographers, and typists, as well as for précis-writers, verbatim reporters, distributions officers, etc. The mimeographing department and the document service must have specially convenient accommodations. Further, there must be offices at the disposal of the secretary in charge of all the material arrangements and the secretary in charge of the liaison with the press. If sufficient space is available, offices must be put at the disposal of each delegation.

4. Lobby.

The rôle of the lobby during a conference is very important. Here delegates, experts, secretaries, and journalists meet freely, and it is important that the lobby and its annexes offer all facilities for the comfort and convenience of the conferees. A post office, a telegraph office, booths for local and long distance telephone calls, a banking counter, a newspaper and tobacco stand — all these facilities should be provided for the delegates and journalists. A bar and possibly a restaurant should be at the disposal of all who take part at the conference. Rest rooms and a first aid service should also be available. A special hall with the necessary desks should be provided for the journalists where they can draft and type their reports. It is also desirable that two or three rooms adjacent to the lobby be placed at the disposal of the delegates for receiving and interviewing outside visitors. A place should be reserved for the service in charge of the distribution and dispatch of the official documents of the conference, and it is important to have an information desk set up in a convenient place in the lobby. A notice board should also be provided, on which announcements concerning last-minute changes in the program of meetings and other important communications can be posted. If necessary, a map of the premises where the prospective conference is to meet should be printed and distributed to the conference members.

In the United States, the problem of housing a conference is relatively simple, since most of the big hotels have special accommodations for large conventions. In Europe, Latin America, and Asia the task of improvising adequate arrangements for housing a conference is often fraught with difficulties. Frequently, luxurious official premises are offered and must be accepted for reasons of courtesy; but only too often these quarters are very inconvenient for the work of the conference, and it is then the duty of the secretariat of the conference, by closely collaborating with the local authorities, to do its best under the circumstances, utilizing past experience which has been gained in the housing of conferences in places not exactly suitable for them.

DATE OF THE CONFERENCE

The date of the conference is usually fixed after the place of the conference has been selected. Sometimes, however, the date is fixed simultaneously with the place of the conference, or is decided upon before the place of meeting has been chosen.

(a) *Meetings of Standing Bodies of International Organizations.*

Generally the date of the periodical meetings of standing international bodies is set well in advance. Often the rules of procedure of the body contain a special provision dealing simultaneously with the place and the date of the meeting. Thus, the Rules of Procedure of the Assembly of the League (Rule I, paragraph 1) provide that: "The Assembly shall meet in general session every year at the seat of the League of Nations, commencing on the Monday which falls in the period September 10th to September 16th inclusive." The Labor Conference met traditionally on the first Thursday of June. The Rules of Procedure of the Council of the League provide for periodical ordinary sessions.[39]

The sessions of the standing committees of the League also took

[39] Originally, no fixed date was laid down for these meetings of the Council. Certain fixed periods were, however, very soon established. On August 31, 1923, the Council decided to hold thenceforward four ordinary sessions each year; in December, March, June, and September — i.e., at intervals of three months. On September 6, 1929, the Council adopted the system which was embodied in the Rules of Procedure of the Council and which made the interval between the sessions of the Council one of four months, except in the case of the third and fourth sessions held in succession during the Assembly.

place at dates fixed by regulations or tradition. Thus, the Permanent Mandates Commission met in May and October, the Advisory Committee on Traffic in Opium in May, etc. If no specific date is provided in the rules of procedure, the standing body often takes a decision at the end of its session concerning the date of the next session.

The authorization for holding extraordinary sessions is generally specifically provided for in the rules of procedure of the body; but in order to avoid any abuse the fulfilment of several conditions is often prescribed before calling an extraordinary session.[40]

Sometimes the rules of procedure are silent concerning the summoning of extraordinary sessions and it is tacitly agreed that in a case of emergency the body may be convoked by its chairman or by the secretary general of the organization. In such circumstances the members of the body ordinarily are consulted to secure their agreement regarding the extraordinary meeting.

(b) *Meetings of "ad hoc" Conferences.*

If an *ad hoc* conference is sponsored by a permanent international organization, the date of the conference is generally fixed by the policy-making body of the organization. It often occurs that the date is fixed in accordance with a proposal made by the special committee to which the preparatory work of the conference has been entrusted. The Preparatory Committee of the Disarmament Conference, however, refused to fix the date of the Conference, as proposed by the German delegation, stating that it was up to the Council to make such a decision.

[40] The Rules of Procedure of the Assembly of the League of Nations provide that (Rule I, paragraphs 2 and 3):

"2. Sessions may also be held at such times as the Assembly at a previous meeting decides, and at such times as the Council, by a majority vote, decides.

"3. If a Member of the League considers a session to be desirable, it may request the Secretary-General to summon a special session of the Assembly. The Secretary-General shall thereupon inform the other Members of the League of the request, and enquire whether they concur in it. If, within a period of one month from the date of the communication of the Secretary-General, a majority of the Members concur in the request, a special session of the Assembly shall be summoned."

Similarly Article I, paragraphs 1 and 2, of the Rules of Procedure of the Council of the United Nations Relief and Rehabilitation Administration provides:

"1. In accordance with Article III, section 2, of the Agreement, the Council shall be convened in regular session by the Central Committee not less than twice a year. It may be convened in special session whenever the Central Committee shall deem necessary, and shall be so convened within thirty days after the request therefor by one-third of the members of the Council. Such request shall be communicated to the Director General who shall transmit it forthwith to the Central Committee.

"2. The Director General, after consultation with the Central Committee, shall fix the time and place of the first meeting of each session of the Council and shall notify the member governments not less than sixty days in advance of a regular session and not less than three weeks in advance of a special session."

When a conference is convoked by a single government or by a group of governments, the date of the conference is set by the sponsoring authorities, the decision being reached on the basis of the same semi-official consultations through diplomatic channels as were employed for determining the place of the conference.

(c) *Circumstances to be Taken into Account in Setting the Date of a Conference.*

The date fixed for an international conference, whether a periodical gathering or a special meeting, must be that which is most convenient for the greatest possible number of delegates. It must interfere as little as possible with the work of other international or national bodies. It is desirable, too, that consideration be given to climatic conditions. Finally, the times of religious or national festivals, periods tradition-ally devoted to vacation, etc., must be taken into account. Thus, in fixing the ordinary session of the Assembly of the League during the month of September, three main considerations were the determining factors in reaching the decision: (1) September is a month during which the European parliaments are generally on vacation; (2) September is a month which follows the traditional summer vacation and precedes the renewal of national political activities in the autumn; (3) September is the best season at Geneva. Many delegates or members of com-missions had apprehensions about coming to Geneva during the winter when the terrible *bise* (north wind) blows. Thus the Council decided in 1928 to hold its winter session at Lugano, instead of Geneva, in order to spare the health of the German Foreign Minister, Dr. Strese-mann.

The date of the conference must fit into the general schedule of all the other projected meetings. It is the duty of the standing secretariat of an international organization to advise, in due course, the different bodies of the organization in order to eliminate any avoidable over-lapping of meetings. Indeed, care must be taken that the strain put on the secretariat by simultaneous meetings does not result in a lessen-ing of its efficiency. As a rule, no *ad hoc* conferences were summoned by the League simultaneously with the session of the Assembly.[41] A pro-vision of a resolution adopted by the Assembly of the League of Nations on September 25, 1931, stated that "The Council, in fixing the date for the convocation of a conference, shall endeavour, as far as possible, to avoid two League of Nations conferences being held simultaneously,

---

[41] Sometimes, *ad hoc* conferences were summoned immediately before the Assembly session (Inter-Governmental Conference for the Conclusion of an International Con-vention concerning the Use of Broadcasting in the Cause of Peace, September, 1936).

and to ensure the lapse of reasonable interval between two conferences." There are, of course, cases of emergency when a certain date must be chosen in spite of inconveniences.

(d) *Change of Date.*

When a date has been set, all efforts must be made to hold the meeting on the day fixed for it. Nothing is more inconvenient, both for the delegates and the secretariat, than a change of the date of the opening of a conference. As a matter of fact this was seldom done. The Rules of Procedure of the Assembly were silent concerning this point, but as far as the sessions of the Council were concerned, detailed rules existed. Thus, paragraph 5 of Article I of the Rules of Procedure of the Council stated:

The President of the Council, after consulting his colleagues and with the consent of the majority, may, where necessary, advance or retard the date of the opening of a session of the Council. The President may not, however, without the consent of all his colleagues, advance or retard by more than seven days the opening of an ordinary session.

The Council laid down detailed rules for the application of these provisions in a resolution which it adopted on January 11, 1935, as follows:

(*a*) Except in cases of real emergency, the President of the Council should not propose a change in the date fixed for a session of the Council if the session is already due to commence in five days.

(*b*) In the communication by which he consults his colleagues as to a change in the date of a session of the Council, the President should, if possible, state the new date proposed for the opening of the session or, if this is not possible, should indicate the earliest date at which the Council will be convened.

(*c*) Except in cases of real emergency, the President of the Council should give his colleagues at least twelve days' notice of the date which he proposes to substitute for the date originally fixed for a session of the Council.[42]

The care taken by the Council to draw up strict regulations concerning changes in the date of its session may be taken as proof of the difficulties which experience has shown to result from such changes.

15. DISPATCH OF SUMMONS

The next step, after fixing the place and the date of the conference, is the dispatch of the letters of invitation. The letters of invitation sent each year for the ordinary session of the Assembly of the League were of a very simple form, of which the following is an example:

[42] L.N., *Official Journal*, 1935, p. 88.

I have the honour, in accordance with Rules 1 and 3 of the Rules of Procedure of the Assembly of the League of Nations, to summon the Assembly to convene at Geneva at 11 A.M. on Monday, September 2nd, 1929.

(Signed) V. SCIALOJA

This letter was sent by the Secretary General of the League, on behalf of the Acting President of the Council, to all the Members of the League.

For Council meetings, a simpler procedure was in use. Paragraph 6 of Article 1 of the Rules of Procedure of the Council stated: "The Secretary-General shall give notice to the Members of the Council of the date at which a session is to begin, unless the session is to be held at a date provided by the present Rules or fixed by the Council." When the date of the session of the Council was provided by the Rules of Procedure or was fixed in advance by the Council, the Secretary General simply mailed to the members of the Council a copy of the agenda of the forthcoming session. The date and the hour of the opening of the session of the Council appeared at the top of the agenda. If the Secretary General had to give notification of a session to be convoked at a date not provided for by the Rules of Procedure, he generally sent a telegram to the members of the Council stating briefly by whom and why he had been requested to convoke the Council, and specifying the date of the opening of the Council session.

Among the standing committees of the League the practice of sending a copy of the agenda of the forthcoming session, mentioning the place and date of the meeting, in lieu of a more formal letter of invitation, was generally adopted. To avoid any misunderstanding, the Secretariat took the precaution to stamp the word "convocation" in large black letters, on the copy of the agenda, and to send it by registered mail.

In all the above-mentioned cases the authority for issuing the letter of invitation rests with the Secretary General acting by virtue of his own powers or on behalf of the President of a policy-making body of the organization.

The situation is more complicated in the case of *ad hoc* conferences or committees. In this contingency the letter of invitation must be more formal and more detailed.[43] It must state clearly whether the projected meeting is summoned under the auspices of an international

---

[43] This is also the practice of the International Conferences of American States. As an example, the invitation for the Seventh International Conference of American States sent by the Government of Uruguay is to be found as Appendix III, *infra*.

organization, or convoked by a single government or a group of governments. In addition to indicating the name of the conference or the committee and the date and place of the meeting, the letter of invitation may contain references to the decisions which led to the summoning of the meeting. The motives for the decisions may also be explained. Further information may be included concerning:

Number of delegates which each government is expected to send.
Names of the other governments invited.
Provisional agenda of the meeting.
Preparatory documentation.
Questions of finance (by whom financed and in what proportion).
Time limit for answering the invitation, etc.

In the case of a meeting composed of individuals sitting in their private capacity, the above procedure applies with certain modifications. Thus the form and the contents of the letter of invitation depend upon the character of the committee or the conference as well as upon that of the authority issuing the letter of invitation. In the case of an international organization, the authority is usually lodged in the secretary general; and in the case of a government, in the minister for foreign affairs. The letter of invitation sometimes takes the form of a communication drafted in the third person.

Similarly, the question to whom the letter of invitation shall be addressed depends on the practice evolved by each international organization or government and on the character of the conference. Obviously, for periodical gatherings convoked by international organizations, such as the Assemblies of the League of Nations, the International Labor Conferences, the International Conferences of American States, invitations must be sent to all member states. Invitations to non-member states, to observers, or to experts are extended only exceptionally.[44] In the case of *ad hoc* conferences summoned under the auspices of an international organization the situation is somewhat different, the range of invitees depending on the purpose and scope of the conference. Often non-member states are also invited. Non-member states invited to a conference held under the auspices of the League were as a rule designated *nominatim* in a Council resolution. In the case of conferences summoned at the initiative of a particular government or of a group of governments, the states initiating the gathering should be free "to invite such other states as they please, without being bound to invite all states having a possible interest in the subject

[44] See "Composition of Public Conferences," *infra*, pp. 68–69 and 75–77.

matter. The only rule in the matter that finds support in custom is that the invited states shall not impose the results of their deliberations upon other states against their will. Hence it is important that all states whose concurrent action is necessary to achieve a particular result should be given an opportunity to attend, or at least to adhere to the results." [45] While almost all the authors in the field of international law agree on the principle, examples of failure to observe this rule are, unfortunately, abundant.

It is outside the scope of this handbook to examine the different systems adopted for addressing the letters of invitation to a conference or a committee. The Secretariat of the League adopted the practice of sending the invitation directly to a member of a conference or a committee when such member was sitting in his personal capacity, and to the government concerned when the member was representing a government. But there were exceptions to this general rule. The Distribution Branch of the Secretariat of the League always kept an up-to-date list of addresses of recipients of such official correspondence. In doubtful cases, the Distribution Branch consulted the section of the Secretariat in charge of the preparation of the conference or of the committee meeting and, if necessary, the Central and the Legal Sections.

16. Staffing

In the case of a conference convoked at the initiative of a particular government, the competent department of the foreign office of the inviting government — and in the case of a conference summoned under the auspices of an international organization, the standing secretariat of that organization — has generally taken care of all the arrangements discussed above.

An international conference, however, must be provided with its own secretarial staff. The methods for supplying such a staff vary according to the procedure adopted in summoning the conference. For instance:

---

[45] Dunn, *op. cit.*, p. 200. Dr. Dunn, *ibid.*, p. 196, says that "The eligibility of political entities to representation in international conferences is in fact purely within the discretion of the governments initiating a conference." And in a footnote he adds, "Apart, of course, from any local constitutional limitation that would prevent a particular subdivision from participating in foreign intercourse, as exists, for instance, in the case of the various states of the United States." It seems that no such limitation would exist for the different republics which are the component parts of the Union of the Soviet Socialist Republics.

1. In the case of a conference summoned at the initiative of a particular government, that government generally furnishes the necessary secretarial staff.

2. In the case of a conference summoned at the initiative of a particular government, in conjunction with a group of states, or of a conference convoked by a group of states, the interested governments will jointly supply the secretarial staff of the conference.

3. The secretarial staff will be selected from among all the participating states.

4. In the case of a standing international organization, the secretarial staff of the conference will be supplied by the permanent secretariat of the organization.[46]

Obviously it is not always possible to make use of the fourth method; in which case, any of the first three methods may be resorted to. Several foreign offices have had considerable experience in organizing international gatherings; and they may be in a position to supply an excellent personnel for the secretariat of a conference. The degree of efficiency of an improvised secretariat of this kind depends, to a great extent, on its leadership.[47] It will not be forgotten that the Secretariat of the Paris Peace Conference was severely criticized by Harold Nicolson, who attributed its defects to the Secretary General of the Conference. "By some mischance M. Dutasta — a weak, flustered, surprised but not unamiable man — was chosen for this high position. . . . That supreme capacity for secretarial organisation, which is a by-product of the French genius, was not apparent at the Conference of Paris. . . ."[48]

Indeed, the rôle of the secretary general of a conference is of prime importance. It is comparable to that of a Chief of a General Staff, while the President of the Conference performs the duties of a Com-

[46] The Pan American conferences select their secretariat in accordance with the third method. However, the Eighth International Conference of American States, held at Lima in December, 1938, adopted the following resolution: "In order to unify the technical organization of the Secretariat of Pan American conferences, and the publication of their proceedings and agreements, The Eighth International Conference of American States Resolves: To recommend to the Governing Board of the Pan American Union the preparation of a project for the organization of a technical secretariat for the conferences, the services of which would be at the disposal of the Governments acting as host of the conferences, and which, during the interval between these meetings, would effect the uniform and coordinated publication, with suitable indices, of the proceedings and agreements of the conferences held under the auspices of the Pan American Union." (Resolution CIII.)

[47] According to an age-old custom a national of the state responsible for the convocation of a conference is usually selected as its secretary general.

[48] Harold Nicolson, *Peacemaking, 1919* (Boston and New York: Houghton, Mifflin Co., 1933), pp. 119–20.

mander in Chief. If the secretary general is qualified and if he has at his disposal a highly trained personnel, thoroughly experienced in the technique of the organization of international gatherings, he will be able to facilitate greatly the work of the conference. For this reason, even in the second or the third of the methods listed above, it frequently happens that the inviting powers ask for the assistance of a member of the secretariat of an international organization in the organizing of a proposed international conference. Thus, M. Aghnides, at that time Director of the Disarmament Section of the Secretariat of the League of Nations, was appointed Secretary General of three international conferences which were not held under the auspices of the League.[49]

Permanent international organizations with an experienced secretariat undoubtedly have the best trained personnel for giving technical assistance in the organization of an international conference. The practice of the League of Nations in this field is therefore of special value. The Covenant of the League of Nations stipulates that the Secretary General of the League shall be at the same time Secretary of the Assembly and the Council.[50] Likewise, the Standing Orders of the International Labor Organization provide that the Director of the International Labor Office shall be the Secretary General of the International Labor Conferences.

From the outset it was decided that the Secretary General of the League should be the secretary of all the League committees or bodies.[51] The same practice with respect to its committees was adopted by the International Labor Organization. It was also understood that the Secretary General should be the secretary of all the *ad hoc* conferences held under the auspices of the League. The Secretary General naturally delegated his powers, but he was, in the final analysis, responsible for the organization of the secretariat of all gatherings held under the auspices of the League. The Secretary General of the League and the Director of the International Labor Office were therefore in a position to exercise at all stages continuous influence upon the preparation and the work of all committees and conferences functioning under those organizations.[52]

---

[49] The Conference concerning the Turkish Straits, Montreux, 1936; the Conference concerning the Suppression of Capitulations in Egypt, Montreux, April, 1937; and the Conference on Security in the Mediterranean, Nyon, September, 1937.

[50] See Article 6, section 4, of the Covenant.

[51] An exception is the Permanent Opium Board.

[52] The Secretary General of the League was assisted in his task by the Deputy Secre-

The most elaborate arrangements were made each year in connection with the organization of the Secretariat of the Assembly of the League. According to its Internal Regulations and tradition, the Assembly appointed a Chairman, a General Committee (Bureau), an Agenda Committee, and a Credentials Committee. In addition, six or seven large committees were set up which dealt with the different items of the agenda. Finally, during the last years preceding World War II the Assembly appointed a Nominations Committee. To the Chairman and to each of these committees a secretary was assigned beforehand, the Secretary General himself acting as Secretary of the Nominations Committee. Numerous secretaries performed such duties for many years and therefore gained considerable experience in the work. Thus, for a period of seventeen years M. de Montenach acted as secretary to the chair [53] of the League Assembly and acquired a notable virtuosity in assisting the different chairmen of the Assembly. The secretaries of the large committees were directors or members of the different sections of the Secretariat specially concerned with the work of each of these committees. For instance, the secretary of the Fourth Committee dealing with the budget of the League was a member of the Treasury and the secretary of the Sixth dealing with political questions was a member of the Political Section.

The rôle of these secretaries (hereinafter called executive secretaries) is of paramount importance. On their experience, skill, and administrative abilities depends, in a great measure, the smooth functioning of the intricate machinery of an international conference. The executive secretaries must have a thorough knowledge of the questions discussed, and for this reason they must from the outset be associated with the preparatory work of the gathering.

It happened quite frequently that a committee of the Assembly would discuss a variety of questions. On the agenda of the Sixth Committee, for instance, figured for many years the subjects of Minorities, Mandates, and Intellectual Cooperation. Obviously, the secretary of the Committee was unable to cope with all these problems. He acted chiefly in an administrative capacity, and was assisted in the technical work by officials of the respective sections charged with the handling of such questions.

---

taries General and the Under Secretaries General. Their duties were chiefly of a political character and they seldom intervened in the technical or administrative side of the preparation or of the functioning of the conferences.

[53] In the practice of the International Labor Conference the secretary of the chair is called "clerk" of the Conference.

All the arrangements described above could easily be applied, *mutatis mutandis*, to other large conferences. Here again the existence of a standing international organization able to provide secretarial facilities and services assumes signal importance. Its permanent staff is already trained for the tasks required for a smooth-running conference. If additional personnel must be hired, the permanent officials can guide and advise the temporary staff.

A rapid review of the kind of administrative personnel needed for a large international conference (whether the conference be at Geneva or elsewhere) may not be out of place. As soon as an appropriate date for a conference was decided upon in the League, the section of the Secretariat primarily concerned with the proposed gathering filled out a questionnaire [54] stating, *inter alia:* (1) the date and place of the meeting; (2) the approximate duration of the conference; (3) the number of delegates expected; (4) an approximate estimate of the number of committees and subcommittees to be created; and (5) the manner of recording the minutes. This questionnaire was sent to the Director of Internal Administration. The Director of Internal Administration and the Central Section saw to it that the various meetings scheduled [55] did not conflict with one another. As a general rule no other meetings were allowed to take place while the Assembly was in session. According to the data supplied by the questionnaire the Director of Internal Administration, in agreement with the heads of the different Internal Services, selected the personnel required for the planned conference.[56] Generally this personnel included:

Précis-writers and Translators. In the Secretariat of the League the two services of précis-writing and translating were combined. A translator was often obliged to perform the duties of a précis-writer or vice versa. Both types of officials generally specialized in certain fields of activity in the League, and consequently preference for attending the meeting was given to the one who was more intimately conversant with the problems to be discussed at that meeting. As a rule two précis-writers were attached to each League committee, one for the French language and the other for the English.[57]

[54] Of course, no such questionnaire was required in the case of the Assembly or Council, for the arrangements there were more definite.

[55] The Information Section of the Secretariat of the League published every fortnight a *calendar* giving a list of all forthcoming meetings of the League scheduled for the next two or three months.

[56] The relevant extract of the *Office Rules* of the Secretariat of the League is given in Appendix IV, *infra*.

[57] The practice of the International Labor Office is slightly different. The com-

Interpreters. These must be highly qualified officials and they should possess a thorough knowledge of the questions to be discussed. According to Mr. Jesu Sanz, professor at the Ecole Normale of Barcelona, who made a serious study in Geneva of the work and the aptitudes of parliamentary interpreters, knowledge is not enough. An interpreter must in addition possess the following talents and qualifications: rapidity of comprehension and association of ideas; intuitive perception; a good voice and clear pronunciation; the ability to express himself with facility and ease; imagination and observation; a good memory for words and ideas. The interpreter must be capable of more than ordinary concentration. Like the orator, he composes his discourse. His task is not to give a textual transcript but a synthesized transposition. The interpreter must have presence of mind, poise, and emotional self-control. Excellent translators have failed as interpreters because of congenital timidity and lack of emotional control.[58] Interpreters of the Secretariat of the League and of the International Labor Office are unusually capable and skilful individuals. Sometimes they succeed in transforming what might be termed a dull and colorless speech into a brilliant piece of eloquence. The duties of an interpreter during a conference are quite strenuous. For this reason it is advisable that at least one interpreter for each language be attached to each committee.

Stenographers and Typists. If the recording of the discussions of the conference requires verbatim records, it is necessary to include special stenographers in the staff ("parliamentary" stenographers; court reporters). In the interest of a smooth-working conference the parliamentary stenographers must be sufficiently numerous (for each language in use) so that they need take notes only for fifteen minutes at a

mittee secretaries perform the duties of the précis-writers in addition to certain administrative functions. As a rule there are three secretaries (*secrétaires au procès-verbal*) for each of the main committees of the Conference: one French-speaking, one English-speaking, and one Spanish-speaking. The rôle of the "executive secretaries" of the League is performed by one or several Representatives of the Director attached to each committee of the Labor Conference. On the whole the I.L.O. system works as well as the system which was in force in the League.

The United Nations Relief and Rehabilitation Administration makes use of a system similar to the I.L.O. practice. However, the committee secretaries, who are senior members of the staff of the Bureau or Division specially concerned with the work of the committee, are relieved of the burden of taking notes during the meeting, this being done by stenographers. In large committees one or two assistant secretaries are appointed in addition to the chief secretary. As a rule the Representative of the Director General is one of the Deputy Directors General or the Director of the Division specially concerned with the work of the committee. More personnel is necessary with the system employed by the Relief and Rehabilitation Administration, but the expense is still less than in the practice of the League or the Labor Organization since only one language is used.

[58] *Anals d'orientació professional,* Year 4, No. 4 (Barcelona, 1931).

time and then may be replaced by another team. Like the interpreters and the précis-writers, the parliamentary stenographers must have some knowledge of the questions to be discussed, or at least a very good training in parliamentary work. Thus, the League of Nations often asked for the help of the stenographers of the French Chamber of Deputies when these stenographers were available. Besides parliamentary stenographers, a sufficient number of regular stenographers and typists must be available for each of the languages in use. Their number, varying in accordance with the importance of the conference, will sometimes be very large. They must be organized in separate teams in order to permit shift-work, and must be placed under the orders of a single officer responsible to the administration for all the arrangements made.

A sufficient number of mimeograph operators is also needed to assure the efficient operation of this very useful service.

Officers of the Distribution Service. It is the task of the distribution branch to supply the members of the conference with the printed or mimeographed documentation. In the case of a conference held outside the headquarters of the permanent international organization, a sufficient number of all important reference documents must be shipped to the meeting place by the Distribution Service. Clerks of that service must be attached to each committee to supply the members of the conference with documents not only during the meetings but also, when necessary, at their personal quarters. The staff of the Distribution Branch of the League Secretariat was highly efficient: documents printed during the night were distributed early in the morning to all the members of the conference at their homes or at their hotels. This of course is possible only by the organization of teamwork.

A *Document Officer* is selected who is in charge of the liaison between all the services enumerated above and the secretaries of the chair and of the committees. The duties of this official, who is either a member of the section primarily concerned with the conference in session (for instance, for the Disarmament Conference, the Secretary of the Disarmament Section), or an official selected *ad hoc*, are important. To the Document Officer are handed in all the proposals, amendments, and reports to be translated and duplicated. In the League practice of the past the task was usually entrusted to a woman official who was responsible for timing the translation, the typing, printing, and distribution of all documents. Each evening she gave to the Distribution Branch a list of the documents to be distributed the next morning.

Archivists. In a very large conference it is useful to have, in addition, one or two secretaries especially entrusted with registering all incoming documents for their proper classification in the archives of the conference. If it is not possible to secure the services of trained archivists, the registry of the conference may be entrusted to an assistant of the Document Officer or to a senior clerk of the Distribution Service.

Ushers and Messengers. The number of ushers and messengers required must be proportionate to the size of the conference. Some of the ushers must be specially trained for emergency tasks, such as extinguishing fires, or administering first aid. They should be placed under the orders of a "supervisor" who is responsible for all the arrangements in the main hall, the committee rooms, and the lobby. He takes care, in particular, that signs indicating the names of each country are placed on the desks in the assembly hall and in committee rooms, and that the necessary writing paper, pencils, etc., are supplied to the delegates. The ushers should also control admission cards issued to the delegates and their collaborators and to the public. If the conference is held outside the usual seat of the organization it is highly desirable that at least the supervisor with two or three of the most experienced ushers be included in the staff taken from headquarters in order to train and direct the additional locally recruited personnel.

In the Secretariat of the League of Nations all the above-mentioned personnel, from the précis-writers to the ushers, were under the orders of the Director of Internal Administration. In practice, however, the heads of the services of précis-writing, translation, typewriting, and reporting, as well as those of the Distribution Branch, were allowed considerable liberty of action, and most of the arrangements were made directly between them and the "executive secretaries" or the Document Officer of the conference.[59] The Director of the Internal Administration intervened only when agreement could not be reached. Most of the time, however, he and his assistants devoted their efforts to supervising purely material arrangements such as housing and the upkeep of conference quarters, distribution of admission cards, and maintenance of order.

The maintenance of order is always a delicate question since it involves the relationship between the chair and the secretariat of the conference and the local police authorities. A governmental interna-

[59] In recent times, the précis-writing, translation, typewriting, and reporting, as well as the mimeograph services, were all supervised by the "Chief of the Document Service." This arrangement resulted in a more rational utilization of the personnel of these services.

tional conference as a rule enjoys diplomatic immunity. The local police may not enter the meeting rooms of the conference without specific
authorization from the chair or from the secretary general of the conference acting on behalf of the chairman. Police in civilian clothes are,
however, often admitted at least to the lobby and the Assembly Hall.
Sometimes private detectives are hired. In any event, arrangements
concerning police protection must be worked out in collaboration with
the local authorities. In order to safeguard all the rights and privileges
of the conference the representatives of the chair and of the secretary
general will have to be possessed of tact and firmness.

Another task entrusted in the League of Nations practice to the
assistants of the Director of Internal Administration was the organization of an *Information Office*. This office has always been a weak spot of
the otherwise excellent arrangements made by the League for international conferences. Indeed, the Information Office (not to be confounded
with the services of the Information Section or Public Relations Department) was chiefly an office for the distribution of admission cards;
it also served as a "lost and found" bureau and a place where information could be secured on hotel and restaurant accommodations. Information of a more important character, such as the name of an official
of the Secretariat competent to deal with a specific question, could not
as a rule be obtained through the Information Office. Evidently, it was
an unwise practice to entrust the Information Office to officials who,
though perfectly willing to be helpful, and unusually kind and courte-
ous, lacked a thorough knowledge of the intricate machinery of the
Secretariat and of an international conference. For this reason delegates
who were seeking information of a technical nature were prone to ignore
the Information Office and to rely instead upon their fellow-countrymen
within the Secretariat, or on the members of the Central or Legal
Section. Undoubtedly, a well-informed official placed at the head of the
Information Office would have facilitated both the work of the delegates and the Secretariat.

Another shortcoming of the Secretariat was the absence of an organized *Protocol Service*. There were, of course, political reasons for this
situation. Nevertheless, the lack of such a service often gave rise to
serious drawbacks. A protocol service had to be improvised for special
occasions, and sometimes an official of the Central Section or the Political Section or even of the Internal Administration acted as *chef du
protocole*. This meant unexpected responsibilities without proper preliminary arrangements having been made. A much better procedure is

to select in advance an official who has a thorough knowledge of international etiquette and to entrust to him all questions of protocol during
the preparation and the progress of the conference.

Arrangements should also be made for the services of a *physician*
who must be available immediately in the event of an emergency.

The establishment of a *press-relations service* is of the utmost importance. Details regarding this service will be given in the section
dealing with the question of publicity in relation to meetings of the
conference.

When the conference is held outside headquarters, an official must
be responsible for all arrangements pertaining to the care of the personnel during the journey to the place of meeting. He is responsible not
only for tickets, passports, and customs formalities, but also for registering official luggage and looking after its safe arrival. Important documents must never be checked as baggage, but should be entrusted to a
reliable official who will be held personally responsible for them. A
similar procedure must be employed regarding the keys of official
luggage. Cooperation of local authorities is generally easily secured.
Unless adequate arrangements are made in advance, confusion and
difficulties invariably arise.

It is important that international conferences have at their disposal
adequate *library* facilities. As Miss Helen Lawrence Scanlon, Librarian
of the Carnegie Endowment for International Peace, points out, "The
inclusion of a reference library within the facilities offered the delegates, while not revolutionary, is certainly noteworthy. One is im-
pressed by the almost complete absence of the word library in studies
dealing with international conferences. . . . If meetings are held in
cities with adequate library facilities a special conference library is not
necessary. For example, the Washington Conference on the Limitation
of Armaments had at its disposal the library resources of Washington.
On the other hand, in planning the arrangements for the United Nations Conference on Food and Agriculture, held at Hot Springs in 1943,
the Department [of State] recognized that a special library would be
required." [60] Similarly, a special library was organized for the First
Council Session of the United Nations Relief and Rehabilitation Administration held at Atlantic City, New Jersey, in November–December, 1943, and on a smaller scale, since the local conditions were more

---

[60] Helen Lawrence Scanlon, "The Library of the First Council Session, United
Nations Relief and Rehabilitation Administration," *Special Libraries*, Vol. 35 (1944),
pp. 166–69.

favorable, for the Second Session of this Council held at Montreal in September, 1944. The League of Nations Secretariat and the International Labor Office provided excellent library service for the delegates and the staff of international conferences held in Geneva. Since League of Nations and International Labor Conferences were as a rule held in Geneva, and since sessions of the League Council and the Governing Body of the International Labor Office, when held outside Geneva, took place generally in a capital, the problem of setting up an *ad hoc* library service did not arise except in a very few cases.

When it is necessary to build up a special library service for an international conference, it is advisable that such a service should be separated from the document service and that it should be run by specialized librarians. Publications should include works on international organizations in general and on special problems dealt with by the conference. In addition, general encyclopedias, biographical, historical, and geographical dictionaries, as well as bilingual or multilingual dictionaries, and map collections when required, must be assembled.

It has been recently recognized that it is very useful to have a *historian* attached to every important international gathering, who can record with accuracy the preparation and proceedings of the conference, having access not only to public information but also to official documents which are not otherwise disclosed immediately to the public.

17. BUDGETING

Conferences involve expenditure. In the case of periodical meetings of permanent international organizations some of the disbursements of the conference are provided for in the general budget of the organization. Most of the personnel is carried on its payroll as standing officials, and expenditures such as rent of premises, lighting, heating, etc., likewise form part of the regular budget.

In the League, appropriations for conferences were as a rule divided into two items: (1) meetings of the conference; (2) printing expenses. For the purpose of the budget of the League the expenses figuring under the first item (meetings of the conference) were not subdivided. For instance, in the case of the Disarmament Conference, the amount shown alongside the item "meetings of the conference" was as high as one million Swiss francs. It was in this manner that conference budgets were presented to the Assembly for approval. Before establishing this lump sum the Treasury of the League invariably made a detailed study of the estimates by breaking them down into a series of subitems.

To illustrate the kind of preliminary work falling upon the Treasury, the following items of expense for a conference held outside the seat of the organization may be mentioned:

1. Subsistence allowances to delegates. Provisions on this count are made only if the delegates to a conference are indemnified by the international agency. In the case of intergovernmental conferences the costs of delegations fall generally upon the sending government.[61]

2. Traveling expenses of delegates. The rules and provisions governing traveling expenses are practically identical with those regarding subsistence allowances (see above, 1).

3. Special compensation to delegates. As stated above, all expenses of governmental delegates are as a rule paid by their governments. Nevertheless, it sometimes happens that an international organization will pay certain compensation to the members of a conference held at a place far from the seat of the organization. These payments may take the form of a special salary or of outfit allowances, etc.

4. Special compensation to the chairman of the conference. The chairman of a conference, even if he receives an allowance from his own government in his capacity as a delegate to the conference, may at times also receive a special compensation from the international organization. This may take the form of an appropriation for entertainment expenses.

[61] F. P. Walters, former Director of the Political Section and Under Secretary General of the League of Nations, discussing the question of subsistence allowances and traveling expenses paid to delegates to the League, points out that: "the practice of the League was far from being consistent in this matter. Thus the expenses of the Delegates to the Governing Body of the International Labour Office were paid from the League Budget, while those of Delegates to its annual Conference were borne by their Governments. The cost of Delegations to the Council, Assembly, and all Conferences was borne by the Governments, but in regard to the various standing committees the practice varied. Naturally those such as the Mandates Commission which were composed of individual experts had their expenses paid from League funds, while those which were composed of Government representatives were regularly but not invariably paid for by the Governments concerned." In Mr. Walter's mind the proper course in the future "would be to include in the League budget appropriations to cover the travelling cost of a certain number of Delegates from every Member for each meeting of the Assembly and the I.L.O. Conference; and to do the same for Council meetings and meetings of the Governing Body of the I.L.O. for those States which are Members or are invited to attend. The same principle should be applied to all the standing committees of both organisations, and these committees should be enlarged so as to give all members a chance to take part in them at reasonably frequent intervals." *Op. cit.*, pp. 11–12. It seems, however, that the trend has been recently in the opposite direction. Article III, Section 7 of the Agreement of the United Nations Relief and Rehabilitation Administration provides that "The travel and other expenses of members of the Council and of members of its committees shall be borne by the governments which they represent."

Moreover, the chairman of a conference is generally entitled to a private secretary, whose salary is included in the budget of the conference.

5. Subsistence allowances for the permanent staff.

6. Traveling expenses for the permanent staff.

7. Outfit allowances for the permanent staff in the case of a conference held in a remote place.

8. Allowances for life insurance premiums for the delegates and the staff, if the conference is held in a remote or dangerous place.

9. Luggage.

10. Insurance of luggage.

11. Rent of premises in those cases where no free quarters are offered.

12. Lighting, heating, cleaning (if no service is provided).

13. Motor cars (sometimes also provided as a free service).

14. Postage, cables, telephone.

15. Temporary personnel hired on the spot. For instance, stenotypists, ushers, messengers.

16. Purchase of books, newspapers, furniture, typewriters, stationery, etc.

17. Entertainment fund.

18. Miscellaneous. To these items must be added the printing expenses, which in some cases may be considerable.

If the conference is held in a remote place the allowances and compensations of the secretarial staff must be estimated on a more generous basis. Conditions of life — for instance, in the Far East — often require that the personnel of an international agency maintain a high living standard. The prestige of the secretariat and of the institution itself may be involved. Sufficient allowances for traveling and housing expenses must be provided to enable the personnel, even in the category of stenographers, to travel in first-class compartments on boats and railways and to live in first-rate hotels.[62] All expenses must, of course, be carefully supervised and kept within the limits of budgetary appropriations. A treasury official of the international organization should therefore be detailed to the conference for this purpose. In the case of a small conference it will be sufficient to make one of the members of the secretariat an *ad hoc* comptroller. Such an arrangement is not fully satisfactory unless this official possesses some knowledge of bookkeeping and is

[62] The Rules pertaining to Traveling and Removal Expenses and Subsistence Allowances (Appendix III (paragraph 13), *Staff Regulations* of the Secretariat of the League of Nations) specifically state that "A secretary travelling with his Chief will be entitled to travel in the same conditions as the latter if required to work during the journey. . . ."

familiar with the problems of converting appropriations or payments into foreign currencies.

18. NECESSITY OF PREPARATION; DANGER OF OVER-PREPARATION

The success of an international conference depends to a great extent upon the type of preparation described in the foregoing pages. For meetings held under the auspices of the League and the International Labor Organization, this preparatory work was in later years facilitated by the existence of permanent secretarial bodies. A great number of questions were settled as a matter of routine: trained personnel was available, preparatory documents were drafted, printed, and distributed without major difficulties; housing problems were simplified, etc. Emphasis has been placed on the skill acquired by standing committees of the League or of the International Labor Organization in preparing draft conventions with the aid of the Secretariat of the League or of the International Labor Office. The same advance arrangements and preparations are needed for international conferences held under the auspices of a particular state or a group of states.

For such conferences preliminary negotiations must be made through the regular diplomatic channels rather than through the agency of the secretariat. As for material arrangements, these must often be improvised by the states, since they lack the established facilities and machinery of a permanent secretariat. The material arrangements of the Secretariat of the League of Nations and of the International Labor Organization were almost perfect. Long-range experience enabled the Secretariat of the League to codify, so to speak, all the essential provisions concerning the material arrangements of the Assembly Meetings. These provisions were regularly published in the first issue of the "*Assembly Journal*."[63]

In addition to the information so published, an *Official Guide* was often circulated to the delegations at the Assembly sessions and at the important *ad hoc* conferences convened under the auspices of the League of Nations. Sometimes these Guides furnished very detailed information concerning material arrangements made for the gathering. For instance, the *Official Guide* prepared for the Disarmament Conference in

---

[63] As an example, the first issue of the "Journal of the Nineteenth Session of the Assembly" is reproduced as Appendix V, *infra*. Compare the League arrangements with those made for the Seventh International Conference of American States (Appendix VI, *infra*). For more details concerning the "*Assembly Journal*" of the League, see *infra*, p. 154, n.

1932 was a booklet of thirty-seven pages.[64] As a rule, an *Official Guide* containing information concerning the arrangements made for the session is distributed to the members of the International Labor Conference. The Guide prepared for the session held in Philadelphia in 1944 had a very attractive covering page.

There is a danger, however, that the political or technical preparations, or the combination of both, may unduly delay the summoning of the conference or tend to force decisions on the conference. Without going into detail, it may be mentioned that there was much criticism of the endless discussions at the Preparatory Commission for the Disarmament Conference. Suffice it to say here that it was in session from May, 1926, to December, 1930. Obviously, the subject was complicated and the aims of the projected Conference of utmost importance. Nevertheless, it may be questioned whether the delay in convoking the Conference was due only to the complexity of the problem, or whether, for reasons of national policy, some governments did not prolong purposely the work of the Preparatory Commission.

Another example is seen in the preparations for the Conference for Limiting the Manufacture and Regulating the Distribution of Narcotic

---

[64] The Table of Contents of the *Guide* was as follows:
I. GENERAL ARRANGEMENTS. (A) *Plenary Meetings of the Conference:* 1. Entrances; 2. Instructions for Motor Traffic; 3. Inside Arrangements. (B) *Committee Meetings:* 1. Entrances; 2. Instructions for Motor Traffic; 3. Inside Arrangements; 4. Publicity of Committees. (C) *President and General Committee.* (D) *Secretariat:* 1. Secretariat Offices; 2. Allotment of the Work of the Conference. (E) *Library.* (F) *Printing and Publishing Department.* (G) *Photographs.* (H) *Local Facilities for the Conference:* 1. Genevese Organization Committee for the Conference; 2. Association des Intérêts de Genève.
II. SPECIAL INFORMATION FOR THE DELEGATIONS. (A) *Members of the Delegations:* 1. Credentials; 2. Names of Delegates, Deputy-Delegates and Experts; 3. Admission Cards. (B) *Arrangements for Delegations:* 1. Languages and Translations; 2. Minutes; 3. Receipt of Documents; 4. Distribution of Documents; 5. Journal of the Conference. (C) *Customs Facilities.* (D) *Telegrams.* (E) *Telephone Service.* (F) *Wireless Telegraphy.* (G) *Postal Arrangements.* (H) *Travel Office.* (I) *Tickers.* (J) *Cars.*
III. SPECIAL INFORMATION FOR THE PRESS. (A) *Admission Cards.* (B) *Press Arrangements:* 1. Plenary Meetings of the Conference; 2. Committee Meetings. (C) *Telegrams:* 1. Press Telegrams; 2. Handing-in of Telegrams and Payment; 3. Drafting of Press Telegrams; 4. Teleprinters. (D) *Telephone Service:* 1. Priority; 2. Time-Limit for Calls and Payments. (E) *Wireless Telegraphy:* 1. Press Wireless Service; 2. Broadcast Reports. (F) *Cinema.* (G) *Photographs.* (H) *Broadcasting.* (I) *Tickers, Postal Service, and Travel Office.*
IV. SPECIAL INFORMATION FOR THE PUBLIC. (A) *Admission Cards.* (B) *Public Entrances.* (C) *Rules.* (D) *International Organizations.* (E) *Sale of Publications and Photographs.*
ANNEXED PLANS: I. *Salle du Conseil Général:* Entrances, Circulation, and Parking of Cars. II. *Salle du Conseil Général; Inside-Arrangements.* III. *Committee Building:* Entrances, Circulation, and Parking of Cars. IV. *Committee Building:* Lower Ground Floor. V. *Committee Building:* Upper Ground Floor. VI. *Plan of Reading-Room.* L.N. Document Conf.D.46.

Drugs, held in 1931. The most important manufacturing countries held a Preparatory Conference in London in 1930 and framed a scheme, which was elaborated by the Advisory Committee on Traffic in Opium, for the future production of narcotic drugs based on a quota system. This scheme was open to the criticism that it would perpetuate the privileged position of these countries and was therefore rejected by the Conference, which resolved itself into a technical committee and worked out a convention based upon completely different principles.

Thus, psychological contingencies must not be disregarded in preparing a conference. It may at times be advisable to speed the preparation of a conference in order to hold it under the most auspicious conditions, and it is often a wise policy to allow the parties concerned liberty of action rather than to force the issue by presenting too rigid a scheme which would be the cause of serious friction during the conference.

PART II

ORGANIZING — DIRECTING — COORDINATING

The first meetings of a conference are generally devoted to the organization of the gathering proper. The essential organs are created and the machinery of the conference starts functioning. This work must be directed and coordinated.

As a rule, the task of creating the organs of the conference falls upon the conference itself; the direction and coordination of the work of the conference is incumbent upon the Chair and the steering committee or Bureau. The secretary general of the conference assists the conference in the creation of the necessary organs; and he assists the Chair and the Bureau in directing and coordinating the work of the conference. Since the boundary lines of the three processes are not clearly defined, a certain amount of overlapping is unavoidable. Frequently, steps arc taken for the organization of a conference before the conference actually takes place. And as the conference progresses the organization is continually perfected by the conference itself, and by the Chair and the steering committee — all assisted by the secretary general. Similarly, during sessions situations may arise which will call for new methods of direction and coordination. The interrelation of the three processes will become clearer upon studying the organs, procedures, and functions of international conferences. It will also become clear that in an international meeting the functions of the leader, the director, and the supervisor cannot always be separated.

Parts II and III of this handbook are devoted to the study of the interrelation of the three processes; Part II dealing more specifically with the organs of an international conference and Part III with problems of procedure which may arise during the meetings of an international gathering.

Organs of International Conferences

The most important organ of the conference is the conference itself sitting in plenary meeting. Consequently, the composition of international conferences must be investigated first.

19. COMPOSITION OF PUBLIC CONFERENCES

As has been pointed out at the beginning of this study, the composition of international public conferences varies extensively, and a purely governmental representation is not an absolute criterion for this kind of conference.[1] A study of the composition of international public conferences would by itself comprise a bulky volume, and for even a mere enquiry into the composition of the conferences held under the auspices of the League of Nations and the International Labor Organization a lengthy monograph would be required. For this reason only the most important characteristics of the composition of the Assembly and the Council of the League, of the International Labor Conferences and of the Governing Body of the International Labor Office, and of the *ad hoc* international conferences held under the auspices of these institutions will be studied below. Brief reference will also be made to the International Conferences of American States and the Council of the United Nations Relief and Rehabilitation Administration.

Space is lacking here for a study of the Congresses of the International Postal Union,[2] in which representatives of certain protectorates and colonies take part with the same rights as the delegates of sovereign states, and of the Permanent Committee of the Office International d'Hygiène Publique, in which certain protectorates and colonies have full membership.

ASSEMBLY OF THE LEAGUE

The pertinent provisions of the Covenant of the League read as follows:

The Assembly shall consist of Representatives of the Members of the League. (Article 3, paragraph 1.)

At meetings of the Assembly, each Member of the League shall have one vote, and may have not more than three Representatives. (Article 3, paragraph 4.)

The relevant provisions of the Rules of Procedure of the Assembly were an amplification of the principles laid down in the Covenant. Their purpose was to regulate the appointment and the rights of substitute representatives and to provide for the possible appointment of deputy delegates and technical advisers. The text follows:

RULE 5. — 1. Each Member shall communicate to the Secretary-General, if

[1] See *supra*, pp. 12–13.
[2] For a study of this question, see Benjamin Akzin, "Membership in the Universal Postal Union," *American Journal of International Law*, Vol. 27 (1933), pp. 651–74.

possible one week before the date fixed for the opening of the session, the names of its representatives, of whom there shall be not more than three. The names of substitute-representatives may be added. . . .

RULE 6. — 1. In addition to the substitute-representatives mentioned in paragraph 1 of Rule 5, the representatives of a Member of the League attending the Assembly, acting together as a delegation, may appoint substitutes. Any such appointment shall be communicated in writing to the President.

2. A substitute-representative appointed by a Member of the League may take the place of a representative without nomination by the representatives.

3. A substitute-representative or substitute may take the place of a representative who is absent from a meeting of the Assembly, or is temporarily prevented from taking part in its deliberations, but, if the representative is present at the meeting, the substitute-representative or substitute is only entitled to assist him.

4. A delegation may appoint for service on a committee a deputy or technical adviser other than those referred to in the above paragraphs of this Rule; but a deputy or adviser so appointed shall not be eligible for appointment as Chairman or Rapporteur, or for a seat in the Assembly.

A detailed study of the composition of the delegations to the Assembly may not be attempted here. Suffice it to say that they frequently consisted of highly placed officials, dignitaries, or parliamentary leaders. Even the heads of state (like the Emperor of Ethiopia or the President of the Republic of Switzerland) at one time led their delegations. Sometimes, however, states were represented by individuals holding very modest positions, such as that of vice consul, etc.

The representatives were classified according to their duties in the Assembly, and not in consideration of the position they occupied in their own countries. Thus, for example, in the "List of Delegates and Members of Delegations" of the nineteenth ordinary session of the Assembly of the League of Nations (1938) the representatives of the member states were classified under the following headings: Delegate, Substitute Delegate, Assistant Delegate, Adviser, Technical Adviser, Legal Adviser, Expert, Assistant Expert, Secretary General, Assistant Secretary General, Secretary, Assistant Secretary, Private Secretary, Press Officer, and "Rédacteur."

The size of the delegations at any one session of the Assembly varied from forty to forty-five members for the British and the French delegations to two members for the delegations from Liberia or Luxemburg.

There is only one case on record where a representative of a non-member state was permitted to sit in a plenary meeting of the Assembly, and that was at a meeting convoked for the election of a judge to the Permanent Court of International Justice. But in 1931, the Assembly invited several non-member states to send representatives to the Third

Committee of the Assembly in order "to assist in an advisory capacity in the Third Committee's discussions on the resolution relating to an armaments truce." [3] More often representatives of standing or *ad hoc* committees of the League were invited as technicians to attend committee meetings of the Assembly. Thus, M. Loudon, Chairman of the Preparatory Commission for the Disarmament Conference, was invited in 1931 to sit in the Third Committee of the Assembly. In 1938, representatives of the Financial and Economic Committees attended the meetings of the Second Committee. A Committee of the Assembly might even invite representatives of semipublic organizations to appear. In 1933, the Secretary General of the Penal and Penitentiary Commission took part in the discussion of the Fifth Committee.

COUNCIL OF THE LEAGUE

Under the Covenant, the Council comprised two kinds of members: permanent members, consisting of the Great Powers, and non-permanent members elected by the Assembly for a limited period.

(a) *Permanent Members*.

The Covenant provided for two categories of permanent members: In the first were the powers described in Article 4, paragraph 1, as the "Principal Allied and Associated Powers"; these were five in number — the United States of America, the British Empire, France, Italy, and Japan. The United States, as is well known, did not occupy the seat reserved for her. The second category included the powers to which the Council and Assembly conjointly were authorized to grant a permanent seat on the Council (Article 4, paragraph 2). A seat was created for Germany on September 8, 1926, and another for the Union of the Soviet Socialist Republics on September 18, 1934.

Certain members of the League demanded, without success, the creation of permanent seats for themselves. Thus, Brazil, having failed to obtain satisfaction, gave notice of withdrawal on June 10, 1926.

(b) *Non-permanent Members*.

Non-permanent seats were created under the same conditions as permanent seats (Article 4, paragraph 2), that is, subject to agreement between the Council and the Assembly.

Article 4, paragraph 1, provided that non-permanent members should "be selected by the Assembly from time to time in its discretion."

The Assembly adopted, first in recommendations and subsequently

[3] L.N., *Official Journal*, Special Supplement No. 93, p. 100.

in actual practice, a system designed to ensure that the Council should always represent the various parts or regions of the world and the different races, religions, and civilizations.

Article 4 of the Covenant provided for four non-permanent members. This number was increased to six in 1922, to nine in 1926, to ten in 1933, and to eleven by the creation of a further provisional seat in 1936. Article 1, paragraph 1, of the Rules adopted by the Assembly on September 15, 1926, fixed the term of office of non-permanent members at three years. These Rules provided for the renewal of the Council by thirds by the election of three of its members each year. Under certain conditions a retiring member could be reelected. Nevertheless, the number of members reelected was limited to the extent that no more than three so elected could sit on the Council at any one time. The Rule of September 15, 1926, provided also that the Assembly should be empowered to decide at any time, by a two-thirds majority, to proceed to a new election of all the non-permanent members of the Council.

Article 4, paragraph 6, of the Covenant provided that, at meetings of the Council, each member of the League represented on the Council should have one vote, and might have not more than one representative. If, during a meeting of the Council, a designated representative was temporarily absent an alternate automatically took his place; this alternate being sometimes a secretary. The unwritten rule was, however, that a seat at the Council table should never be empty during a meeting.

Apart from the representatives of the states which were either permanent or non-permanent members of the Council, other representatives might be called upon from time to time to sit as members of the Council. Several cases can be distinguished:

(a) *The case covered by Article 4, paragraph 5, of the Covenant.* This article reads:

Any Member of the League not represented on the Council shall be invited to send a Representative to sit as a Member at any meeting of the Council during the consideration of matters specially affecting the interests of that Member of the League.

In such an instance, an invitation was sent to the state concerned. The latter sat with the Council and enjoyed the same rights as a regular member of the Council, that is to say, the representative in question took part in the discussion and in the voting.

On several occasions the Council examined the nature of the interests justifying the issuance of the invitation provided for in Article 4, paragraph 5. The practice followed was somewhat complex. The mere fact of a state being particularly interested in a given question was not looked upon as sufficient. It was the view of the Council that the problem dealt with should, upon objective appraisal, be one of particular concern to the state desiring to be represented at a meeting of the Council. A state which was not a member of the Council but was considered as being particularly interested in a given question might be allowed to take part in the work of the Council both when the inclusion of the question in the agenda was discussed, and when the Council was dealing with the question itself.

(b) *The Case of a Special Convention.*

Some conventions provided for participation in the Council's work by a state which was not a member of the Council. The Opium Convention signed at Geneva on February 19, 1925, provides that the members of the Permanent Central Opium Board are to be appointed by the Council and that the United States of America and Germany should each be invited to nominate one person to participate in these appointments. This raised the point whether, in such a case, it was by the Council that the election should be made or by a special electoral body with the Council as its chief component.

(c) *The Case of a Decision by the Assembly.*

The Assembly, by a resolution dated October 3, 1936, decided to admit Germany, Brazil, and Japan to sit in the Council at any election of members of the Permanent Court of International Justice that might take place before January 1, 1940.

(d) *Invitation Addressed by the Council to a State.*

Apart from the cases mentioned above, the Council was entitled to invite a state not a member of the Council or even of the League of Nations to sit at the Council table. In such cases the state thus invited [4] did not as a rule take part in the voting.

Article XIII of the Rules of Procedure of the Council stated, in addition:

The Chairmen and Members of Committees, experts and officials of the League may be admitted to give information or assistance at meetings of the Council.

On September 29, 1937, the Council took the following decision:

It is generally unnecessary for the chairmen or other representatives of League Committees to come to the Council table for the discussion of their Committees' reports. Nevertheless, it is open to the Rapporteur for the particular question on

[4] An invitation of this kind was, in virtue of Article II, addressed by the Council to the United States, on October 15, 1931, in connection with the Sino-Japanese conflict.

the agenda to ask the Secretary-General to arrange for the representation of the Committee, should special circumstances appear to the Rapporteur to warrant such action.[5]

STANDING AND PROVISIONAL COMMITTEES OF THE LEAGUE

Space is lacking for a full description of the composition of the standing and provisional committees appointed by the League. They were composed either of members sitting as representatives of their governments or of members appointed in their individual capacity. Reference may be made here simply to the Report of the Secretary General concerning the League Committees published in 1934 [5a] and to the General Regulations for League Committees adopted by the Council on January 24, 1936.[6]

INTERNATIONAL LABOR CONFERENCES

The composition of the International Labor Conferences is well known. They are composed of the representatives of the states members of the Organization, each country being represented by four delegates, two for the government and two for the employers and the employees respectively. Each delegate may be accompanied by not more than two advisers for each item on the agenda of the meeting. The peculiarity of the system of the International Labor Conference is that every delegate is entitled to vote individually on all matters treated by the Conference. This is an important departure from the generally accepted principle that each state shall have only one vote regardless of the number of its delegates at an international meeting.

GOVERNING BODY OF THE INTERNATIONAL LABOR OFFICE

The Governing Body of the International Labor Office, which consists of thirty-two members, is also composed of representatives of governments, employers, and workers, i.e., sixteen persons representing governments, eight representing the employers, and eight representing the workers.

Of the sixteen persons representing governments, eight are appointed by the members of the Organization of chief industrial importance, and eight are appointed by the members of the Organization selected for that purpose by the government delegates to the International Labor Conference, excluding the delegates of the eight members of the Organ-

---

[5] L.N., *Official Journal*, 1937, p. 1169.   [5a] L.N., Document C.287.M.125.1934.
[6] L.N., *Official Journal*, 1936, pp. 131–33.

ization mentioned above. Of the sixteen members of the Organization represented, six must be non-European states.

The persons representing the employers and the persons representing the workers are elected respectively by the employers' delegates and the workers' delegates to the Conference. Two employers' representatives and two workers' representatives must belong to non-European states.

The duration of the office of the Governing Body is three years.

PAN AMERICAN CONFERENCES

The number of delegates which each government is entitled to send to the Pan American conferences is not limited by a formal provision as in the case of the Assembly of the League or the International Labor Conferences. Thus, at the Seventh International Conference of American States the United States of America had six full delegates, Uruguay sixteen, etc. The conference was composed of nearly two hundred representatives of twenty American republics who were classified under headings such as: President of the Delegation; Delegate; Counselor; Adviser; Technical Adviser; Secretary General; Secretary; Assistant Secretary; Press Officer. Several former presidents of American republics were among the delegates as well as ten ministers for foreign affairs in office.

COUNCIL OF THE UNITED NATIONS RELIEF AND REHABILITATION ADMINISTRATION

Article III, paragraph 1, of the agreement setting up the United Nations Relief and Rehabilitation Administration provides that each member government shall name one representative, and such alternates as may be necessary, upon the Council of the United Nations Relief and Rehabilitation Administration. As Dr. Philip C. Jessup remarks rightly, "the Council of UNRRA is in fact comparable rather to the Assembly than to the Council of the League." [7] It is true that on the Council of the United Nations Relief and Rehabilitation Administration all the member governments [8] of the Administration are repre-

[7] Jessup, "The First Session of the Council of UNRRA," op. cit., p. 103, n. 6.

[8] Article II of the agreement of the United Nations Relief and Rehabilitation Administration which deals with membership in the Administration is as follows: "The members of the United Nations Relief and Rehabilitation Administration shall be the governments or authorities signatory hereto and such other governments or authorities as may upon application for membership be admitted thereto by action of the Council. The Council may, if it desires, authorize the Central Committee to accept new members between sessions of the Council.

sented. Moreover, the number of alternates, advisers, secretaries, etc., attending the meetings of the Council is very large (more than two hundred at the second session of the Council held in Montreal in September, 1944).

LEAGUE "AD HOC" CONFERENCES

Most of the conferences sponsored by the League were *general conferences*. The Council instructed the Secretary General to issue invitations to all members of the League; at the same time the Council usually set up a list of non-member states which should also be invited. Sixty-four states were invited to send delegations to the Disarmament Conference and sixty of them actually sent representatives. Other conferences were similarly attended by a large number of states as, for instance, the Conference on Narcotic Drugs of 1931, the World Economic Conference of 1927, and the Monetary and Economic Conference held in London in 1933. Sometimes League conferences were *limited conferences*, and invitations were issued only to the governments of countries belonging to a certain geographic area or having a special interest in a particular subject. For instance, the Statute of the Organization for Communications and Transit (Article 24, paragraph 1) provided that:

Limited conferences, to which only the representatives of the States concerned are invited with a view to the conclusion or revision of conventions specially affecting them may be convened by the Council on the proposal of the Committee, which shall append to its proposal a list of the States that should in its opinion be invited.

The League convened limited conferences to deal with subjects in various fields. The First Opium Conference held at Geneva in 1925 and the Bangkok Opium Conference held in 1931, were attended only by the representatives of governments specially interested in the regulation or suppression of the habit of smoking opium.

The *ad hoc* conferences held under the auspices of the League of Nations were almost always composed of government representatives. For this reason they were often called intergovernmental conferences. However, there were exceptions. Reference has been made in the first

---

"Wherever the term 'member government' is used in this Agreement it shall be construed to mean a member of the Administration whether a government or an authority." The reason for employing the term "authority" in the agreement is that at the time of the signing of the agreement the French Committee of National Liberation was not recognized as the *de jure* government of France.

part of this handbook to the Conference of Press Experts convoked by the League in 1927, in which governmental, semipublic, and private interests were represented.

No attempt was made in the case of intergovernmental League conferences to set up rigid rules concerning the size of the delegations attending such meetings. On the contrary the Rules of Procedure of these conferences displayed great flexibility in this respect. For instance, the Rules of Procedure of the Disarmament Conference (Article I) provided that:

1. The Conference shall consist of the delegations appointed by the Governments invited to the Conference.
2. Each delegation shall consist of one or more Delegates who may be accompanied by substitute delegates, advisers, experts and secretaries.

The Statute of the Organization for Communications and Transit adopted by the Council of the League of Nations on January 29, 1938, provided in Article 18, paragraph 1, that:

Delegations to the [general] conference may include one or more representatives, deputies and experts, each delegation having only one vote.

At the Disarmament Conference some states (as for instance, Denmark) had as many as ten full delegates. As for the sessions of the Assembly, delegations at important League conferences included a large number of substitute and assistant delegates as well as advisers, experts, secretaries, etc.

OBSERVERS

States which are not entitled to take an active part in the work of a conference or which do not wish to take an active part may send observers. Naturally, if a state which has not been selected as a member of the conference desires to send an observer, authorization must be given to it to do so. In the practice of the League of Nations this authorization was given either beforehand by the Council or by the conference itself.

Apart from governmental delegations and observers, League conferences were often attended by experts appointed in an individual capacity or by representatives of national or international organizations invited to take part in the work of the conference.

As stated before, the competent authority for appointing such experts or inviting such representatives was usually either the Council of the League or the conference itself. However, other methods were occasionally employed;[9] thus, the Monetary and Economic Conference held in London in 1933 was attended by experts appointed both by the Council of the League and by the President of the Conference. Article 18 of the Constitution of the International Labor Organization provides that the International Labor Conference may add to any committee which it appoints, technical experts who shall be assessors without being entitled to vote. In fact, observers, experts, and representatives of national or international organizations are as a rule not entitled to vote.

In its twenty years of active existence the League of Nations has been cautious not to adopt general rules applying to all observers.[10]

The Rules of Procedure of the Council of the United Nations Relief and Rehabilitation Administration contain a special provision concerning observers. Article VII of these Rules reads:

> The Council and the Central Committee may invite observers or may invite public international organizations, non-member governments or authorities, relief and welfare agencies or others to send observers, to attend all or any of their meetings or parts thereof, or to participate in such meetings or parts thereof, without vote, under such conditions as the Council or the Central Committee, respectively, shall determine. All such invitations shall be transmitted by the Director General.

So far the Council and the Central Committee of the United Nations Relief and Rehabilitation Administration have not determined the "conditions" under which observers may participate in the meetings of the United Nations Relief and Rehabilitation Administration.

The International Conferences of American States have in recent times adopted a negative policy concerning "official observers." Thus the Governing Board of the Pan American Union submitted to the Eighth International Conference of American States held at Lima in December, 1938, a report in which it stated that, in view of the fact that the sessions of the conferences as well as those of the committees had been public since the Sixth Conference of 1928, there was no reason for establishing a category of "official observers." This view was concurred in by the reporting delegate, who, in his report, expressed himself as

[9] For instance, the Statute of the Organization for Communications and Transit provides (Article 19):
"1. The Committee may appoint either persons who are members of the Committee or persons who do not belong to the Committee to take part in the work of the conference in an advisory capacity and on behalf of the Committee.
"2. The Council or the conference may invite qualified international or national organisations to appoint representatives to take part in an advisory capacity in the work of the conference."

[10] For a discussion of the rôle of the observers of international conferences, see Genet, *op. cit.*, Vol. III, pp. 160–61.

follows: "In our opinion no reason exists to counsel the creation of this special category (of official observers). Foreign or extracontinental nations may fully inform themselves of the deliberations and resolutions in the publications of the International Conferences of American States, and also of the trends of Pan Americanism. Furthermore, we have no interest in the participation in this essentially continental work of countries that are not linked by the ideal of Pan Americanism; which is not a policy of exclusion, but one of definition of collective ideals of peace and of continental juridical, social and economic organization." The report was approved by the committee, as was also the opinion of the reporting delegate that no resolution on the subject was necessary.

INTERNAL ORGANIZATION OF DELEGATIONS

Each delegation must have a leader who speaks and votes in plenary meetings on behalf of the whole delegation.[11] This leader of a delegation is sometimes called first delegate, president, or chairman of the delegation. It of course falls upon each government to organize its own delegation within the general framework of the constitution of the international organization or of the rules of procedure of the international gathering. In the practice of the League neither the chair nor the Secretary General intervened in this field. It is conceivable, however, that a government sometimes consulted the Secretary General semiofficially concerning certain questions, such as, for instance, the number of personnel to be included in the delegation in order that its own delegation might be of approximately the same size as that of the other governments.

This chapter would not be complete without mention of certain features emphasizing the rights of a state to send a delegation of its own choosing. Referring again to the practice of the League, in several instances a government has found it expedient to send a delegate who was not a national of its own state. Liberia, for example, was successively represented by a Dutchman, an Italian, and a Belgian. In some instances a delegate represented two states at the same time. Thus, the Italian mentioned above who represented Liberia also claimed to have full power to represent a certain Central American state. The practice of dual representation was looked upon with disfavor by the Secretariat and was finally discouraged altogether.[12]

[11] This is, of course, not the case in the International Labor Organization.
[12] Nevertheless, historical precedents do exist for dual representation, and the practice is not inconsistent with international law. Thus at the Hague Conferences of 1899 and 1907, Montenegro was represented by the Russian delegation.
Article 13 of the Universal Postal Convention, signed at Buenos Aires, on May 23,

LIST OF DELEGATES

The names of the representatives, deputies, experts, advisers, secretaries, etc., appointed to attend the international gathering by their respective governments must be communicated to the secretary general of the international organization or the conference. If the conference has been convoked by a particular state the names should be communicated to the government of that state.

The Office Rules of the Secretariat of the League (Rule 113 c) provide that "Copies of communications from Governments announcing the nomination of their delegates to the Assembly and to the more important conferences are made by the Registry and sent to the Sections mainly concerned." As the officer preparing the list of delegates was not necessarily identical with the officer charged with the preparatory work for the Credentials Committee (see next section of this Part concerning credentials), it considered essential that each letter giving the names of the delegates, etc., should be copied immediately on receipt and a copy sent to both officers. The person responsible throughout for the preparation of the list of delegates saw to it that he received the original letter as well as the copy so as to check the names and ensure that they were correct. Provisional mimeographed lists were compiled and circulated within the Secretariat. Officials of the Secretariat who acted as "liaison officers" with their governments carefully scrutinized these provisional lists since they were an indication of the importance given by the other governments to the forthcoming meeting. On the eve of the conference a provisional printed list was made available to the public. In case the list of names of a delegation was not available at the moment of the printing of the provisional list corresponding space was left open for the insertion of the name of the country and its delegates. A revised list was printed and circulated after the conference had been in session for several days.[13] At the first plenary meeting of the conference, special forms were distributed on which members of the delegations were requested to write their names, official titles, and

---

1939, provides, *inter alia:* "Each country is represented at the Congress by one or more plenipotentiary delegates, provided with the necessary credentials, by their Government. It may, if necessary, be represented by the delegation of another country. However, it is understood that a delegation may be charged with representing only two countries, including the one by which it was originally accredited. In the deliberations, each country has but one vote."

[13] The Secretariat of the League subjected the lists of delegates to the Assembly or *ad hoc* conferences to certain limitations. Clerical staff, typists, etc., accompanying delegations were never included in the list regardless of the title they might be given in the communications forwarded by the delegations to the Secretariat.

addresses so that the final list of delegates might be prepared. The special forms which were distributed at the first meeting were seldom adequately filled in except for the names of the delegates. A note was therefore inserted in the provisional list and published in the *Journal* of the Assembly or of the conference in question requesting delegations to send in their corrections within a stated time.

Governments are entitled to alter the composition of their delegations during the sessions of international gatherings. But all such changes must, of course, be communicated to the Secretary General or the chair.[14] In the practice of the League these changes were immediately published in the *Assembly Journal* or in the Journal of the conference. A supplement to the list was subsequently circulated. Editing the list of delegates is not always an easy task. The official in charge of this task must have a broad knowledge of international conferences in order to give some unity of presentation to the list and check the translation of unusual titles as well as the qualifications of the conferees. He must also possess some diplomatic skill. The author of this study remembers the case of a state insisting on having four full delegates at an Assembly session instead of the three as stipulated by the regulations. The case was exceptional as one of the delegates of that state was the Chairman of the Assembly, and a formula for giving satisfaction to his government had to be discovered. Many hours of deliberation as well as the help of the Legal Section were needed in order to draft an appropriate footnote explaining the infringement of the rules.[15]

The final list of delegates containing all the corrections and additions is subsequently published on the front pages of the minutes of the international conference.

PRECEDENCE

A question which arises in connection with the preparation of a list of delegates and which must be taken into account when planning the distribution of seats in the meeting room is that of precedence among the delegations. In the practice of the League, the precedence adopted for intergovernmental meetings was the French alphabetical order of the names of the states represented at the conference. If some states were represented by observers their names were printed on the list

---

[14] The Statute of the Organization for Communications and Transit (Article 18, paragraph 3) provides: "The names of the deputies and experts may also be communicated in the course of the conference to the Secretary-General of the League through the intermediary of the delegation concerned."

[15] See L.N., *Official Journal*, Special Supplement No. 155, p. 11 n.

immediately following the names of the delegates of states regularly represented.[16] The same precedence was observed for roll-calls and for allotting seats in the meeting rooms, where the delegates of the states the names of which, in French, were at the beginning of the alphabet, sat in the first row facing the chairman.

The practice of the International Labor Conferences was to arrange the seats in accordance with the names of the countries in the French alphabetical order, and to reverse this order at the following session so that the same delegates would not always be seated in the back rows.

The seating arrangements of delegates around ordinary tables are different from those adopted where the tables are in the form of a horseshoe. A peculiar custom existed for allocating seats at the Council table. The President sat in the middle, at his left the Secretary General; the representatives of the permanent members of the Council sat immediately at the right and at the left of the President and the Secretary General; next, also at the right and left, came the so-called semi-permanent members of the Council; and then the other members in the order of the seniority of their election to the Council. If representatives of states which were non-members of the Council were invited to sit at the Council table, they sat at both ends of the table arranged in the form of a horseshoe, or at the ends of the semicircular table which was used in recent years.

At the United Nations Conference on Food and Agriculture, the order of precedence adopted was the English alphabetical order. The same method is being adopted for the sessions of the Council of the United Nations Relief and Rehabilitation Administration.

In the practice of the Pan American Conferences lots are drawn by the Secretary General of the Conference at the first meeting to establish the order of precedence of the delegations.[17]

According to an account of Dr. James Brown Scott, the United States representatives took their places at the table at the First Peace Conference at The Hague in 1899 under the letter E (Etats-Unis) but at the Second Peace Conference of 1907 under the letter A (Amérique),

---

[16] In the list of delegates appended to the minutes of the second session of the Council of the Relief and Rehabilitation Administration, in addition to names of observers, the admission of which had been decided by the Council, the names of the representatives of Switzerland and Sweden (non-members of the Administration) have been inserted under the heading "Representatives of Non-Member States attending in the capacity of visitors." Such a mention seems to be without precedent.

[17] The practice of establishing the order of precedence by lots has its origin in a decision of the Vienna Congress of 1814–15. Apart from the Pan American Conference it has found very little favor in diplomatic and conference practice of recent times.

it having in the meantime been remembered that United States of America was the official title. Dr. Scott observes that this happy philological discovery enabled the United States delegates to claim at the latter conference the benefit of the first letter of the alphabet and to take precedence over other American states.[18]

The United States of America was classified under the letter A when seats were assigned to her delegates during *ad hoc* conferences held under the auspices of the League of Nations. Similarly, at the sessions of the International Labor Conference the United States of America is classified under the letter A. In the early days of the League the British delegates, as representatives of the British Empire, had their places assigned to them under the letter B. This alphabetic classification was maintained even after the adoption of the Statute of Westminster, when they became delegates of the United Kingdom of Great Britain and Northern Ireland. The International Labor Organization continues to classify the British delegates under British Empire. Representatives of the Union of South Africa took their places in the Assembly of the League and at *ad hoc* League conferences under the letter A, but at International Labor Conferences they are classified under U.

At the meetings of the United Nations Relief and Rehabilitation Administration the representatives of the United States of America take their places under the letter U, next to the representatives of the Union of South Africa and the United Kingdom of Great Britain and Northern Ireland. The representatives of Brazil and Mexico, which are officially listed among the signatories of the agreement setting up the United Nations Relief and Rehabilitation Administration as United States of Brazil and United Mexican States, take their respective places under the letters B and M. The places assigned to the representatives of El Salvador are under the letter E, whereas in League of Nations meetings their seats were reserved under the letter S.

20. CREDENTIALS AND FULL POWERS

As a rule delegates to an international public conference should be provided with credentials or full powers attesting that they have been appointed by their governments to attend the conference, to conduct negotiations, and possibly to conclude and sign the international agree-

---

[18] James Brown Scott, *Le français, langue diplomatique moderne; Etude critique de conciliation internationale* (Paris: A. Pédone, 1924), p. 19, as referred to by Sir Ernest Satow, *A Guide to Diplomatic Practice*, 3d edition (London, etc.: Longmans, Green and Co., 1932), p. 30.

ment which may result from the conference. Space is here lacking for an exhaustive study of the form and content of full powers. Even if only the practice of the League were taken into account a long chapter would be required for a full explanation of the various problems with which the Secretariat was confronted in this field. A few comments, however, may be made on the subject. Rule 5, paragraph 2, of the Rules of Procedure of the Assembly of the League provided that:

The full powers of the representatives shall be delivered to the Secretary-General, if possible, one week before the date fixed for the opening of the session. They shall be issued either by the Head of the State or by the Minister for Foreign Affairs.

It was explained in a footnote to this provision that:

It is obvious that, in the case of countries which do not possess a Minister for Foreign Affairs, the full powers may be issued by an authority possessing similar or equivalent powers.

Furthermore, the Rules of Procedure stipulated that a committee of nine members entrusted with the examination of the full powers be elected by the Assembly on the proposal of the President [19] and that this committee appoint its own chairman and vice chairman. The committee had to report without delay. Any representative whose admission had been questioned was allowed to sit provisionally with the same rights as other representatives, unless the Assembly decided otherwise.

The provisions concerning full powers contained in the Rules of Procedure of *ad hoc* conferences were very similar to those contained in the Rules of Procedure of the Assembly.[20] Sometimes a provision concerning the full powers was omitted in the Rules of Procedure of the conference, it being assumed that the practice of the Assembly would be followed.

The Secretariat carefully prepared beforehand the work of the credentials committee. Separate "dossiers" for each state were set up

---

[19] As a rule the Assembly accepted the names proposed by the President without voting by secret ballot.

[20] For instance, the relevant provisions of the Rules of Procedure of the Disarmament Conference (Article IV) read as follows:

"1. A committee of five members nominated by the President and appointed by the Conference shall be set up to examine the delegates' credentials and shall report to the Conference without delay.

"2. Any plenipotentiaries whose admission cannot be decided upon forthwith shall sit provisionally with the same rights as other plenipotentiaries, unless the Conference decides otherwise."

by the Registry in which all the relevant documents concerning the representation of the members of the Assembly or the conference were gathered. These dossiers were sent to the Legal Section, which studied them and drafted a preliminary report for the committee on credentials. Telegrams or letters emanating from Prime Ministers, Ministers for Foreign Affairs, or Permanent Delegates accredited to the League were usually accepted as credentials. If the signing of a convention or an agreement was contemplated, the Secretariat and the credentials committee saw to it that the delegates were empowered to do so.

Serious difficulties in connection with the examination of full powers very seldom arose. As the members of the credentials committee had to be appointed at the beginning of the first meeting, the list of its members, which was suggested for approval to the Assembly or conference by the President, was set up by the Secretariat. Among the suggested members were always included the names of jurists who were thoroughly grounded in the work of international conferences, and hence the task entrusted to the committee was completed in a very short time.

The situation is different for the International Labor Conferences where, owing to the peculiar representation of the members by government delegates and by delegates representing employers and workers, it often occurs that the credentials of delegates belonging to one of the two last categories are challenged. The standing orders of the International Labor Conferences therefore contain detailed provisions concerning the verification of credentials.

But even in the practice of the League it happened from time to time that both the Secretariat and the credentials committee had to face exceptional difficulties.

The best illustration of the kind of complications which may arise is probably the case of the Ethiopian delegation at the Assembly sessions of July and September, 1936. At the July session the Negus decided to place himself at the head of the Ethiopian delegation. The credentials committee, with the help of the Secretariat, had to determine the point whether a head of state who has signed his own full powers can sit as a delegate in the Assembly. The question was quickly settled in favor of the Negus since nothing either in the rules of the League or in the laws of Ethiopia prevented such a course of action. Moreover, there were ample historical precedents for heads of states leading delegations of their countries at international conferences.

The situation was more complicated at the September session, as it

had become doubtful whether Ethiopia still fulfilled the statutory requirements governing League membership since the country had been
almost completely overrun by the Italian Army. It had been planned
among the representatives of certain agencies and of the Italian Government to prevent the Ethiopian delegation from sitting at the Assembly by challenging the validity of its full powers. Ethiopia, they
said, was no longer a "fully self-governing State" as required by
Article I of the Covenant. For the first time in the history of the League
the membership of the credentials committee included a majority of
foreign ministers and political personalities instead of specialized
jurists,[21] and in lieu of appraising the form of the full powers of the
Ethiopian delegation, the committee discussed during several meetings
the highly political issue of the international status of Ethiopia. Ethiopia won the case but prudently refrained from sending a delegation to
subsequent Assemblies.

Oddly enough, the Rules of Procedure of the Council are silent regarding the full powers of the Council's members. In May, 1938, the
Emperor of Ethiopia sat at the Council table without encountering
any opposition. The following declaration was, however, read by the
President of the Council:

It was the desire of the Council to assure the participation of delegates of the
Emperor Haile Selassie in the Council's discussions on Item 18 of the agenda of
the session, without prejudice to questions of principle and irrespective of the
precise character of their full powers.[22]

In the practice of the Council a mere telegram or letter emanating
from the government of a Council member, informing the Secretary
General of its choice of a representative, was considered a sufficient
notification of the latter's appointment and authorization. However,
frequently even this formality was dispensed with. The Secretary General was simply informed of the appointment by a letter emanating
from the permanent delegate of the state member of the Council or by
a telephone call. There was no inconvenience in this practice, under
normal conditions, but sometimes difficulties did arise. Thus, in the
early thirties a revolution broke out in a Latin American state a few
days before the opening of a session of the Council. The permanent
delegate of that state, who happened to be its representative on the
Council, insisted that he attend the session and sit at the Council table

[21] At this session of the Assembly, at the request of the Ethiopian delegation, the
credentials committee, for the first and only time, was elected by secret ballot.
[22] L.N., *Official Journal*, 1938, p. 333.

in spite of the fact that the new régime in his country would no longer delegate any power to him. It was only with the greatest difficulty that his South American colleagues persuaded him not to persevere; had he continued to insist that he was in fact a permanent delegate, and had he taken his seat at the meetings, the President of the Council and the Secretary General would have been placed in a very embarrassing situation. His presence at the meetings would probably have had to be tolerated until an official notification of dismissal had been received from the new government.

In the case of the standing and *ad hoc* committees of the League, a distinction must be made between committees composed of members appointed in an individual capacity and committees composed of government representatives. For the members of the first category of committees the letter of appointment was equivalent to credentials. In the committees composed of representatives of governments the practice was similar to the practice in force for the Council; and the same kind of incidents which occurred in the Council occurred from time to time in this type of committee.

21. THE PRESIDENT OR CHAIRMAN

The assembled delegates are the most important organ of an international conference. The organ next in importance is the chairman. Indeed, a conference in session without leadership is hardly imaginable.

There are undoubtedly various methods for selecting the chairman — or as he is frequently termed — the president of a conference.[23]

(*a*) He may be elected by acclamation or by secret ballot.
(*b*) He may be designated by casting lots.
(*c*) He may be designated in accordance with an automatic rule of rotation by seniority or alphabetical order, etc.

[23] There is no clear distinction between the use of the terms "chairman" and "president" for the purpose of designating the presiding officer of an international gathering. The tendency seems to be to use the term president for the presiding officer of a large international gathering, such as the Assembly of the League, the International Labor Conference, or an *ad hoc* conference attended by a great number of delegates. The use of the term chairman for the presiding officer of the Council of the United Nations Relief and Rehabilitation Administration, composed of the representatives of forty-four states, appears to be a departure from the foregoing tendency.

On the other hand, the presiding officer of smaller international gatherings, such as the Governing Body of the International Labor Organization and an international committee or commission, is usually called chairman. Yet, the presiding officer of the League Council, which never comprised more than fifteen members, is called president in the Rules of Procedure of the Council. In French and Spanish, as well as in Russian, the distinction between chairman and president does not exist, for the word corresponding to president (président, presidente, predsedatel, respectively) is used in all cases.

(d) He may be selected beforehand by a body or a person external to the conference.

(e) He may be designated by a previous conference.

If the president has been designated or appointed beforehand, he will open the first meeting of the conference. If he is to be elected, the first meeting will be opened by a temporary president.

TEMPORARY PRESIDENT

The Rules of Procedure of the Assembly provide that "Until the election of the President, the President of the Council shall act as President of the Assembly." (Rule 7, paragraph 3.)

A similar provision exists in the Standing Orders of the International Labor Conferences.

The tradition for the Pan American Conferences is that the head of state of the country in which the conference is held designates the temporary president. Thus, Article 1 of the Regulations of the Seventh International Conference of American States reads:

The President of the Republic of Uruguay shall designate the temporary President who shall preside at the opening session and shall continue to preside until the Conference elects a permanent President.

The tradition of the Pan American Conferences is in agreement with a well-established international practice to which, in Number 1 of the Journal of the United Nations Conference on Food and Agriculture, the following reference was made:

In accordance with established international practice, the President of the United States of America, as Chief of State of the Country serving as host to the Conference, has designated the Chairman of the Delegation of the United States, the Honorable Marvin Jones, as temporary President of the Conference, to serve until the election of the Permanent President.

The first meetings of the main committees of the League Assembly were opened by a Deputy Secretary General who proposed the appointment of a former chairman of the respective committee as temporary chairman. This temporary chairman then presided over the election, by secret ballot, of the chairman of the session.

When a new League committee was set up, its first meeting was often presided over by the Secretary General until the committee elected its chairman.

Article II, paragraph 1, of the Rules of Procedure of the Council of the United Nations Relief and Rehabilitation Administration provides that "at the opening of each session of the Council, the Director General shall preside until the Council has elected a Chairman for the session."

Similarly, the Rules of Procedure of the Standing Committees of the United Nations Relief and Rehabilitation Administration provide that "the Director General shall fix the time and place of the first meeting of each standing committee and he or his representative shall preside at the meeting until the committee has elected its chairman."

The parliamentary practice according to which the oldest member of the gathering automatically becomes temporary president is sometimes used in international conferences.

PERMANENT PRESIDENT

(a) *President Designated or Appointed Beforehand.*

The Rules of Procedure of the Council provide that the representatives on the Council shall preside over its sessions in rotation, according to the French alphabetical order of the names of the countries.[24] It

---

[24] The rules concerning the President of the Council were as follows:

1. *Ordinary session.* — Article IV of the Rules of Procedure of the Council reads as follows:
"1. The representatives on the Council shall preside over its sessions in rotation in the alphabetical order in French of the names of the countries which they represent.
"2. A President shall, in principle, enter into office at the beginning of an ordinary session and remain in office until the opening of the next ordinary session."
Previously, the practice was that the two autumn sessions of the Council were presided over by the same president. In order to ensure effective rotation, the Council decided, on September 29, 1937, to discontinue this practice and to have each of the four regular sessions of the Council presided over by a new president.

2. *Extraordinary sessions.* — Article IV, paragraph 3, of the Rules reads as follows:
"3. Extraordinary sessions shall be presided over by the President for the time being in Office."

3. *Replacement of the President.*
(*a*) During a session. Article IV, paragraph 4, reads as follows:
"4. If the representative who should act as President considers that he should decline to do so during a particular session, or during the consideration of a particular matter, the Council shall arrange for another member to act as President."
Such a case arose on several occasions (for instance when the country which the president represented was party to a dispute) and the practice was that the President last in office took the place of the president in office. This practice followed the principle embodied in Article V of the Rules of Procedure quoted below:

(*b*) During intervals between sessions. Article V, reads as follows:
"Where during the interval between sessions of the Council, the Secretary-General, for the purposes of the application of the provisions of the present Rules or for any other purpose, has occasion to apply to the President of the Council and the President is prevented from acting, the Secretary-General shall apply to the last President, if the country which he represents continues to belong to the Council. If the last President is unable to act, the Secretary-General shall apply, subject to the same condition, to his predecessor, and, thereafter, in accordance with the same system, to earlier Presidents of the Council."

would have been difficult for political reasons to choose the president of the Council by any other means. But the shortcomings of the method employed are obvious. The Council might be presided over during a grave political crisis by the representative of a small country subject to pressure by a great power involved in the dispute. Such a system also allows accession to the chairmanship of incompetent persons. The Council, which had established this system for itself, condemned it in other bodies of the League. Thus, the General Regulations on Commissions (Article 6) drawn up by the Council provided that "each committee shall appoint its chairman," and this provision was based on the following statement contained in the report of the "Committee on Committees" approved by the Council: "The Committee considers that a Committee should normally elect its own chairman. Committees should be asked *not* to lay down an automatic rule of rotation by seniority or alphabetical order, etc." [25]

Another procedure for filling the permanent presidency of a conference held under the auspices of the League was for the Council to appoint the president of a forthcoming conference. The Statute of the Organization for Communications and Transit (Article 21) formally recognizes this method by stating: "should the Council not have appointed the president of the conference, the latter shall itself make the appointment." The willingness of the Transit Organization to abide by such a procedure was not always shared by other League bodies. Conferees often complained privately that the appointment of the president of the conference by the Council was an infringement upon the sovereign powers of the conference.[26]

Nevertheless, this sytem has manifold advantages. As a result of his appointment in advance of the meeting the president-to-be has an unusual opportunity to acquaint himself with the preparatory work of

---

4. *Case in which the President of the Council ceases to represent his country on the Council.* — Article VI reads as follows:

"1. If the person who is President ceases to represent his country on the Council, he shall be replaced by the new representative.

"2. In like manner, if a former President has ceased to represent his country on the Council, the new representative shall act in his place for the purposes of Article V of the present Rules."

This provision was intended to indicate that the presidency of the Council was not a personal office and that when the occupant of this office ceased to represent his country, he vacated the presidency. He was then succeeded by the new representative of the country in question.

[25] L.N. Document A.16.1935., p. 3. (Suggestion 7, 2nd paragraph of the Committee suggestions.)

[26] Some authors have questioned the right of the Council of the League to appoint the presiding officer of a conference at which states not members of the League were present. See Dunn, *op. cit.*, pp. 210–11.

the conference. Thus, when taking the chair, he is in a much better position to carry on successfully, for he is already familiar with the problems that may come up for discussion. Time is saved at the beginning of the conference, because the formalities of an election are avoided. Finally, and this is the main advantage, it is possible for the Council to select the most qualified person for the chairmanship of the conference.[27]

(b) *Elected President.*

The normal procedure for a conference is to elect its president. It was in conformity with this procedure that presidents of the Assemblies of the League and presidents of the International Labor Conferences were appointed. Presidents of *ad hoc* conferences convoked under the auspices of the League were also frequently chosen in accordance with this system.

In the case of conferences convoked by a particular state or by a group of states, the prevalent practice is that the country serving as host to the conference supplies the president of the conference. Such has been the practice of the Pan American Conferences, and this was also the case at the United Nations Conference on Food and Agriculture, the United Nations Monetary and Financial Conference, and the International Civil Aviation Conference. Significant deviations from this rule have, however, taken place. Thus, the two Hague Conferences of 1899 and 1907 elected the first delegates of Russia as presidents of the gatherings in view of the rôle Russia had played in making these two conferences possible. As a rule, the presidents of this last type of conference are elected by acclamation.

The Assembly of the League always elected its president by secret ballot.[28] The rules of procedure of many standing committees of the League provide expressly that the election of the chairman must be effected by secret ballot.

HONORARY PRESIDENT

When a large international conference does not select as its chair-

[27] When a conference was held outside Geneva, the Council often yielded to the custom that the president must be a national of the country serving as host to the conference and appointed the president in accordance with this usage. For instance, the Council appointed a Dutchman, M. Heemskerk, as president of the Conference for the Codification of International Law held at The Hague in 1930, and an Englishman, Mr. Ramsay MacDonald, as president of the London Monetary and Economic Conference of 1933. This, of course, need not be construed as a reflection upon the competence and high ability of these two statesmen.

[28] The only exception was the election of M. Hambro in December, 1939, by acclamation.

man a national of the country which is host to the conference, it frequently elects by acclamation a prominent individual of that country as honorary president of the gathering. Thus, for instance, the Disarmament Conference in 1932 elected M. Motta, President of the Swiss Confederation, as Honorary President of the Conference.

The Assembly of the League twice elected M. Motta as Honorary President.[29] It also elected, at its second session in 1921, an older statesman of Switzerland, Gustave Ador, as Honorary President. Generally, an honorary president is entitled to sit in the "Bureau" of the gathering. Several precedents could be cited from conference history in support of the custom of electing an honorary president, but for immediate purposes it may suffice to refer to the two Hague Peace Conferences. Both were presided over by the first delegates of Russia, but in each instance the Minister for Foreign Affairs of the Netherlands was elected honorary president of the gathering.

QUALIFICATIONS OF THE PRESIDENT

Political factors cannot be disregarded in the selection of a president of an international conference. They also had to be taken into account in connection with League conferences. Nevertheless, the abilities of the candidate under consideration were taken into account by the Council in appointing the president of an *ad hoc* conference or by the other League bodies which chose their chairmen themselves.

An unwritten rule existed according to which the President of the Assembly could not be the national of a country permanently represented on the Council. Except for this custom there was nothing to prevent the Assembly from selecting its president from among any of the members of the League.[30] True, the Assembly endeavored to introduce a kind of rotation by giving an opportunity to each region of the world to be represented in turn in the office of president, but it did not hesitate to reelect former presidents when that was deemed necessary.[31] A similar practice prevailed in the International Labor Conferences.

[29] At the first session of the Assembly in 1920 and again in 1937 on the occasion of the twenty-fifth anniversary of the entry of M. Motta in the Swiss Federal Council.

[30] An interesting light is thrown on this question by Margaret E. Burton, *The Assembly of the League of Nations* (Chicago: The University of Chicago Press, 1941), pp. 102 ff.

[31] Thus, in 1930, the Assembly adopted a report of its General Committee in which the following statement was made: "The Assembly will, however, no doubt endorse the view that the post of President is one for which the individual most qualified should be chosen, irrespective of his nationality, and that personal ability is the first quality of which account should be taken." See L.N., *Official Journal*, Special Supplement No. 84, p. 497.

The president of an international conference must inspire confidence and respect; hence he must be impartial and he must have qualities of leadership. Thorough technical knowledge of the problems discussed by a large international conference is not essential for a president. His skill in conducting the discussions is far more important, and in this respect parliamentary experience is of the greatest value. The Assembly of the League and the International Labor Conferences have had highly qualified presidents. Two names will be cited here as examples: M. Hymans and Lord Burnham.

One of the best presidents of an *ad hoc* conference held under the auspices of the League was M. de Brouckère who, in 1931, presided over the Conference for Limiting the Manufacture and Regulating the Distribution of Narcotic Drugs. M. de Brouckère certainly had no detailed knowledge of the highly technical problems under discussion, when he took over the chair, but his tact, his skill, and his authority performed miracles, and in spite of all the difficulties which the conference had to face it achieved a remarkable success.

In a smaller body, technical knowledge of the problem is more necessary but there, also, character is of high importance.

RIGHTS AND DUTIES OF THE PRESIDENT

The president opens, suspends, and closes the meetings; he brings to the attention of the conference all communications of sufficient importance to justify their submission to the gathering. He watches over the observation of the rules of procedure, calls upon the speakers, pronounces the closing of discussions, puts questions to a vote, and announces the result of the vote. These principal rights and duties of the president are included, in a more or less detailed form, in all the rules of procedure of international conferences.

Apart from summarizing and clarifying statements or trying to reconcile opposing viewpoints, the president of a large conference usually does not himself take a stand in the discussions. However, in the case of smaller bodies, such as the Council or the standing and *ad hoc* committees, it was the League practice for the chairman to take part in the discussion and sometimes to vote. Article II, paragraph 5, of the Rules of Procedure of the Council of the United Nations Relief and Rehabilitation Administration provides that the chairman, or a vice chairman acting as chairman of the Council, shall not vote but may appoint an alternate to act as the representative of his government on the Council.

An important task incumbent upon the President is the maintenance of order and dignity of the proceedings. He must act in this respect with tact, energy, and swiftness. The most striking and unfortunate case when disturbance during a meeting of the Assembly of the League of Nations occurred was in July, 1936. The Emperor of Ethiopia, who had assumed the functions of the First Delegate of his country, had decided to bring his plea for help personally before the Assembly of the League. No sooner had he begun his speech when Italian journalists, seated in the galleries, began to whistle and to hoot. The President of the Assembly requested the Swiss police in uniform to enter the galleries and to expel the disturbers,[32] which was done with celerity. The next day the President made the following pronouncement:

Before passing to the agenda, I have to make a short communication. Yesterday, the order and dignity of your proceedings were disturbed by a most regrettable external incident, an incident deeply deplored by every Member of the Assembly. In order, if possible, to prevent its repetition or, in any event, to define its precise significance, I think I should draw your attention to one of the fundamental rules of any deliberative assembly: nothing counts or exists for it, except what occurs in the course of its proceedings; no attitude, no gesture coming from outside — especially from the galleries — can affect its own position as a corporate body or that of any of its members. But there is an elementary duty incumbent upon those who are privileged to witness your debates — to refrain from demonstrations of any kind. That is why orders were immediately given yesterday to remove the demonstrators. It is not my business to address the galleries from the platform; but I can assure the Assembly that, should there be any further attempt of any kind to interrupt its discussions, steps will at once be taken, with the same decisiveness and celerity as yesterday, to put an end to the disturbance and to prevent any recurrence of it.[33]

Space is lacking here to describe in detail other tasks occasionally entrusted to a president either on the basis of special regulations and resolutions or by usage. Thus, it fell to the presidents of the Assembly, the International Labor Conferences, and *ad hoc* conferences held under the auspices of the League, to receive deputations of bodies which had no official status at the conference. The Report of the Committee on Council procedure, adopted by the Council on September 29, 1937, provided, however, that the President of the Council could not speak in the name of the Council unless specially authorized by the latter, and that therefore he should not, in that capacity, receive deputations. The report added that any statement made to him should be ad-

[32] As a matter of fact, the Geneva *gendarmes* had entered the galleries before the order of the President had been transmitted to them.
[33] Meeting of July 1, 1936, L.N., *Official Journal*, Special Supplement No. 151, p. 26.

dressed to him in his capacity as a member of the Council. No similar rule existed in the case of the Assembly, but in doubtful or delicate cases the president usually consulted the Bureau before receiving a deputation.

The president of a body meeting at regular and fixed intervals, like the League Council, was sometimes empowered to take administrative, financial, or even political measures between the sessions.

According to an unwritten rule the president delivers a formal address at the beginning of a conference and the final address. In another chapter reference will be made to other presidential functions, such as certain social duties usually incumbent upon chairmen of international conferences.

22. VICE PRESIDENTS OR VICE CHAIRMEN

International conferences elect as a rule one or more vice presidents or vice chairmen. Their duty is to assist the chairman in his task; occasionally one of them may be called upon to occupy the chair in the absence of the president.

The number of the vice presidents varies in accordance with circumstances. The Rules of Procedure of the Assembly of the League provide for eight vice presidents; the Standing Orders of the International Labor Conferences, for three. The Disarmament Conference, which was considered one of the most important conferences held under the auspices of the League, had fourteen vice presidents.[34]

It is not essential for the functioning of an international meeting to have vice chairmen. The Council of the League, for instance, had no vice president. This was also the case with many standing or *ad hoc* committees of the League. But it is always advisable to designate somebody in advance as a substitute for the chairman in case of his absence.[35]

[34] Compare the system of electing vice presidents with the system of the Pan American Conferences, at which the presidents of the delegations attending the conference are *ex officio* vice presidents of the conference and may be called upon to occupy the chair in the absence of the president. The order in which they are called is determined by the casting of lots. See Appendix VII, "Regulations of the Eighth International Conference of American States," Article 4, *infra*.

Compare this procedure also with the system of the International Labor Conference, in accordance with which the groups representing governments, employers, and workers each have the right to nominate one of their members as vice president subject to the approval of the Conference.

[35] Thus, Article III, Section 4, of the Rules of Procedure of the Standing Committees of the Council of the United Nations Relief and Rehabilitation Administration provides that:

23. STEERING COMMITTEES

Usually the president and the vice presidents constitute the directing and coordinating body of the conference. To these officers may be added, in accordance with the Rules of Procedure of the gathering in question or in conformity with a decision of the conference, a certain number of other conferees who will form the Bureau or General Committee of the conference. The Bureau of the Assembly of the League was composed of the President of the Assembly, eight vice presidents, and the chairmen of the main committees of the Assembly, the Agenda Committee, and the Credentials Committee — altogether a total of seventeen or eighteen members, with the Secretary General of the League as a member *ex officio*.

The rôle of the General Committee is to assist the president in the general direction of the conference, in regulating the composition of all such committees as the gathering may decide to create, in deciding on the communications to be made to the conference, in the framing of the agenda for each meeting, in determining the order of priority for its various items, etc. Thus, questions of procedure are the principal concern of the Bureau under ordinary circumstances. However, it is not unusual for questions of high political importance to be brought before this body. Indeed, in recent years the Bureau of the Assembly of the League of Nations tended more and more to become the central political committee of the Assembly. It will suffice to mention by way of illustration the discussions which took place in the Bureau of the Assembly concerning the Ethiopian affair.[36] Similarly, the Bureau of the Disarmament Conference discussed important political problems.

Other names may be used for steering committees of conferences and other methods employed for selecting their members. The Pan American Conferences organize a Committee on Initiatives composed of the presidents of delegations and presided over by the president of the conference. This committee may meet even before the first plenary meeting

---

"Upon the death, resignation, or inability to serve of the chairman of any standing committee, the first vice chairman, or, if he is not available the second vice chairman shall serve as chairman *ad interim* until a new chairman is elected. In the event of the temporary absence of the chairman during a meeting or any part thereof, the first vice chairman, or, if he is not available, the second vice chairman, shall preside. A vice chairman acting as chairman shall have the same powers and duties as the chairman."

[36] For a more detailed study of the political rôle of the Bureau of the Assembly, see Burton, *op. cit.*, pp. 110 ff. See also Howard B. Calderwood, "The General Committee and Other Auxiliary Committees of the League Assembly," *American Journal of International Law*, Vol. 38 (1944), pp. 74-94.

of the conference preparing proposals concerning the work of the conference.[37]

Article VI, paragraph 2, of the Rules of Procedure of the Council of the United Nations Relief and Rehabilitation Administration provides that at the opening of each session the Council shall establish a General Committee consisting of the chairman and vice chairmen of the Council (the Council has three vice chairmen), the members of the Central Committee (composed of four members: the representatives of the United States of America, the United Kingdom, the Union of the Soviet Socialist Republics, and China), and four other members elected by the Council. The General Committee shall, subject to the concurrence of the Council and in consultation with the Director General, determine the order of business of the Council, set the date of adjournment of the session, fix the time and place of each meeting during the session, decide what matters are to be considered at each meeting, pass upon the provisional agenda before its approval by the Council, coordinate the work of all committees of the Council during the session, and otherwise facilitate the orderly dispatch of the business of the Council and its committees. The chairman of the Council convenes and presides at the meetings of the General Committee.

Because of the tripartite structure of the International Labor Conference, the problems involved in steering its work are more complicated than in the case of conferences consisting solely of government representatives. The latter, even if they have to defend divergent interests, are trained in a technique of discussion which does not markedly differ from one country to another. The employers' and workers' representatives at the International Labor Conference, on the other hand, are concerned with aspects of the problems under discussion which often differ sharply from those of concern to government representatives, and, as a result of their background and working methods, tend to approach these problems from a different angle and in a less stereotyped way. Thus the steering machinery of the Conference is specially important as a means of ensuring continuity in the work of the Organization and smoothness in its operation. It may be profitable to consider the methods which have been adopted for this purpose in the light of experience.

The International Labor Conference first appoints its officers, who include the President of the Conference, traditionally a government

[37] Seventh International Conference of American States, *Plenary Sessions, Minutes and Antecedents*, Montevideo, 1933, p. 30.

delegate, and three Vice Presidents appointed by the government and the employers' and workers' groups, respectively. The officers deal primarily with questions of a general or political nature which do not directly affect the working of the Conference.

The main steering and coordinating agency of the International Labor Conference is the Committee of Selection, consisting of 32 members, including 16 government representatives and 8 representatives for each of the other two groups. In contrast to all the other committees of the Conference, on which the three groups are equally represented, the Selection Committee exactly reflects the composition of the Conference itself, in which each delegation consists of two government delegates and one representative each of employers and workers.

It is the Selection Committee which determines the order of the Conference's work and which deals with all the varied and often delicate questions which arise from day to day in the course of the proceedings. The Committee acts as the intermediary between the Conference and the three groups; it is through the representatives of the groups, especially in the case of the employers' and workers' groups, that the matters referred to the Selection Committee are brought to the knowledge of the groups, and that the matters of concern to the groups are brought before the Conference.

A tradition which is not based on the Standing Orders has grown up in the course of time; the Selection Committee, which has the same number of members as the Governing Body, consists basically of the members of the Governing Body. It happens at every session of the Conference that certain members of the Governing Body are not present as delegates, and are therefore replaced on the Selection Committee by other members of their group; but in practice the Selection Committee is able to benefit by the experience and authority of practically all the members of the executive body of the Organization, which normally meets four times a year. This very greatly facilitates the settlement of the often complicated and contentious problems with which the Committee has to deal. Familiar as they are with the constitutional procedure and practice of the Organization, the members of the Selection Committee, who are also members of the Governing Body, are eminently competent to solve each particular problem in a manner consonant with the general interest of the Organization and with the continuity of its work. On the other hand — and this applies especially to the employers' and workers' groups — the members who have been regularly associated with the work of the Organization over a long period of years enjoy unquestioned authority and are better able than casual members to secure the acceptance of solutions which they can show to be sound.

The part played by the Selection Committee as thus constituted at successive sessions of the Conference has contributed very materially to overcoming the inevitable difficulties involved in the operation of so complex a mechanism as the International Labor Conference. As the representative of the groups and as the steering agency, the Committee may be said to be the nerve center of the International Labor Conference.[38]

24. OTHER CENTRAL COMMITTEES

Frequently, besides the steering committee, international conferences possess several other central committees.

CREDENTIALS COMMITTEE

One of these central committees is almost indispensable in all conferences in which the delegates are provided with full powers; this committee is the credentials committee, to which reference has been made in a previous chapter where its functions have already been described.

AGENDA COMMITTEE

At the beginning of each session, the Assembly of the League set up an Agenda Committee which consisted of seven members appointed by the Assembly on the nomination of the President. The Committee elected its own Chairman and Vice Chairman; its task was to consider applications for the inclusion of new questions in the agenda of the Assembly and to report to the Assembly thereon. However, the Assembly decided without previous reference to the Agenda Committee upon proposals for the mere reference to one of the main committees of portions of the Report on the Work of the League.

Paragraph 4 of Article 4 of the Rules of Procedure of the Assembly reduced further the rôle of the Agenda Committee. Its provisions read as follows:

The Assembly may in exceptional circumstances place additional items on the agenda; but all consideration of such items shall, unless otherwise ordered by a

[38] The author of the handbook owes a special debt of gratitude to Mr. Robert La-france, Chief of the Diplomatic Division of the International Labor Office, who has written the above section concerning the Committee of Selection of the International Labor Conference.

two-thirds majority of the Assembly, be postponed until four days after they have been placed on the agenda, and until a committee has reported upon them.

Thanks to this provision, it was possible for the Assembly to discuss questions of real importance without undue delay.

Reference by the Assembly of a question to the Agenda Committee served as an expedient method of putting a given question in "cold storage," as the Agenda Committee was prone to recommend the postponement of the examination of new items to a forthcoming session.

Most of the *ad hoc* conferences held under the auspices of the League had no agenda committees, their task being performed by the bureaus or steering committees of the conferences.

Similarly, if a delegation at a Pan American Conference proposes a topic not included in the program, the topic is referred to the Committee on Initiatives of the Conference. Then, after the submission of the report by the Committee on Initiatives and its acceptance by a two-thirds vote of the delegations,[39] the topic is referred to the appropriate technical committee or, if the topic warrants, to a new *ad hoc* committee specially created.

The task of the Agenda Committee or of the steering committee in considering the addition of new items to the agenda of an international conference is closely related to the adoption of the final agenda of the conference and the delimitation of the scope of its work.

Reference has been made in Part I of this study to the special care taken in setting up the draft agenda of an international conference. However, it is difficult to avoid changes in the draft agenda or to prevent the proposal of new topics during the session. The Secretariat of the League has always adhered to the doctrine that an international conference is sovereign and that it may take whatever decisions it thinks fit concerning the scope of its work.[40]

[39] A similar system was adopted by the recent United Nations Conference on Food and Agriculture. The relevant provisions of the Regulations of the Conference are as follows:

"ART. 10. The agenda of the Conference shall be that previously agreed upon by the participating governments.

"ART. 11. New topics that may be proposed during the sessions shall be admitted to the agenda only if they pertain to the immediate purposes of the Conference and then only with the consent of three-fourths of the Executive Committee.

"All proposals for the inclusion of additional topics in the agenda shall be presented to the Executive Committee as soon as possible, and in any event within one week after the opening of the Conference, thereby affording adequate time for the consideration of all subjects presented to the Conference."

[40] See the exchange of letters between the Government of the United States and the Secretary General of the League concerning the scope of the work of the Conference for the Suppression of Illicit Traffic in Dangerous Drugs. Appendix IX, *infra*.

DRAFTING COMMITTEE

The Standing Orders of the International Labor Conferences contain formal provisions for the setting up of a central Drafting Committee of the Conference. Its task is to draw up in the form of draft conventions or recommendations the decisions adopted by the Conference. It must also ensure the identity of the contents of the French and English texts of all draft conventions or recommendations, the translation of which is undertaken by the Secretariat. No similar provision exists in the Rules of Procedure of the Assembly, but it was customary for any *ad hoc* conference held under the auspices of the League to set up a central drafting committee when the conference had to draft an international convention or agreement.

It has been the practice of the International Conferences of American States to appoint a Drafting Committee "consisting of one representative for each of the official languages of the conference" (i.e., English, French, Spanish, and Portuguese). Article 14 of the Regulations of the Eighth International Conference of American States, held in Lima in December, 1938, provided that —

Following approval by the committee, and before submission to the plenary session, all treaties, conventions, resolutions and other conclusions shall be referred to the Drafting Committee for the addition of the Protocolary clauses indicated in the Annex to these Regulations,[41] and for coordination of the text in the several languages of the Conference.

Article 37 of the same Regulations provided that —

after approval by the respective committees and before presentation to the plenary session, the treaties, conventions, resolutions, recommendations, votes and agreements shall be submitted to the Drafting Committee for purposes of coordination in the several official languages.

COMMITTEE ON RESOLUTIONS

This type of committee is peculiar to the International Labor Conferences. Its task is to examine resolutions submitted other than those relating to items on the agenda. In the case of other conferences such proposals would usually be examined by the steering committee.

NOMINATION COMMITTEE

Prior to 1937 the Assembly of the League elected its President, Vice Presidents, and committee chairmen without any preliminary nomination of an official character, and it is no secret that the Secretariat

[41] See Appendix VII, *infra*.

played a prominent part in the preparations for the election of the Assembly's officers.[42]

Since 1937 new regulations have been applied which read as follows:

RULE 7 (*b*). — 1. At the commencement of each session, the Assembly shall appoint a committee of eleven members whose duty shall be to nominate candidates for functions which carry with them a seat on the General Committee.

2. The provisional President of the Assembly shall submit proposals to it regarding the composition of this Committee.

3. The Members of the Assembly and the Committees shall retain the right to vote for persons other than those proposed by the above-mentioned Committee.

The aim of these provisions was to diminish the influence of the Secretariat in the elections of the Assembly, and to increase the influence of the small powers upon the choice of the members of the General Committee.

It is difficult to express a definite opinion concerning this new procedure as it was in force only during a short period. At first sight it had obvious advantages. But it is well known that the Secretariat had for some twenty years used its influence with tact and impartiality and that the suggestions it made concerning the choice of the officers of the Assembly corresponded generally with the wishes of the gathering. In any event rivalries, when they existed, were never brought out in the open even before such a small body as the Nomination Committee consisting of eleven members. Furthermore, the Secretariat still was able under the new provisions to exercise its influence in suggesting to the provisional President the names of the candidates for the Nomination Committee.

As to the influence of the small powers, the creation of the Nomination Committee took place at a moment especially favorable for the small powers. Obviously, the great powers had also to be represented on the Nomination Committee. But it happened that only three great powers were actually members of the League when the Nomination Committee was created. Under these circumstances the small powers had an overwhelming majority in the Committee. If, however, the membership of the great powers in the League had been six or seven, as it would have been under normal circumstances, the influence of the small powers would have been materially reduced. In order to prevent this, it would have been necessary to enlarge the committee, as was the case with the Council of the League, where a similar situation arose.

[42] For more details, see Burton, *op. cit.*, pp. 109-18.

Thus the membership of the Nomination Committee would have had to be increased to eighteen or twenty. It is doubtful if a Nomination Committee of this size would have been able to reach any decision without the help of the Secretariat.

Article VI, paragraph 1, of the Rules of Procedure of the Council of the United Nations Relief and Rehabilitation Administration provides for the election by the Council, at the opening of each session, of a Committee on Nominations consisting of eleven members. This committee submits to the Council nominations for the offices of chairman and vice chairmen of the Council, for the four members of the General Committee to be elected by the Council, and for appointments to each standing or other committee of the Council for which new appointments may be required. The experience is too recent to be conclusive.

25. THE MAIN COMMITTEES AND TECHNICAL COMMITTEES

TASK OF THE COMMITTEES

The work of a large international conference cannot be accomplished wholly in plenary meetings. Most of the major international public conferences held after World War I were attended by a great number of conferees. The plenum of a conference of this type is too cumbersome a body to undertake the detailed preparation of the decisions of the gathering. Moreover, the tasks which conferences are confronted with are frequently complicated and technical. The topics figuring on the agenda of the conference should therefore be distributed among several committees, whose number and membership depend largely on the quantity and nature of the business on hand. The task of the committees is to study attentively the questions referred to them and to report to the conference. Items belonging to related subjects should be referred, as far as possible, to the same committees. Generally speaking, it will be the steering committee of the conference which makes proposals to the conference concerning the distribution of the topics on the agenda among the different committees.

NUMBER OF COMMITTEES

Division of work must not lead to undue fragmentation. The committees of a conference should not be too numerous, but their number must be sufficient to ensure smooth and efficient work.[43]

[43] At the Paris Peace Conference 58 committees and subcommittees were created which held 1646 meetings. André Tardieu, *La Paix* (Paris: Payot et Cie., 1921), pp.

Traditionally, the Assembly of the League appointed six main committees.[44] In 1938, by way of experiment, the Assembly added a seventh committee to the existing six. These committees dealt with the following items:

1. Legal and constitutional questions
2. Technical organizations
3. The reduction of armaments
4. Budgetary questions
5. Social and general questions
6. Political questions
7. Health, opium, and questions on intellectual cooperation

The Pan American Conferences generally appoint almost as many main committees as the Assembly of the League.

The London Monetary and Economic Conference held in 1933 appointed only two main committees, an Economic Committee and a Financial Committee, in spite of the complexity of its task and the huge number of delegates attending.

COMMITTEE OF THE WHOLE

A conference sometimes sits as a committee of the whole. This procedure is frequently used by conferences with a smaller attendance than those mentioned above, and also when the agenda of the conference is relatively simple such as, for instance, the discussion of an existing draft convention. In this case, after a general discussion in plenary meeting, the conference will sit as a committee of the whole in order to discuss the articles of the draft convention separately.

Drafting committees are appointed for the task of drawing up in a convenient form the decisions of the conference. The conference then meets again in plenary session for the formal adoption of the texts prepared by the drafting committee.

But even in the case of a very large conference, a system similar to that of the committee of the whole may be employed. Thus, the Disarmament Conference constituted a General Commission of the Confer-

95–108. For an interesting comparison of the preparation and organization of the Paris Peace Conference with the preparation and organization of the Congress of Vienna, see Paul You, *Die Friedens-Warte*, Vol. 43 (1943), pp. 146–59. For a recent and detailed study of the procedure and organization of the Paris Peace Conference, see F. Marston, *The Peace Conference of 1919; Organization and Procedure* (London, etc.: Oxford University Press, 1944).

[44] For a general study of the committees of the Assembly of the League of Nations and their procedure, see Marcel Henri Prévost, *Les commissions de l'Assemblée de la Société des Nations* (Paris: Editions A. Pedone, 1936).

ence consisting of one representative for each delegation. The Conference authorized the General Commission to constitute, as and when the need arose, such commissions, subcommissions, and committees as it might consider desirable. These bodies were to report to the General Commission on the matters which it referred to them. The General Commission elected as its president the President of the Conference. Thus the General Commission was the Conference sitting in a less formal and solemn way.

COMPOSITION OF COMMITTEES

According to custom, all delegations are entitled to be represented on each main committee of an international conference. In many cases the rules of procedure specify that the members of the committee may be accompanied by advisers, experts, and secretaries. The delegations to the Assembly of the League had full freedom to designate their representatives in the main committees.[45] Special forms were distributed to the delegations at the opening of the first meeting of the session, requesting them to fill in the names of the delegates who were to take part in the work of the various committees.[46] These forms were collected without delay, and a list of members of committees was compiled by the Secretariat and distributed in mimeographed form at the first meeting of the committees of the Assembly when the chairmen were appointed.[47] They were printed in the *Assembly Journal* the same night for permanent reference throughout the Assembly session.

The procedure followed by the Seventh International Conference of American States held in Montevideo in 1933 was slightly different. The President of the Conference determined the membership of the committees in accordance with the lists submitted by the presidents of delegations, indicating the members of the delegations who were to

[45] The United Nations Conference on Food and Agriculture adopted a similar procedure. The relevant provisions of the Regulations of this Conference were:

"ART. 12. The Conference shall be divided into the following four Technical Sections and such Committees as the respective Sections shall determine. . . .

"ART. 14. Each delegation shall be entitled to be represented by one or more of its members in each of the Technical Sections. The names of such members shall be transmitted by each delegation to the Secretary-General as soon as possible and in any event before the first regular meeting of each Section."

[46] See pp. 78–79.

[47] As a rule a delegation is under no obligation to retain the same representative in a committee throughout the whole session of a conference. In the practice of the League, there was no difficulty in replacing one representative in a committee of the Assembly or of an *ad hoc* conference by another representative; the only formality consisted in advising the Secretary General of the change. The fulfilment of this formality was, however, essential.

serve on each committee. But this practice was changed at the Eighth
Pan American Conference, held at Lima in December, 1938, and a
procedure similar to the procedure of the League of Nations adopted.
Article 9 of the Regulations of this Conference provided that "There
shall also be organized committees for each chapter into which the program of the Conference is divided, to study, report, and formulate projects on the topics of the agenda. Each delegation shall be entitled to be
represented by one or more of its members on each committee, the
names of such members to be transmitted by each delegation to the
Secretary-General as soon as possible and in any event before the first
meetings of the committees."

At its second session, held in September, 1944, at Montreal, the
Council of the United Nations Relief and Rehabilitation Administration created two *ad hoc* committees on policy and procedure for the
duration of the session. The Council decided that these committees
"shall consist of such members of the Council or their alternates as desire to participate in the work of the respective committees."

If a conference is of a highly technical character, the main committees may be composed of members especially appointed for their
knowledge of the problems under discussion or their interest in them.
Thus, the members of the committees of the International Labor Conferences are selected by the Committee of Selection from lists furnished
by the government groups and the employers' and the workers' groups.

OFFICERS OF COMMITTEES, "RAPPORTEURS"

As a rule committees have the right to appoint their chairmen[48]
and, if necessary, one or several vice chairmen. Whatever may be said
concerning the qualifications of a committee chairman would merely be
a repetition of what has already been said in connection with the president of the conference itself. However, more technical knowledge of the
problems under discussion is usually required from the chairman of a
committee than from the president of the conference.

The continental custom of appointing a *rapporteur* charged with the
task of submitting the conclusions of a committee to the main body has

---

[48] There are, however, examples of presidents of a conference choosing the committees' chairmen. The Council of the United Nations Relief and Rehabilitation
Administration at its second session appointed the chairmen of the Committees on
Credentials, on Observers, and on Nominations upon suggestions made in plenary
session from the floor when the other members of these three committees were appointed. The chairmen and the vice chairmen of the two *ad hoc* committees created at
the same session were also directly appointed by the Council on the basis of their
selection by the Committee on Nominations.

been accepted by almost all international conferences. Very seldom does the chairman of the committee undertake the task of reporting the committee's findings to the conference.[49] The rôle of the rapporteur is rarely defined in the regulations of an international conference.[50] For this reason it may be of interest to quote the provisions concerning rapporteurs embodied in the Regulations of the Seventh International Conference of American States:

ART. 10. The chairman of each committee shall appoint a reporting delegate for each topic or each group of related topics. The functions of the reporting delegates shall be:

1. To initiate the discussion of the question under consideration and present a report containing the antecedents and an analysis of the various aspects of the question, which shall serve as a basis of discussion.

2. At the conclusion of the discussion, the reporting delegate shall summarize

[49] Generally the chairman of the "central" committee of the conference acts as rapporteur. Thus, the president of the conference, who as a rule acts *ex officio* as chairman of the Bureau, reports to the conference in the name of the steering committee.

[50] Reference to rapporteurs is made only briefly in two provisions of the Rules of Procedure of the Assembly of the League of Nations. Rule 14, paragraph 4, provided that "Each committee shall appoint its Chairman and Rapporteurs," and Rule 15, paragraph 2, states that "The Chairman and the Rapporteur of a committee may be accorded precedence for the purpose of defending or explaining the conclusions arrived at by their committee."

The Standing Orders for Committees of the International Labor Conference are slightly more explicit. Article 2, paragraphs 3 and 4, provide that each committee shall elect from among its members one or more reporters to present the result of its deliberations to the Conference on its behalf and that before presenting a report to the committee for its approval, the reporter or reporters shall submit it to the officers of the committee. It is added that the reporters may be either delegates or advisers.

The Council of the League of Nations had two kinds of rapporteurs — permanent rapporteurs and special rapporteurs. Permanent rapporteurs were appointed each year by the Council for certain categories of questions with which the Council was habitually called upon to deal. These appointments were made in pursuance of Article III, paragraph 4, of the Rules of Procedure of the Council, which provided that "At the last ordinary session of each year, the Council shall draw up a list of rapporteurs for the various matters with which it is habitually called upon to deal." Special rapporteurs were appointed by the Council when it deemed this to be expedient for the study of matters brought before it and for which there was no permanent rapporteur. The number of special rapporteurs varied according to cases; the Council called on one or more rapporteurs. Usually, however, when several persons (generally three) were called upon, only one of them acted as rapporteur, and it was the duty of the other two to assist him in his task. When the special rapporteurs were not appointed by the Council they were appointed by its President in pursuance of Article III, paragraph 5, of the Rules of Procedure of the Council, which reads as follows: "Where rapporteurs have not been appointed by the Council, they shall be appointed by the President."

The Rules of Procedure of the Council of the United Nations Relief and Rehabilitation Administration do not contain special provisions concerning rapporteurs. Reference, however, is incidentally made to rapporteurs in Article IX, paragraph 2, of these Rules, to the following effect: "The chairman or rapporteur of a committee shall be accorded preference for the purpose of explaining or defending the report of the committee." It is customary for *ad hoc* committees of the Council of the United Nations Relief and Rehabilitation Administration to call on a rapporteur.

the debate in a report and shall formulate, in accordance with the opinion of the majority of the committee, the project which, after approval by the committee, shall be submitted to the Conference. A general reporting delegate may be appointed to submit the conclusions of the committee to the Conference.

3. The minority group of a committee shall have the right to designate a reporting delegate to present their views to the Conference, and the project which they may formulate.[51]

The duties of the rapporteurs of the conferences held under the auspices of the League, and of the committees of the Assembly, were very close to those defined by the above-quoted provisions of the Seventh Pan American Conference.

In the practice of the League the rôle of the rapporteur was very important. Indeed, the conclusions of his report were generally accepted by the committee and thereafter by the main body. It was not exceptional for a rapporteur to be a very able conferee with a thorough knowledge of the problems under discussion. Sometimes, however, a rapporteur would be selected merely to satisfy a delegation or an individual. In such a case the report was drafted by the Secretariat and the name of the rapporteur had no particular significance.[52] But it would be a mistake to assert that the influence of the Secretariat was always paramount. There are many instances in which drafts of the so-called Rapporteur's Report, prepared by the Secretariat, were replaced by texts actually drawn up by the rapporteur or a small committee of delegates convoked privately by the rapporteur.[53]

SUBCOMMITTEES

Committees themselves often set up subcommittees, which generally elect their own officers. Subcommittees seldom comprise representatives of all the delegations attending the conference. Indeed, they are almost always concerned with technical or legal aspects of a problem and expert knowledge is usually the criterion for the choice of subcommittee

---

[51] Compare the above-quoted provisions with the slightly different provisions adopted for the Eighth International Conference of American States. See Appendix VII, *infra*.

[52] Reviewing a pamphlet by R. J. P. Mortished, entitled *Problems of International Organisation*, recently published in the Workers' Educational Association, *Study Outlines*, No. 12, London, 1944, Mr. J V. Wilson, former Chief of the Central Section of the Secretariat of the League of Nations, says that the author, an official of the International Labor Office, "makes an interesting comparison between the practice of the I.L.O., where the Office itself made proposals, and that of the League, where this responsibility was taken by a Delegate acting as Rapporteur. The distinction is perhaps more formal than real, because it was known and accepted that the proposals of League Rapporteurs were usually drafted by the Secretariat." *International Affairs*, London, Vol. XX (1944), p. 563.   [53] See *infra*, pp. 152–53.

members. Subcommittees in their turn may create subordinate organs. However, no abuse must be made of the device of subcommittees and subordinate organs, for if they become too numerous the machinery of a conference jams.

26. THE SECRETARIAT

As has been pointed out, there are two organs which are essential for an international conference: the conference itself sitting in plenary meeting, and the presiding officer of the conference. The third organ of importance is the secretariat of the conference.

In Part I of this study, the manifold advantages resulting from the existence of a permanent secretariat have been explored. It has been stated that the Secretary General of the League and the Director of the International Labor Office were *ex-officio* secretaries of almost all the meetings held under the auspices of these two organizations. For this reason it was unnecessary to describe in detail the duties of the secretariat in the regulations of the conferences dependent on the League or the International Labor organizations.

If the services of a permanent secretariat are not available, the rules governing the functions of the secretary general of the conference and of his staff must be laid down with greater precision. For instance, the Regulations of the Eighth International Conference of American States provided that:

ARTICLE 6. The duties of the secretary general are:

1. To organize, direct, and coordinate the work of the assistant secretaries, secretaries of committees, interpreters, clerks, and other employees which the Government of Peru may appoint for service with the secretariat of the Conference.

2. To receive, distribute, and answer the official correspondence of the Conference in conformity with the resolutions of that body.

3. To prepare, or cause to be prepared under his supervision, the minutes of the meeting in conformity with the notes the secretaries shall furnish him; and to distribute among the delegates, before each session, printed or mimeographed copies of the minutes of the previous session, for the consideration of the Conference.

4. To revise the translations made by the interpreters of the Conference.

5. To distribute among the committees the matters on which they are required to present reports, and place at the disposal of the committees everything that may be necessary for the discharge of their duties.

6. To prepare the order of the day in conformity with the instructions of the president.

7. To be the intermediary between the delegations or their respective members

in matters relating to the Conference and between the delegates and the Peruvian authorities.

8. To transmit the original minutes of the Conference and of the committees to the Director General of the Pan American Union for preservation in the archives of the Union.

9. To perform such other functions as may be assigned to him by the regulations, by the Conference, or by the President.

This listing of functions shows clearly the many-sided character of the duties of the secretary general of an international conference; it is, however, far from being complete, though lack of space does not permit extending it here. For present purposes it will perhaps be sufficient to mention some of the methods employed by the Secretariat of the League and the International Labor Office during international conferences.

In accordance with the Rules of Procedure of the Assembly (Article 4, paragraph 2a) and the Standing Orders of the International Labor Conferences (Article 6, paragraph 3), both the Secretary General and the Director of the International Labor Office (whose functions correspond to those of the Secretary General) were required to submit to the respective bodies an annual report on the work of the Secretariat and the Office respectively, and on the steps taken to give effect to the decisions of previous sessions.

The manner in which these reports were submitted to the two bodies and discussed by them was reflected in the rôle played by the secretaries of the two organizations.

The dynamic personality of the first Director of the International Labor Office exerted the most profound influence upon the relationship between the International Labor Conference and its secretary general. M. Albert Thomas was not satisfied with presenting a written report on the work of the organization since the last session of the conference. He dwelt upon it at great length in a brilliant speech which was always one of the high lights of the whole session. He did not hesitate to request permission to speak whenever he deemed it necessary. His was a powerful influence upon the Conference, and he made full use of it.

The report of the Secretary General of the League was usually a formal and detailed account of the work of the League since the previous meeting of the Assembly. The last peacetime report of that official was the only one written in a more vivid form. The Secretary General never added oral explanations to his report and he sat by silently throughout the session. This was consistent with the traditions of the congresses and conferences before World War I. But one may well regret that the voice of the official to whom had been entrusted the safekeeping of the Covenant did not rise from time to time to warn the delegations of the dangers threatening the peace. It would seem that a middle course could have been found which would have afforded the Secretary General an opportunity to expound before a large audience the principles underlying the Covenant of the League.

The Secretary General of the League did not hesitate, however, to take part in the discussions of the Bureau and of the main committees of the Assembly. But the meetings of the Bureau were not public and the Secretary General spent the greater part of his time participating in the discussions of the Fourth Committee of the Assembly in order to defend his budget. It was regrettable that the Secretary General had to devote the best of his efforts, at the time when the Assembly was in session, to securing the appropriation of credits, which often amounted to ridiculously small sums. This practice prevented him from giving all the necessary attention to important political and technical problems.

It was not unusual, in addition, for the Secretary General to intervene during meetings of the Council. Nor was it unusual for him to speak during a plenary meeting of an *ad hoc* conference held under the auspices of the League, and to give advice to the conferees. He spoke even more frequently during sessions of standing and *ad hoc* committees of the League.

Passing to another aspect of the work of the Secretariat of the League during international conferences, it may be of interest to describe in more detail the ways and means by which the chair was assisted by the officials of the League.

The most elaborate preparation was made for the plenary meetings of the Assembly. For these meetings the Secretary of the Chair prepared a real "scenario," i.e., a complete outline of what was supposed to happen during the meeting. Such an outline, for instance, would contain passages like the following:

The President says: The agenda of the present meeting involves a number of preliminary formalities, which I now call upon you to fulfill, etc. If no one has any objection to offer, I shall consider these proposals adopted.

The President says: The next item on the agenda is, etc. If no one has any remarks to offer, I shall take it that the Assembly agrees to the proposal, and the request will accordingly be referred to the . . . Committee for examination, the Assembly deciding in the meantime to suspend the application of rule . . . of the Rules of Procedure.

The President says: . . . The Proposal is adopted. . . .

The President says: The next item on the agenda is the general discussion of the report on the work of the League since the . . . session of the Assembly.

Mr. X, first delegate of . . . will address the Assembly, etc.

When it was expected that the discussion would be complicated several drafts were prepared in order to enable the President to cope with hypothetical developments. Previous experience enabled the Secretary of the Chair in most cases to foresee what would happen under certain circumstances. One of the drafts prepared in advance usually fitted the situation that actually arose. When an unexpected proposal was made, the time needed for the translation of the proposal was generally sufficient for the hurried preparation of a special draft for the President. These cases were, however, exceptional. As a rule, the draft was discussed beforehand with the President, who offered his comments and gave his instructions to the Secretariat. One copy of the draft was submitted for approval to the Secretary General, another was given to the interpreter attached to the chair. A third copy was placed in the hands of the stenographers in order to facilitate their task.

It was this careful preparation that was largely responsible for the smoothness and dignity which characterized the plenary meetings of the Assembly and which could not fail to make a profound impression upon the audience. To presidents who were thoroughly experienced in the work of international conferences and who were skilled in the art of parliamentary procedure, the draft prepared by the Secretariat served merely as a means of orientation. For other presidents it was an indispensable guide and text, especially for those who lacked sufficient knowledge of the French and English languages.

The drafts prepared for the President of the Assembly on the occasion of a meeting of the Bureau were less elaborate. They indicated briefly what were the different topics on the agenda of the meeting of the Bureau, the decisions suggested, and the communications to be made.

For the meetings of the Council the draft prepared for the President indicated for each topic of the agenda whether the President must ask anyone not a member of the Council to sit at the Council table. The draft indicated also whom the President must call upon to speak in relation to the topic to be discussed, and it likewise contained the formula according to which the decision of the Council was to be recorded.

In recent years it has been customary to hold a private meeting of the Council prior to the first public meeting. During this private meeting the President of the Council informed his colleagues of the manner in which he intended to conduct the public meeting. The members of the

Council had an opportunity to make observations or suggestions and the Secretary General to express his opinion.[54]

In the case of very large *ad hoc* conferences, detailed drafts were occasionally prepared by the Secretariat for the guidance of the president during the meeting. Usually, however, no drafts were prepared; the secretary of the conference would currently advise the presiding officer in a low voice as the meeting went on. The same was true in the case of the meetings of the main committees of the Assembly and of most of the standing and *ad hoc* committees. The Secretariat not only assisted the chair in conducting the discussions during the meeting but it also helped the president and the Bureau to coordinate the work.

During the session of the Assembly several meetings of the "executive secretaries" of all the committees were held under the chairmanship of a Deputy Secretary General. Each executive secretary informed his colleagues of the number of meetings which were necessary for his committee to finish its work. Time-limits were set and plenary meetings fixed. The Secretary General was informed by the executive secretaries of all important political or administrative difficulties which arose in the committees. The Treasurer was informed as early as was possible of decisions involving possible new expenditures.

To describe here in detail the functions of the staff attached to the conference, would be repeating what has already been said in Part I of the present study. It will be sufficient to reiterate that the success of a conference depends to a considerable extent upon the efficiency of the work of all the members of its secretariat.

[54] This afforded the Secretary General an opportunity to exert his influence upon the decisions of the Council, since he himself felt more free to speak during a private meeting of the Council than in a public meeting. One could have welcomed this influence if it had always been in favor of the principles set up by the Covenant. Unfortunately, this was not always the case. For instance, in May, 1939, the Secretary General, by his intervention in a private meeting on the Council, prevented the reading by the President of the Council in the public Council meeting of a telegram from Dr. Beneš protesting against the occupation of Ruthenia by Hungarian troops.

Theoretically the Secretary General might have been right in warning the President of the Council that the reading of a communication emanating from a private person (Dr. Beneš had at that time not yet been recognized as President of the Czechoslovak Republic) was contrary to the established custom. It would seem, however, that the political situation would have justified the making of an exception. It is obvious that the Secretary General would never have expressed himself in the same manner during a public meeting.

PART III

ORGANIZING—DIRECTING—COORDINATING

(*Continued*)

Meetings of the Conference and the Committees

In Part II of this handbook, considerable space has been devoted to an examination of the organs of an international conference. These organs are, as a rule, created in accordance with a set of official rules which either already exist (if the conference is a regular feature of a permanent international organization), or are specially drawn up (if the conference has been convoked for a specific purpose).[1] The business of the conference, either in plenary meetings or in committees, will therefore generally be conducted in accordance with the provisions of existing rules established for the occasion.

The organization and the business of the Assembly of the League of Nations were regulated by its Rules of Procedure.[2] International Labor Conferences are guided by Standing Orders. The sets of rules governing the organization and proceedings of both these bodies were set up in the early days of their existence and afterwards amended and perfected. They are somewhat bulky and complicated, being to a certain extent a compilation of various systems used in different parliaments. Some of the rules of procedure of the standing committees of the League were rather detailed. Other committees had no rules whatsoever, in the strict sense of the term. Their procedure was governed by the basic texts of their whole organization; this was the case, for instance, with the Commission of Enquiry for European Union.

Many commissions settled questions of procedure as they arose, in the light of the rules of the Assembly. Similarly, many commissions with rules of procedure of their own had recourse to the rules of the Assembly whenever their own rules were found to be obscure, incomplete, or inadequate.

The adoption of the League's General Regulations on Committees in 1936 brought more unity in the rules of procedure of the standing committees. Moreover, the Council decided that committees to be set up

---

[1] It was not the practice of diplomatic conferences held prior to the twentieth century to adopt formal rules of procedure for conducting their business.

[2] See Appendix VIII, *infra*.

in the future should submit their draft rules of procedure to the Council for endorsement.

Ad hoc conferences held under the auspices of the League generally adopted special rules of procedure at an early stage of their work.[3] Usually, draft rules of procedure were prepared by the Secretariat and submitted for approval to the conference by the chair. Sometimes, however, the conference appointed a special committee charged with the task of drawing up the rules of procedure.[4] There was a tendency to make these rules less complicated than those of the Assembly and in doubtful cases to have recourse, like the standing committees, to the rules of the Assembly.

The rules of procedure of the Pan American Conferences are drafted by the Governing Board of the Pan American Union before the opening of the session.[5]

The Rules of Procedure of the Council and of the Standing Committees of the United Nations Relief and Rehabilitation Administration, adopted at the First Session of the Council of the Administration, held at Atlantic City, are undoubtedly influenced by the rules of procedure of the League, the International Labor Organization, and the International Conferences of American States.

An international conference, as a rule, is at liberty to change its rules of procedure at any time, provided, of course, in the case of an international organization, that the changes made shall not be inconsistent with the charter of the organization. A provision is generally embodied in the rules, however, laying down special conditions for the adoption of any modifications. Thus, the Rules of Procedure of the Assembly provided that no alteration should be made "except upon a majority vote of the Assembly, taken after a committee has reported on the proposed alteration." The Regulations of the Eighth International Conference of American States provided that the rules might be subject to such modifications "as may be determined by a vote of two thirds of the delegations at the Conference." Article XIV of the Rules of Procedure of the Council of the United Nations Relief and Rehabilitation Administration provides that the Rules of Procedure of the Council may be suspended by a two-thirds majority of the members of the

[3] However, the Organization for Communications and Transit set up rules of procedure which were valid for all general and limited conferences on communications and transit.

[4] For instance, the Disarmament Conference of 1932.

[5] The Rules of Procedure of the Eighth International Conference of American States are given in Appendix VII, *infra.*

Council present at any meeting and that amendments may be adopted by a simple majority of the members present at any meeting subject to the proposal having first been reported upon by a Committee of the Council.

The work of international public conferences is conducted in plenary meetings and in committee and subcommittee meetings. If the conference is large the number of plenary meetings will be reduced to a minimum because of the impossibility or inadvisability of carrying on detailed discussions in a body sometimes comprising several hundred conferees. General principles may be formulated, broad directives given, and decisions recorded in the large meetings, but problems cannot be scrutinized and documents drafted by a multitude of delegates. Conferences of smaller proportions can conduct a good proportion of business in plenary meetings, but the drafting of texts is referred to a drafting committee or to the Bureau of the gathering.

27. PLENARY MEETINGS

At least two plenary meetings are indispensable in any international conference, one for initiating the work of the conference, the other for concluding it. At the first meeting the conference will create its organs and organize its work, at the last it will record the results of the session. As a rule, however, more than two plenary meetings are needed.

The opening meeting of a conference has almost always a solemn character. Preparation for it will be carefully made by the temporary or permanent secretariat. All material arrangements in the meeting room will be checked not only by the official in charge of the internal administration but also by the official appointed for assisting the chair in the Bureau. Indeed, such arrangements as the allocation of seats sometimes has a political significance.[6]

When the conference has been convoked at the initiative of the government which acts as host to the gathering, or when a conference held under the auspices of an international organization is held outside the seat of the organization, the head of state of the receiving country or one of his representatives will sometimes formally open the conference.

At the inaugural session of an International Conference of American

---

[6] No seats were reserved for Czechoslovakia at the Assembly held in December, 1939. The removal of the posters bearing the name of that country from the meeting room on order of the Secretary General was not justifiable.

States the chief of state of the country in which the conference is held solemnly addresses the conferees. Thus, among the League conferences, the London Monetary and Economic Conference of 1933 was opened personally by the King of England, who addressed the members of the Conference in French and English. The Conference of Central Authorities of Eastern Countries dealing with the suppression of traffic in women and children, held at Bandoeng in 1937, was inaugurated by a speech of the head of the Department of Justice of the Netherlands Indies, acting as substitute for the Governor General.

This inaugural session is sometimes held in a place different from the one where the conference meets for its business meetings, such as the residence of the head of a state.

The first meetings of a session of the Assembly of the League or of an International Labor Conference were opened by the President of the Council of the League or by the Chairman of the Governing Body, respectively.

In the practice of the Assembly of the League the temporary President, immediately on taking the chair, proposed the appointment of the Credentials Committee. As soon as that committee was appointed he delivered his opening address.

The opening address delivered by the President of the Council was usually prepared by the Secretariat and consisted of a brief review of the events relating to the League which had occurred since the last session of the Assembly. To this review the President of the Council frequently added a personal touch by referring to the position of his country towards international problems. He then outlined the work of the forthcoming session and expressed the hope that it would be successful.

Following the opening address, the Assembly heard the report of the Credentials Committee. Under the new procedure which went into effect in 1936, the Assembly, upon adopting this Committee's report, appointed the Nominations Committee and thereafter adjourned. Upon resumption of the meeting the Chairman of the Nominations Committee proposed the nomination of one of the delegates as President of the Assembly. The election of the President then took place followed immediately by a speech of the elected President. This address was supposed to be an improvisation; in reality the election of the permanent President was seldom a complete surprise to the nominee. The extemporaneous speech had frequently been well prepared in advance.

The Nominations Committee submitted its proposals concerning the composition of the Bureau of the Assembly, and the election of the Vice Presidents took place. Next came the appointment of the Agenda Committee and the adoption of the agenda of the session.

In Part I of this handbook it has been stated that the Assembly was practically under no limitation in the choice of its subjects for discussion. The length of the session depended therefore upon the number and the nature of the topics to be considered by the Assembly. Nevertheless, it was possible to predict that with some twenty or twenty-five routine items figuring on the agenda, the Assembly would last about three weeks unless the discussion of the report of the Secretary General was unexpectedly prolonged. Obviously, if some important political question came up for discussion, other arrangements had to be made as to the duration of the session.

Upon the adoption of the agenda,[7] the Assembly adjourned again and the main committees, as well as the Agenda Committee, met in order to elect their chairmen.

At the following meeting of the Assembly the President informed the delegations of the composition of the Bureau, and in the name of the latter he made proposals concerning the distribution among the main committees of the items on the agenda. With this all the preliminaries were completed and the Assembly entered into the general discussion of the work of the League since its last session.

If it has been deemed useful to describe in detail how the Assembly of the League was put in motion, it is because in this respect the Assembly procedure was the most complicated of all the League conferences. Indeed, frequently the conferences held under the auspices of the League had a president appointed beforehand by the Council, but none of them appointed a Nominations Committee. Frequently also no Agenda Committee was appointed. The preliminaries of the actual work of such conferences were therefore greatly simplified. However, the sequence of events would be, *mutatis mutandis*, almost the same.[8]

As a rule, a general discussion of the problems submitted for consideration takes place in the course of every international conference. The report of the Secretary General served as the basis for this type of dis-

[7] It is customary during the session of a conference to circulate to the members of the gathering a daily agenda. As a rule the agenda of the meeting must be put on the desks of the delegates, with all the relevant documents, before each meeting. The same must be done for the committee meetings.

[8] As has already been pointed out, a set of regulations would be adopted at an early stage of the conference; for instance, immediately after the appointment of the Credentials Committee if no previously established rules of procedure had to be followed.

cussion by the Assembly of the League. In other conferences the text of a draft convention or the report of a preparatory committee or some other document would provide the basis for a general exchange of views.

It is the task of the president of the conference to regulate and canalize the general discussion.[9] The secretary of the Chair can be of the greatest help to the president in this respect. It is necessary to find out as soon as possible the names of those who intend to speak as well as the time for the addresses. It was frequently difficult to find speakers for initiating the general discussion at the League Assemblies, because the delegates of the great powers preferred to speak at the end of the discussion and the delegates of the small powers hesitated to speak before the point of view of the great powers had been disclosed.

As it is difficult to begin the committee work before the general discussion has been concluded, it is desirable that such discussion should not last too long. In the practice of the Assembly the general discussion had to be brought to a close at the end of the first week of the session, as each additional day of general deliberation meant a proportionate extension of the length of the whole session, normally limited to three weeks.

After the conclusion of the general discussion the committee work of the conference begins. Unless an important question must be settled by the conference sitting as a whole, no more plenary meetings are then necessary until the committee work is completed, when the conference resumes the plenary meetings in order to approve the final texts of the session.[10]

The last stage of the session of the Assembly, comparatively speaking, was short, thanks to the efficient methods developed for the adoption of the reports and resolutions.[11] Similarly, the last meetings in an *ad hoc* conference held under the auspices of the League were, whatever

[9] In 1922 the Assembly adopted certain proposals of its Bureau concerning the arrangements for the debates on the annual report of the Secretary General. See Appendix X, *infra*.

[10] In the League practice it often happened that the committees met during the period when the report on the work of the League was under discussion. Similarly, the plenary meetings were resumed while the committees were still in action.

[11] Rule 14 (a) of the Rules of Procedure of the Assembly stated:

"1. When the reports and resolutions submitted by the various Committees of the Assembly are brought up for adoption in plenary session, the President, in the cases indicated below, shall read the titles of the reports and put forthwith to the vote the resolutions which are proposed.

"2. The procedure provided for in paragraph 1 shall only apply in cases where the Committee has unanimously declared that it does not consider a discussion of the report in plenary session to be necessary and where no delegation had subsequently asked the President to open a discussion on the report. The report must be circulated to the delegations twenty-four hours before it is brought up in plenary session."

the results, a mere acknowledgment of the work of the committees. Only very seldom would a delegation take a strong stand against committee decisions.[12]

When the session has thus reached its last stage, it is brought to an official conclusion with a speech of the president.

When a conference held under the auspices of the League ended with the signing of an agreement or convention, this usually took place at the last meeting of the conference, before the closing address of the president. The ceremony was often a simple one, the Head of the Treaty Registration Branch of the Legal Section of the Secretariat acting as *Chef du Protocole*. Sometimes, however, the Secretary General and other high officials attended, and a certain amount of pomp marked the occasion. An elaborate inkstand made of gold and ivory, presented to the League by the Emperor of Ethiopia, was used on such occasions.

The president's last address to the conference is a summary of the work of the session and a commendation of the results achieved. Usually the president also expresses thanks for the assistance given to the conference by the secretariat. If the conference has been enjoying the hospitality of a certain country it is customary for the president to pay tribute to the government of that country.[13] He then formally announces the closing of the session.

28. COMMITTEE MEETINGS

The actual work of a conference is performed by its committees and subcommittees.

Committees go about their work in a more simple and direct way than the conference as a whole. After electing its officers (if these are not appointed beforehand), the committee immediately enters into the discussion of its agenda. Frequently a general discussion precedes the

[12] See, for example, the statement of the delegate of the United States of America explaining the reasons for which he was not willing to sign the convention prepared by the Conference for the Suppression of the Illicit Traffic in Dangerous Drugs. League of Nations, *Records of the Conference for the Suppression of the Illicit Traffic in Dangerous Drugs (Geneva, June 8th to 26th, 1936), Text of the Debates*, pp. 174–76.

[13] At its first session, held at Atlantic City in November–December, 1943, the Council of the United Nations Relief and Rehabilitation Administration adopted the following resolutions: (1) Resolution expressing thanks to the Government of the United States of America as the host of the session; (2) Resolution expressing thanks to the Mayor and Commissioners of Atlantic City and to the Manager of the Claridge Hotel in which the Conference was held; (3) Resolution expressing thanks to the representatives of the Press, Radio, and Motion Pictures; (4) Resolution expressing thanks to the officers and staff of the Temporary Secretariat; (5) Resolution expressing thanks to the Chairman of the Council.

detailed examination of the different items of the agenda. Obviously, the rôle of experts in committee discussions is more important than in plenary meetings of the conference. In the former, parliamentary skill must generally give way to technical knowledge.

The importance of the functions of the rapporteur has already been mentioned. The executive secretary who is attached to this officer of the commission will watch closely the discussion and will set up a draft report as the work goes on. At the end of the discussions the rapporteurs for the different items of the agenda submit their draft reports to the committee for approval.

Instead of appointing a rapporteur, a committee sometimes creates a subcommittee or a drafting committee. In such cases the chairmen of these subordinate bodies submit draft reports for the committee's approval.

Proposals and amendments in large volume will then start coming in; these are generally arranged by the president of the committee in a manner that will permit an orderly discussion. The texts finally agreed upon by the committee are submitted to the plenary conference for approval.[14]

29. PUBLICITY

Whether the discussions of the conference take place in plenary sittings or in committee meetings, certain rules for regulating the discussion have to be observed. In the practice of the League the first of these rules was publicity.

The principle was firmly established that plenary meetings of all types of conferences related to the League — whether they were sessions of permanent international institutions, or sessions of *ad hoc* conferences — must be held in public.[15] Private plenary meetings were the exception.

[14] Compare the procedure described *supra*, in the two sections "Plenary Meetings" and "Committee Meetings," with the procedure of the International Labor Conferences as described in No. 1 of the *Provisional Record* of the Twenty-Sixth Session of the International Labor Conference, held in Philadelphia in April–May 1944. See Appendix XI, *infra*.

[15] Compare the procedure of the League with the procedure adopted for the recent United Nations Conference on Food and Agriculture. Article 26 of the Regulations of the Conference stated that: "The opening and closing sessions of the Conference shall be public. Other public sessions may be held when previously agreed upon and so ordered by a majority vote of the delegations." This procedure is more in agreement with the classical procedure adopted for international governmental conferences prior to the first World War.

On the other hand, Article I, paragraph 3, of the Rules of Procedure of the Council of the United Nations Relief and Rehabilitation Administration provides that "as a

As far as League committee meetings were concerned the reverse was true. The rule was that committees should meet in private unless they decided otherwise. However, it was the custom for the main committees of the Assembly to sit in public. Similarly, many standing or *ad hoc* committees sat in public.[16] The General Regulations on Committees (Article 8) allowed the committees of the League full freedom to decide "whether their meetings are to be public." Publicity was secured:

1. By admitting the public [17] to the plenary meeting. Admission cards were distributed by the Secretary General.[18]
2. By an early publication of the records of the conference.
3. By announcing at a public meeting the decisions of the conference taken at a private meeting.
4. By issuing special summaries or communiqués to the press.
5. By granting special facilities to the journalists, photographers, and cinematograph operators.

The Information Section of the Secretariat of the League was in charge of all the arrangements made for helping the journalists in their tasks.

Obviously, everything that happens at an international conference cannot immediately be disclosed. There is danger in too much publicity.

---

general rule, the plenary meetings of the Council shall be public, but the Council may decide that any meeting shall be held in private."

Concerning the publicity of international conferences during the last eighty years, see the interesting study made by Hill, *op. cit.*, pp. 168 ff.

[16] Article II, paragraph 3, of the Rules of Standing Committees of the Council of the United Nations Relief and Rehabilitation Administration provides that "the meetings of each standing committee shall be private unless the committee shall decide by a two-thirds vote of the members present that any meeting shall be public."

[17] Obviously, the public is not admitted in the space reserved for the conferees. Sometimes the Rules of Procedure of conferences contain special provisions concerning the types of persons who are allowed to attend the meetings of the conference in the precincts reserved for the conferees. For instance, the Standing Orders of the International Labor Conferences provide that apart from delegates and advisers the only persons permitted to enter the conference hall are:

"(a) Ministers whose departments deal with the questions discussed by the Conference and who are not Delegates or advisers;

"(b) One secretary or interpreter for each Delegation;

"(c) Representatives on the Governing Body who are not Delegates or advisers at the Conference;

"(d) The Director of the International Labour Office and the officials of the secretariat of the Conference;

"(e) The secretaries of the Employers' and Workers' Groups;

"(f) Persons appointed by Members of the Organisation to occupy advisers' posts which may fall vacant in their delegations;

"(g) Persons appointed as observers by a State invited to attend the Conference."

[18] For the rules in force concerning the distribution of cards to the public during the sessions of the Assembly, see Appendix V, *infra*.

It often leads to the shifting of the discussion from conference and committee rooms to places outside the precincts of the conference. Those negotiations in the rooms of the big hotels of Geneva constituted a revenge of the old-fashioned diplomacy against the "open, just and honourable relations between nations" promised in the Preamble of the Covenant.

Private and even secret meetings may be necessary, but recourse to them must be had sparingly. Leakage of what happens at an international conference in peacetime can be avoided only with the greatest difficulty. Most of the time the responsibility for leakages will not fall upon a member of the secretariat but upon a delegation which will seek a political advantage by disclosing what happened during a secret meeting.[19]

A newspaper published at Geneva, the *Journal des Nations*, which, in spite of its name, had no official connections with the League, at times contained unusually accurate information concerning secret meetings of the League. Officials of the Secretariat could obtain more information by reading this newspaper than by questioning their colleagues who, even if they knew what happened during a secret meeting, were bound to observe complete discretion.

The skill and the personal influence of the head of the press service of a conference are important factors in the relationship between journalists and the international gathering. Generally speaking, the Director of the Information Section of the Secretariat of the League and his staff dealt successfully with the journalists when the meeting of the conference was held at Geneva. Their task became more complicated when a meeting was held outside Geneva because of the different environment and atmosphere.

30. RIGHT TO ADDRESS THE CONFERENCE

The rules of procedure must contain provisions regulating the rights of the conferees to address the conference, and usually also contain a stipulation entitling the Secretary General of the conference or his

[19] Harold Nicolson strongly criticized the methods adopted for dealing with the press at the Paris Peace Conference. In his opinion, "There are only two ways for dealing with a democratic Press. The best way is to tell them everything; that bores them stiff. The second best way is to tell them nothing, which at least provides them with the glory of a 'secrecy' stunt, which provides a highly pleasurable form of news value. The worst method is to tell them half-truths in the form of conciliatory leakages. It was this flabby method which was adopted by the Conference of Paris." Nicolson, *op. cit.*, pp. 123–24.

deputies to make verbal communications to the assembly. As a rule no member of the conference should be allowed to address the gathering without the express permission of the president. Also as a rule, speakers should be called upon in the order in which they have signified their desire to speak. In calling on speakers it is customary in conference practice to accord precedence to the chairmen and rapporteurs of commissions in order that they may have adequate opportunity to defend or explain conclusions arrived at by their commissions.

Sometimes the rules of procedure contain a provision stating that the conference may limit the time allowed to each speaker. Nevertheless, a provision to that effect is very difficult to apply in an intergovernmental conference, since the delegates are the representatives of sovereign states. However, a rule of that kind is easier to apply in conferences of a mixed character. Indeed, the Standing Orders of the International Labor Conferences contain a provision according to which "no speech shall exceed 15 minutes exclusive of the time for translation."

The chairman is entitled to call a speaker to order if his remarks are not relevant to the subject under discussion and, in extreme cases, he may direct the speaker to resume his seat. While the first measure may have to be enforced on some occasions, it would create a sensation if the president of an intergovernmental conference were to resort to the second measure.[20]

Finally, it is a firmly established custom, generally embodied in the rules of procedure of international conferences, that if, when a question is under discussion, a member rises to a point of order, such point of order must immediately be decided upon by the president.

31. LANGUAGES

A very important problem facing international conferences is that of languages. For centuries Latin was the language of international gatherings. Since the seventeenth century it has been gradually replaced by French. At the beginning of the twentieth century the position of French as the official international language was unchallenged. However, since World War I, English, Spanish, and even Italian and German have competed with the predominance of French as a recognized diplomatic language. The problem is further complicated by the fact that national groups wish to see their particular language accepted

[20] The author of this handbook has no recollection of a resort to the measure in question in the course of a conference held under the auspices of the League, but cases of that kind have happened during International Labor Conferences.

as the official language of an international conference. They look upon such acceptance as a recognition of their political importance, enhancing their prestige.[21]

The League of Nations inherited the parity of the French and English languages from the Paris Peace Conference. Nevertheless, there was but one standing rule providing for the use of French and English in speeches and documents. This provision was Rule 16 of the Rules of Procedure of the Assembly:

1. Speeches in French shall be summarised in English, and *vice versa*, by an interpreter belonging to the Secretariat.
2. A representative speaking in another language shall provide for the translation of his speech into one of these two languages.
3. All documents, resolutions and reports circulated by the President or the Secretariat shall be rendered in both French and English.
4. Any representative may have documents circulated in a language other than French and English, but the Secretariat will not be responsible for their translation or printing.
5. Any Member of the League, or any group of Members, may require that all documents and publications of the League shall be regularly translated into, and printed and circulated in, a language other than French and English, but shall in such case defray all the necessary expenses.

Most of the Rules of Procedure of the *ad hoc* conferences held under the auspices of the League contained similar provisions.

At the first and second sessions of the Assembly, the Spanish-speaking delegations made a very serious but unsuccessful effort to have the Spanish idiom recognized as the third language of the League.

The privilege of using languages other than French and English was not denied to speakers. But the provision requiring a representative who speaks in another language to provide for the translation of his speech into one of the two official languages resulted in the privilege being only rarely made use of.[22]

[21] At the conference held on the eve of World War I, in July, 1914, concerning Spitzbergen, the recognized official language was French. As the political situation rapidly deteriorated, the German delegate suddenly began to talk in German, and the Russian delegate immediately answered in Russian.
[22] A statement from the League's Secretariat, bearing on the relation of the language question to the selection of delegates sent to Geneva, is highly significant: "In the League of Nations, there are two official languages: French and English, and all communications must be made in these two languages. The delegates have the right, however, to make communications in other languages on condition that they have an interpreter, which necessitates two translations instead of one. Very few delegates take advantage of this privilege, because no one has time to lose and each interpretation slows up the speed of the work. The States, Members of the League of Nations, therefore renounce what is always a question of prestige and not of necessity, and send delegates who understand and speak French or English." Bibliothèque du

The representatives of Germany on the Council generally spoke German. Similarly, when addressing the Assembly during a plenary meeting, the German delegates spoke German, although they usually spoke French or English at committee meetings. Occasionally, to enhance the prestige of their nation, the Italian and the Polish representatives spoke in their native language.

The Emperor of Ethiopia spoke Amharic when he addressed the Assembly in 1936. In connection with this practice, embarrassing incidents sometimes happened. During a meeting of the Preparatory Commission of the Disarmament Conference a delegate of a Far Eastern country who had never before attended a meeting of the League, addressed the Commission in his national language; his speech was then translated into one of the official languages of the League by his own young secretary. To the bewilderment of two or three conferees who were able to understand the original speech of the Far Eastern delegate the translation did not correspond in the slightest degree with the speech actually delivered by the delegate himself. He had made a flowery peroration and the translation turned out to be a strong piece of nationalistic propaganda.

As a matter of fact most of the speeches made during the Assembly sessions were delivered in French.

In a very valuable study of the language problems of international conferences, Professor Herbert Newhard Shenton, taking into account only speeches made in plenary sessions of the Assembly of the League of Nations, obtained the following factual evidence for the years 1920, 1924, and 1927.

English, which was accepted quite generally at the first session of the Assembly in 1920 (35 per cent of the speeches were made in English, by delegates from twelve countries) on a basis of substantial equality, rapidly slipped into the background in later meetings, until in 1927 only 22 per cent of the speeches were made in English by delegates from six countries, four of these parts of the British Empire.

Percentage of speeches in French and English:

	1920	1924	1927
French................	65	79	77
English...............	35	21	22
German..............			1[23]

Bureau International des Fédérations d'Enseignement Secondaire, Fasc. No. 5, p. 4, quoted by Herbert Newhard Shenton, *Cosmopolitan Conversation; The Language Problems of International Conferences* (New York: Columbia University Press, 1933), pp. 382, 384.   [23] Shenton, *op. cit.*, pp. 380–82.

This trend continued during the following years.

It must be recalled that the question of an auxiliary language has been given serious attention by the League, the subject having been considered from various angles by the first three Assemblies. In pursuance of a decision made by the Second Assembly, the Secretariat prepared a report on "Esperanto as an International Auxiliary Language," which was discussed by the Third Assembly. The matter was then referred to the Committee on Intellectual Cooperation, which reported back with the recommendation of a wider study of national languages. The report of this Committee was accepted without the recommending clauses and no further development occurred.[24]

The Standing Orders of the International Labor Conference (Article 13) provide that:

1. The French and English languages shall be the official languages of the Conference.

2. Speeches in French shall be summarized in English and *vice versa* by an interpreter belonging to the secretariat of the Conference.

3. A Delegate may speak in a non-official language, but his Delegation must provide for a summarized translation of his speech into one of the two official languages by an interpreter attached to the Delegation, unless an interpreter of the Conference for the official languages can be placed at its disposal by the secretariat of the Conference. This summarized translation shall then be rendered in the other official language by an interpreter belonging to the secretariat.

4. The translation and circulation of documents shall be in the hands of the secretariat and the practice adopted at the Washington Conference as regards translation and distribution of documents in the Spanish [25] language shall be continued.

[24] For more details, see *ibid.*, pp. 396–98.
[25] At its twenty-sixth session, held at Philadelphia in April–May, 1944, the International Labor Conference adopted the following resolution:

"Considering that the nations of Latin America have made a substantial contribution to the development and universalisation of the International Labour Organisation;

"Considering that the nations of Latin America have unanimously developed, spontaneously and with exceptional rapidity, a social policy based on the international Conventions and on the generous conceptions of the protection of labour and collective welfare;

"Considering that the prominent position attained by the American Republics and the special social conditions of the Western Hemisphere have been demonstrated at the Labour Conferences of the American States which were held in 1936 and 1939, at Santiago-de-Chile and Havana respectively, and which had far-reaching results;

"Considering that the ethnical unity, historic traditions and Ideals characteristic of the peoples of Latin America demonstrate the existence of an authentic culture, the value of which is all the greater inasmuch as it extends over the whole of the South American Continent and Central America;

"Considering that the social development of Latin America springs from the Iberian civilisation, which is both Spanish and Portuguese and is two-fold in its nature, and still maintains this diversity which so far from being a cause of division, rather serves

The Standing Orders for Committees of the International Labor Conference (Article 7) provide in addition that:

4. In cases where at least one-fifth of the members of a Committee taking an actual part in its work either as regular members or as substitutes declare individually and in writing that it is difficult for them to take part in the proceedings of the Committee in either of the official languages and ask for an additional interpretation into another language with which they are conversant, the Committee shall accede to that request provided that the secretariat of the Conference is able to supply the necessary interpreters.

5. In cases where the number of members of a Committee who ask for an additional interpretation into a non-official language in the conditions laid down in the above paragraph is less than one-fifth of the number of members, the Committee shall decide whether it shall accede to the request as an exceptional measure and provided that the secretariat of the Conference is able to furnish the necessary interpreters.

The current practice of the International Labor Organization is to have all speeches rendered in English, French, and Spanish. During plenary meetings of the International Labor Conference the interpretation is made by simultaneous multiple telephone interpretation of speeches, as described below, but during the meetings of the Governing Body or the committee meetings the interpretation is successively made by interpreters.

As a rule, the official languages of the International Conferences of American States are Spanish, English, Portuguese, and French. The reports, projects, and other documents must be printed and submitted

---

to bind them more closely together for the preservation of the characteristics they derive from a common historic source;

"Considering that the Spanish and Portuguese languages spoken by the nations of Latin America are also the languages of the countries of the Iberian Peninsula, of the peoples of a large part of the Continent of Africa, and of various regions of Asia;

"Considering also that the Spanish and Portuguese languages are regional transformations and progressive adaptations of Latin and at the same time modern, living languages, with a classical etymology, which can be readily understood and acquired;

"Considering that the original root and the manner of development of the Portuguese and Spanish idioms, which development has taken place in geo-political condition presenting substantial similarities, have rendered impossible wide divergences between the two tongues, so that today the peoples who speak them can readily understand one another;

"Considering that the Havana Conference of 1939 in Resolution XXV, expressed itself unanimously in favour of the publication of legal decisions by the International Labour Organisation in Spanish and Portuguese;

"Considering finally that the use of the Spanish language has become an established practice of the International Labour Organisation and that Portuguese has been used for several official publications of the Organisation;

"The Conference requests the Governing Body to consider the possibility of making Spanish and Portuguese official languages of the International Labour Organisation and to submit to the next General Session of the Conference any necessary amendments of the Standing Orders of the Conference and its Committees."

for the consideration of these conferences and their committees at least in Spanish and English. Article 17 of the Regulations of the Eighth International Conference of American States, held at Lima in December, 1938, provided as follows: "Delegates may speak in their own languages from manuscript or otherwise. The interpreters shall render a summary of the speech in the other official languages of the conference unless the speaker or any delegate may request a complete translation of his remarks. The interpreters shall also render in the other official languages the remarks of the president and the secretary general of the Conference."

Between World War I and World War II the position of French as the official language of international diplomatic gatherings remained very strong, the practice adopted by the League of Nations, the International Labor Organization, and the Pan American Conferences being considered rather as an exception.

French was spoken at the Lausanne Peace Conference in 1923 and at the Conference of Locarno in 1925. Article 9 of the Rules of Procedure of the Red Cross Conference held in Geneva in 1929 provided that:

The French language is adopted as the official language for discussions and proceedings of the Conference. A summary in French of speeches made in another language shall be provided by the delegation to which the speaker belongs with the co-operation of the Secretariat, if necessary.

Certain of the British Empire delegations having expressed the wish that, as at League of Nations conferences, English should also be a language of the Red Cross conference, the President (M. Dinichert, head of the Swiss Delegation) maintained that, apart from that exception, French was the language of international conferences; arrangements would, however, be made to present summaries of the proceedings in English.[26]

At the United Nations Food and Agriculture Conference held at Hot Springs, Virginia, in May–June, 1943, the official language was English. The representative of France, however, made a reservation expressing the hope that French, as the traditional language of diplomatic gatherings, would be employed again in forthcoming international conferences.

Article XI of the Rules of Procedure of the Council of the United Nations Relief and Rehabilitation Administration provides that:

[26] Satow, *A Guide to Diplomatic Practice*, 3d edition, *op. cit.*, p. 316.

1. English shall be the official language of the Council and its committees.
2. Upon the request of any member of the Council that the final recommendations and resolutions of the Council and its committees shall be rendered both in English and in his own language, it shall be so provided.

In accepting this provision, the representative of France made a strong reservation stating that it must be clearly understood that he did not renounce in any way the right to claim for French its traditional rôle as the official language in the discussion and formulation of international documents of a diplomatic character.[27]

At the end of the United Nations Monetary and Financial Conference, held at Bretton Woods, New Hampshire, during the summer of 1944, the first delegate of France, Mr. Pierre Mendès-France, in a letter addressed on July 22, 1944, to Mr. Henry Morgenthau, Jr., President of the Conference, wrote "Allow me lastly to express regret that the Conference has not thought appropriate to give more precision to the drafting of its texts by using the French language which because of its clarity is traditionally used in diplomatic relations."

Undoubtedly the use of a single language considerably speeds the proceedings of a conference and greatly simplifies the task of its secre-

[27] The difficulties which occurred in connection with the adoption of this provision have been described by Dr. Francis B. Sayre, Diplomatic Adviser of the United Nations Relief and Rehabilitation Administration, in an address delivered at the Forty-eighth Annual Meeting of the American Academy of Political and Social Sciences, as follows:
"Whenever people come together from the four corners of the earth, difficulties and differences of opinion are bound to arise. The Atlantic City conference was no exception. Even inconsequential differences kept arising to plague us. For instance, there was the question of language. Our original draft of the permanent rules provided that English should be the official language. The French pressed a motion that French should be added as an official language, and secured its adoption. Then the Latin American countries pressed for Spanish. The Brazilian delegate thereupon moved for Portuguese. Finally, the Russian rose to his feet and for ten minutes filled the room with ringing Russian oratory. Then we proceeded to reconsider. . . ." *Annals of the American Academy of Political and Social Science*, Vol. 234 (July, 1944), p. 30.
The reservation made by the representative of France is recorded in the report of the Committee on Organization and Administration of the First Session of the Council of the United Nations Relief and Rehabilitation Administration as follows:
"With reference to Article XI of the proposed Rules of Procedure of the Council, the representative of the French Committee of National Liberation stated that he accepted in principle the use of English as the official language of the Council and its committees in view of the exclusively economic and technical character of the problems with which the Council has to deal, it being clearly understood, however, that he did not renounce in any way the right to claim for French its traditional role as the official language in the discussion and formulation of international documents of a diplomatic character. The representatives of Belgium, Luxembourg and the Netherlands associated themselves with this statement of the representative of the French Committee of National Liberation." *First Session of the Council of the United Nations Relief and Rehabilitation Administration, Atlantic City, New Jersey, November 10–December 1, 1943, Selected Documents*, Department of State, Conference Series 53 (Washington: Government Printing Office, 1944), p. 84.

tariat. From these two advantages results a third benefit, i.e., the expenses of the conference are considerably lessened. However, it is clear that the members of an international conference must be provided with the requisite means of understanding one another, of discussion and of deliberation. For this reason it is difficult to foretell whether the exclusive use of a single language could be enforced in most forthcoming conferences.

It would seem not an easy matter to do away completely with the French language since it is more precise and less apt to involve ambiguities than would be the case with many of the other languages. It is partly for this reason that for centuries French has been the accepted language of diplomacy, and because of that has achieved wide recognition. Even today the language most frequently known by diplomats besides their national language is French. Another reason for the wide use of the French language in diplomacy was the predominant position long held by France in the society of nations. With the growing power of other nations — for instance, Russia — the question of the use of their national languages in international gatherings is likely to arise.[28]

It seems probable that henceforth, as in the past, several languages will be used in international conferences.[29] Indeed, this practice has definite advantages. First, a greater number of conferees may take an active part in the discussions of the conference.[30] Second, the translation

[28] Concerning the richness and the precision of the Russian language, Lomonosov, a Russian author of the eighteenth century, wrote: "Carlos V, King of Spain and Roman Emperor, used to say that with God it is best to speak Spanish; French with friends; German to an enemy; and with women, Italian. Had he known the Russian language also, he might have concluded that it is propitious always to speak Russian with everyone. For in Russian he would have found the majesty of Spanish, the vivacity of French, the vigor of German, the tenderness of Italian, and beyond all this, the richness and strength of precise description of Greek and Latin."

[29] "The question of the official languages of an international institution is charged with dynamite. There is no equitable solution. A compromise has to be found," writes Mr. J. V. Wilson, former Chief of the Central Section of the Secretariat of the League of Nations, discussing the problem of languages at international meetings in a very interesting article, "Problems of an International Secretariat," *International Affairs* (London), Vol. XX (1944), p. 551.

[30] The use of two languages in the practice of the League did not always provide the delegates with these requisite means and, obviously, the use of only one language would further aggravate the situation.

In 1924, Professor Munch, who became later Minister of Foreign Affairs of Denmark, wrote: "The privilege of speaking in a language other than French or English has had but very limited importance. Once one of the Spanish delegates spoke in Spanish in order to establish the right created by rule, and the delegates of Ireland and of Abyssinia made part of their first speeches in their national languages. It goes without saying that the regular employment of French and English is a great advantage for those nations having one of these languages as their mother tongue; it is much easier for their delegates than for the delegates of the other nations to emphasize their arguments in the discussions, and quite naturally their representatives are preof speeches affords to the conferees an opportunity to think over what has been said and to prepare answers. In a diplomatic gathering it is important that after a controversial statement, time should be given to the conferees for cooling off. Third, as far as secretarial work is concerned, the use of several languages would make it possible to employ a personnel selected among a larger number of nationalities.

Thus, it is likely that specialized interpreters will continue to be necessary at international conferences.[31] Mention has already been made in Part I of the present handbook of the skill and the wide knowledge of the interpreters in the Secretariat of the League of Nations and the International Labor Office.

One of the most practical innovations designed to overcome the language barrier which always exists where men of many nationalities gather together has been used at international conferences for the past few years with considerable success. This is the remarkable system of simultaneous, multiple telephone interpretation of speeches, which is made possible by the efficient employment of a corps of competent interpreters, each of whom is enclosed in a sound-proof chamber fitted with a glass partition through which he can follow the proceedings in the conference hall. As he listens to a speech through headphones, he quickly translates it, sentence by sentence, into the microphone, which, along with the receiving apparatus, constitutes the standard equipment in each chamber.

At the other end of the line, the seats of the delegates and their advisers, as well as certain seats in the press and diplomatic galleries, are equipped with a receiving apparatus which makes it possible to hear either an amplification of the speaker's voice or a translation of the speech into a familiar language. This receiving apparatus is relatively simple in construction, consisting merely of a set of headphones, a volume regulator, and a control switch. The control switch may be set by means of a dial to connect the listener's headphones with any one of

---

ferred as rapporteurs." Rask-Orstedfondet, *Les origines et l'œuvre de la Société des Nations* (Copenhague, etc.: Gyldendalske Boghandel, 1923–1924, 2 vols.), Vol. II, p. 366.

[31] It is interesting to note that a School of Interpreters has been created by the University of Geneva for preparing interpreters who specialize in the work of international gatherings. Information concerning this school is given in an article by its administrator, Dr. Antoine Velleman, Professor at the University of Geneva, published in *Die Friedens-Warte*, Vol. 43 (1943), pp. 167–76. An English summary of this article has been annexed to the *Proceedings of a Conference on Training for International Administration, Held at Washington, D. C., August 21–22, 1943, under the Auspices of the Division of International Law of the Carnegie Endowment for International Peace* (Washington, 1944).

eight separate telephone circuits. Each circuit is numbered on the dial according to the telephonic connection it governs. For example, line No. 1 is used only to amplify the speaker's voice, while each of the other lines is used for an interpretation into the language desired by the listener.

This system was more widely used at the International Labor Conferences than at the meetings of the League of Nations.[32] While it has certain obvious advantages, it carries with it a greater danger of faulty

[32] It might be of interest to quote the instructions given by the International Labor Office to the interpreters at the International Labor Conferences:

"In the plenary sittings of the Conference, interpretation will be done either from the platform or through the telephonic interpretation system.

"The interpretation of each speech should be as accurate as possible. The Interpreters should bear in mind that the text of their interpretation will be published in the *Provisional Record* with as little editing as possible; formal statements (the typewritten text of which is generally available) should be translated in full.

"The speeches should be summarised to a certain extent, leaving out repetitions, and bringing out the various points more concisely than in the original speech.

"In certain cases both interpretations of a speech are given from the platform; in other cases the second interpretation is made through the telephonic interpretation system while the first interpretation is being delivered from the platform. The order in which the interpretations are to be given and the division of work between the interpreters will be arranged by the Chief Interpreter, who will also indicate which interpretation should be given by telephone.

"On the platform the Interpreter should face the audience and speak clearly, exactly in front of the microphone. For telephonic interpretation Interpreters should speak clearly, in a fairly low voice, straight into the hush-a-phone, in order not to inconvenience the other Interpreters. When speeches are interpreted by telephone while they are being delivered, the Interpreters should follow as closely as possible the form of the speech, endeavouring at the same time to make complete sentences which can be used for the purposes of the *Provisional Record*.

"The Chief Interpreter or another Interpreter chosen by him should see to it that the interpretation by telephone is completed before another speaker addresses the Conference.

"As far as possible, Interpreters should try to procure in advance the text of speeches to be delivered during the sitting or at the next sitting, more especially in the discussion of the *Director's Report*. They should find out from the Clerk of the Conference who are the speakers on the list. In many cases they may have time to prepare a summarised translation, or at least to study the text of the speech, and thus be able to give by telephone a clearer translation which can be used more readily for the *Provisional Record*.

"Interpreters will be assigned to each Committee by the Chief Interpreter in accordance with the programme for the day as shown in the *Daily Bulletin*, account being taken of further requirements which may occur in the course of the day. As far as possible the same Interpreters will remain assigned to each Committee throughout its proceedings.

"In the Committees the telephonic interpretation system will not be used except, perhaps, as an emergency, in a Committee sitting in the Conference Hall.

"As in the Conference, the speeches should be summarised, the main points, however, being clearly brought out. The Interpreters of each Committee will arrange between themselves the order of the interpretations. In the Committees Interpreters should be careful to face the Officers and Secretariat of the Committee and to speak loudly and clearly enough to be understood from all points of the Committee room.

"Interpreters may be required to assist the Secretaries of Committees or the general Services of the Conference in the translation of urgent documents."

interpretation unless the interpreter has in advance been supplied with the relevant text.

32. PROPOSALS, DRAFT RESOLUTIONS, AND AMENDMENTS

An orderly discussion in a conference presupposes the existence of some rules concerning the submission and the discussion of proposals, resolutions, motions, and amendments.

The Rules of Procedure of the Assembly of the League (Rule 14, paragraph 2) provided that "The Assembly shall not decide items on the agenda in full meeting until the report of a committee upon them has been presented and circulated, unless the Assembly itself, by a two-thirds majority, determines otherwise." [33]

In general, resolutions, motions, and amendments must be introduced in writing and handed to the president or the secretary of the meeting. Copies must be distributed as soon as possible, and copies of reports and resolutions well in advance. The agenda of the meeting and the documents to be discussed during the meeting must, as a rule, be put on the desks of the delegates before the meeting starts. The practice of the Council of the League was slightly different; a special document officer distributed the relevant document or documents during the meeting whenever the discussion passed from one item of the agenda to the next. Sometimes a provision is added in the rules that no proposal shall be discussed or voted upon at any meeting of the conference unless copies of it have been circulated to all representatives not later than the day preceding the meeting. However, compliance with such a provision is not always possible, and therefore this rule is commonly mitigated by another provision to the effect that the president may authorize the discussion and consideration of amendments or of motions relative to the procedure without previous circulation of copies. Sometimes, the rules of procedure provide that in order to give such permission the president must obtain the consent of the conference, which shall decide upon the point by a majority of votes.

[33] Compare this provision with Article IX, paragraph 1, of the Rules of Procedure of the Council of the United Nations Relief and Rehabilitation Administration: "Every proposal which may be introduced into the Council by a member and which involves formal action by the Council on any item of the agenda shall forthwith be referred by the Chairman of the Council to the appropriate committee or committees. No action or vote shall be taken by the Council on any such proposal until a report thereon by such committee or committees has been presented and circulated to the members of the Council, unless the Council shall, by two-thirds vote, determine otherwise. Such reports shall, so far as practicable, be circulated at least twenty-four hours prior to the meeting at which the Council takes action or votes thereon."

In contrast to the practice prevailing at plenary meetings, it was the custom in the League to discuss at once resolutions, amendments, or motions submitted to committee meetings. At these meetings it was not so much a problem to secure the permission of the president or the conferees for such discussion as it was to have the document mimeographed or typed in a sufficient number of copies for immediate distribution. It would have been a great improvement to have the main sitting-rooms equipped with special facilities — such as huge blackboards or bulletin boards as used by newspapers and brokerage houses — for immediate reproduction of the texts submitted to the gathering. A device of this kind was successfully employed during the International Labor Conference held in Philadelphia in April–May, 1944.

33. Previous Questions, Closure

If it is necessary to supply written texts to the delegates in order to acquaint them with the exact content of the question under discussion it is equally important to prevent endless discussions and perorations not relevant to the problems under consideration.

During the discussions, a delegation is entitled to move for consideration of the "previous question" or for adjournment. Any such proposal should be given priority in the debate. In addition to the proposer of the motion, it was the custom of the League for two speakers to address the conference — one in favor of, and one against, the motion if there was any opposition to the proposal.

Further, a delegation might at any time propose the closure of the debate regardless of whether or not other representatives had signified their intention to speak. In the case of a delegate desiring to oppose the closure, the rule mentioned above applied, namely, that two speakers would be called upon, one to speak in favor of, and one against the proposal. The question was finally decided by a majority vote.[34]

In reality, however, such measures are only seldom applied at international conferences and only in exceptional cases were they ever used at meetings of the League of Nations. Indeed, it is the duty of the presi-

[34] For questions of procedure such as those mentioned above, no previous notice of the motion need be given nor need a copy of it be handed in to the chair. The Standing Orders of the International Labor Conference (Article 14, paragraph 5) provide specifically: "5. In the case of motions as to procedure, no previous notice need be given, nor need a copy be handed in to the secretariat of the Conference. Motions as to procedure include the following: a motion to refer the matter back; a motion to postpone consideration of the question; a motion to adjourn the sitting; a motion to adjourn a debate on a particular question; a motion that the Conference proceed with the next item on the agenda for the sitting."

dent never to let matters reach such extremities. If an adjournment is necessary, the president should take the initiative in proposing it. If the president feels that a speech should be cut short, he is free to announce that several delegates have signified their intention to speak. He will then grant them this opportunity, and thereupon, after having himself presented a condensed review of the entire discussion, will close the meeting.

34. VOTING

EQUALITY OF VOTES

At international conferences equality of votes for all states has so far been accepted as a general rule.

This principle is embodied in the Covenant of the League of Nations which states, in paragraph 4 of Article 3, that "at meetings of the Assembly, each Member of the League shall have one vote"; and similarly paragraph 6 of Article 4 provides that "at meetings of the Council, each Member of the League represented on the Council shall have one vote." [35]

Specific recognition of the rule of equality of votes is also contained in the rules of procedure of the intergovernmental conferences. For instance, the Regulations of the Eighth International Conference of American States (Article 23) read as follows:

In the deliberations in the plenary sessions as well as in the committees, the delegation of each Republic represented at the Conference shall have but one vote, and the votes shall be taken separately by countries and shall be recorded in the minutes.

The Rules of Procedure of the Conference for the Suppression of the Illicit Traffic in Dangerous Drugs stated that "Each Government represented shall have one vote."

Article X, paragraph 2, of the Rules of Procedure of the Council of the United Nations Relief and Rehabilitation Administration provides that "Each member government represented on the Council or on any of its committees or subcommittees shall have only one vote."

[35] The Assembly report of December 7, 1920, in discussing "whether a member of the Council, in rendering his decisions on the Council, represented the Member of the League which appointed him or acted in an independent capacity," said: "Representatives on the Council and the Assembly are responsible to their own Governments and to those Governments alone. The Assembly has no right to interfere with the choice which a Member of the League may make of persons to represent it, nor to prevent a Representative from saying what he pleases; but it is essential that it should be thoroughly understood that, when a Representative votes, the vote is that of the Member which he represents, whether the vote be cast in the Council or the Assembly."

However, in the case of international public conferences, where the subject-matter under discussion is not highly controversial, the principle "one state, one vote" [36] is not always respected. Thus, at the International Institute of Agriculture, the great powers have five votes while the other nations have from one to four votes, according to their importance.

The idea of state equality as applied to voting power will obviously be maintained in the forthcoming international conferences, and one cannot help but agree that theoretically, at least, this principle strengthens the position of small nations and is therefore democratic. On the other hand, from the political point of view, two other problems can hardly be avoided: first, the political weight attached to the vote of great powers, and secondly, the pressure exerted by these great powers upon small states compelling them to vote in a given way. Politically speaking, the votes of the United States and of the Republic of San Marino in an international conference will have different weight. Moreover, it is almost unavoidable that great powers will have satellites which will vote in the way indicated by those powers.[37]

MAJORITY AND UNANIMITY

The problem of equality of votes is closely related to that of unanimity and majority.[38] Equality of voting power and unanimous consent have been throughout the centuries the two pillars on which international conferences have rested.

Both the principle of equality and the principle of unanimity were embodied in the Covenant of the League of Nations. But, if unanimity was the general rule, it was mitigated by a number of special exceptions contained in the Covenant itself,[39] and by a general exception concern-

[36] It has already been mentioned that in the International Labor Organization each member of the Organization has actually four votes, since the delegates of the government, the employers, and the workers are entitled to vote individually.
[37] For fuller discussion of the problem of equality of states in international conferences, see Edwin DeWitt Dickinson, *The Equality of States in International Law* (Cambridge: Harvard University Press, 1920), Chapter VIII.
[38] For a study of the majority and unanimity rule in the League of Nations, see Georges T. Éles, *Le principe de l'unanimité dans la Société des Nations et les exceptions de ce principe* (Paris: A. Pedone, Editeur, 1935); Cromwell Adams Riches, *The Unanimity Rule and the League of Nations* (Baltimore: The Johns Hopkins Press, 1933); C. A. Riches, *Majority Rule in International Organization; A Study of the Trend from Unanimity to Majority Decision* (Baltimore: The Johns Hopkins Press, 1940).
[39] They were four in number and may be paraphrased as follows: Article 1, paragraph 2: The admission of new members to the League is to be agreed to by a majority of two thirds of the Assembly. Article 4, paragraph 2 *bis:* The Assembly shall fix by a two-thirds majority the Rules dealing with the election of the non-permanent members of the Council. Article 15, paragraph 10: Where the procedure laid down in Article 15 is applied, a report made by the Assembly, if concurred in by the members

ing questions of procedure at meetings of the Assembly and the Council (Article 5, paragraph 2, of the Covenant). It was specifically indicated that "the appointment of committees to investigate particular matters" is to be considered a "matter of procedure." This provision probably marked the limit of what could be comprised under the term "procedure." Indeed, the distinction between questions of substance and of procedure is sometimes indiscernible and often subject to controversy.

The relevant provisions of the Rules of Procedure of the Assembly were the following (Rule 19):

1. Except where otherwise expressly provided in the Covenant or by the terms of a treaty, decisions of the Assembly shall be taken by a unanimous vote of the Members of the League represented at the meeting.

2. All matters of procedure at a meeting of the Assembly, including the appointment of committees to investigate particular matters, shall be decided by a majority of the Members of the League represented at the meeting.

3. All decisions taken in virtue of these Rules shall be considered as matters of procedure.

4. A majority decision requires the affirmative votes of more than half of the Members of the League represented at the meeting.

5. For the purposes of this Rule, representatives who abstain from voting shall be considered as not present.

In the practice of the Assembly of the League the rule of unanimity was moderated principally by two methods of procedure. First, there was the method evolved by the Assembly under which it adopted a recommendation, or more exactly a *vœu*,[40] instead of adopting a resolution. It was ruled by the Assembly at its first session that for the adoption of a recommendation or *vœu*, unanimity was not necessary and that only a majority was required.[41] Obviously, recommendations had no legal force,[42] but some very important political measures were

of the League represented on the Council and by a majority of the other members of the Assembly, has the same force as a report unanimously adopted by the Council. Article 26: This article, which deals with amendments to the Covenant, is not an exception to the unanimity rule, but provides that the amendments shall come into force only when ratified by the members of the League composing the Council and by a majority of the others. It is moreover generally admitted that Article 15, paragraph 6, departs from the unanimity rule by excluding the vote of the parties to the dispute, as well as Article 16, paragraph 4, which excludes the vote of any member of the League which has violated a covenant of the League.

[40] Frederick Sherwood Dunn points out rightly that "the French word *vœu*, when used in this sense, has no exact equivalent in English. It may be translated as 'recommendation,' 'opinion,' or 'wish,' but none of these expresses the full meaning of the word." *Op. cit.*, p. 119.

[41] On the distinction between decision and *vœu*, see also Burton, *op. cit.*, pp. 182–87.

[42] The term "recommendation" conveys a special meaning in the practice of the International Labor Organization as compared with the practice of the League of

adopted by the Assembly in the form of a *vœu* if unanimity could not be secured otherwise. Thus, on October 11, 1935, the Assembly adopted a *vœu* creating the Committee of Coordination charged with the application of sanctions to Italy. The Italian delegate voted against the measure and the delegates of Austria and Hungary abstained. Nevertheless, the Assembly by this means succeeded in setting up the Committee.

The second of the methods is to be seen in the custom established by the main committees of the League of adopting their decisions by the vote of the majority of the Members of the League represented at the meeting. In 1924, the Netherlands delegation proposed to amend the Rules of Procedure, since it seemed that the practice of the committees was in contradiction to the letter of the Rules. Indeed, Rule 19 of the Rules of Procedure quoted above reproduced the unanimity requirements laid down in the Covenant, and Rule 27 provided that the Rules of Procedure for plenary meetings must also apply to committee proceedings. Nevertheless, the subcommittee of the First Committee of the Assembly which discussed the Netherlands proposal reached the conclusion that the contradiction was more apparent than real, and the Netherlands delegation withdrew its proposal.[43]

Most of the *ad hoc* conferences held under the auspices of the League of Nations followed the practice of the Assembly concerning the unanimity rule even if their rules of procedure was silent on this subject.[44]

Provisions contained in the Constitution of the International Labor Organization constitute a formal departure from the rule of unanimous

---

Nations. Recommendations adopted by the International Labor Organization must be brought by the members of the Organization before competent national authorities in the same manner as international draft labor conventions. A recommendation has therefore more weight than a resolution adopted by International Labor Conferences. In the practice of the Assembly of the League the term recommendation was as a rule employed in a different sense. In the assembly it was used as the English equivalent for the word *vœu*, a literal translation of which would have been misleading. As it has been pointed out, *vœux* adopted by the Assembly had no legal force, in contrast to resolutions. Resolutions adopted by the International Labor Conferences correspond thus rather to *vœux* adopted by the Assembly of the League, and recommendations adopted by the Labor Conference correspond rather to the resolutions adopted by the Assembly of the League.

[43] The report of the subcommittee of the First Committee of the 1924 Assembly has been attached as Appendix XII, *infra*.

[44] Article 22 of the Statute of the Organization for Communications and Transit provided, however:

"Rules as to Majority:

"1. The conference may not validly take a vote unless the representatives of the majority of the delegations are present.

"2. Except as provided in the following paragraph, the decisions of the conference shall be taken by a simple majority of the votes cast by the delegations present.

"3. The final text of conventions and recommendations drawn up by the conference shall be adopted by a majority of two-thirds of the votes cast by the delegations present."

consent. Article 17 of the Constitution (Article 403 of the Treaty of Versailles) provides that "Except as otherwise expressly provided in this Part of the present Treaty, all matters shall be decided by a simple majority of the votes cast by the Delegates present." Article 19, paragraph 2 (Article 405 of the Treaty of Versailles), provides that for adoption of a recommendation or draft convention "a majority of two-thirds of the votes cast by the Delegates present shall be necessary on the final vote."[45]

The practice of the International Conferences of American States is even more elastic. Thus, Article 28 of the Regulations of the Pan American Conference held in Lima in 1938 provided that:

Except in cases expressly indicated in these regulations, proposals, reports, and projects under consideration by the Conference shall be considered approved when they have obtained the affirmative vote of an absolute majority of the delegations represented by one or more of their members at the meeting where the vote is taken.[46]

A similar provision was inserted in the Regulations of the United Nations Conference on Food and Agriculture.

Article X, paragraph 4, of the Rules of Procedure of the Council of the United Nations Relief and Rehabilitation Administration provides that "Except as otherwise provided by the Agreement or by these Rules of Procedure, all decisions of the Council shall require an affirmative majority vote of the members present."

For centuries the principle of unanimity has governed international conferences. In the interwar period a tendency could be observed in favor of abrogating this rule and of promoting the adoption of provisions which would enable international political or technical gatherings to reach decisions in a manner similar to that which has long been accepted in international judicial and arbitral tribunals. Indeed, the work of the Permanent Court of International Justice is founded upon the principle of majority vote, and, as a rule, that is the principle prevailing in all international courts and tribunals.

[45] Decisions of the International Labor Conferences are, however, not binding on the governments, and are subject to ratification. This kind of procedure only transposes the difficulty. If the decisions taken by the majority of an international conference are in no sense binding and have the same force as a *vœu* or a recommendation of the Assembly of the League of Nations, there can be little objection against such a practice on the part of the opponents of majority rule.

[46] A two-thirds majority was necessary in the following cases: (1) for discussing amendments without referring them to a committee; (2) to proceed to the immediate consideration of a motion; (3) for considering a new topic after the report of the Committee on Initiatives; (4) for amending the Regulations.

QUORUM

There is a close relationship between the doctrine of unanimous consent and the problems connected with the quorum required at international conferences.

The Covenant of the League did not specify the presence of a minimum number of members as a condition to be met by the Council or the Assembly in entering into a discussion or taking a vote. But the Rules of Procedure of the Council (Article VIII) state that "The Council shall not discuss or decide upon any matter unless the majority of its members are present." No such provision is contained in the Assembly's Rules of Procedure. Similarly, the rules of procedure of *ad hoc* conferences convoked under the auspices of the League of Nations and the regulations of the standing committees of the League were generally silent on this subject.[47]

While the attendance at the meetings of the main committees of the Assembly was sometimes low, the plenary meetings were, as a matter of fact, generally attended by almost all of the delegates of the states represented at the session. Very seldom was a seat empty at a Council meeting. Similarly, the attendance was high at the meetings of *ad hoc* conferences and at the sessions of standing committees.

At all the meetings of the League, representatives who abstained from voting were, as a general rule, considered as absent.

The Constitution of the International Labor Organization provides (Article 17, paragraph 3) that "the voting is void unless the total number of votes cast is equal to half the number of the Delegates attending the Conference."[48]

The Regulations of the Eighth International Conference of American States provided in Article 21, that "to hold a meeting it is necessary that a majority of the nations attending the Conference be represented

---

[47] There were, however, exceptions. Thus, the Rules of Procedure of the Advisory Committee on Traffic in Opium and Other Dangerous Drugs stated that the quorum at a sitting of the Committee was constituted by a majority of the members of the Committee, and that all decisions of the Committee must be taken by a majority vote of the members present at the meeting. (Article 7.)

[48] This provision of the Constitution is supplemented by the following provision of the Standing Orders of the International Labor Conferences:

ARTICLE 18. — *Quorum.* 1. In accordance with Article 17 of the Constitution of the Organization a vote is not valid if the number of votes cast for and against is less than half the number of Delegates attending the Conference and having the right to vote. This number shall be provisionally fixed after the presentation of the brief report referred to in paragraph 2 of Article 3 (This report deals with the powers of the delegates). It shall then be determined by the Credentials Committee. Any delegate who finally leaves the Conference before its termination and who gives formal notice of his departure to the secretariat without authorizing an adviser to act in his place

by at least one of their delegates." Further, Article 24 of those Regulations provided that "the Conference shall not proceed to vote on any report, project, or proposal relating to any of the subjects included in the program, except when at least two-thirds of the nations attending the Conference are represented by one or more delegates." However, this provision was mitigated by a previous article (Article 18, paragraph 2) which stated that "a delegation not present at the session may deposit or transmit its vote in writing to the secretary, which shall be counted provided it has been transmitted or deposited before the vote is declared closed. In this event, the delegation shall be considered as present and its vote counted."[49]

shall be regarded as no longer attending the Conference for the purpose of calculating the quorum. If any Delegate is not finally admitted the number constituting the quorum shall be modified accordingly for the subsequent sittings.

2. Where a quorum has not been obtained in a vote by a show of hands, the President may immediately take a record vote. He shall be obliged to do so if a record vote is called for by twenty members present.

3. Where a quorum has not been obtained in a vote by a show of hands only or in a record vote, the President may take a record vote on the same question at one of the two next following sittings.

4. The preceding paragraph does not apply to a final vote for the adoption of a Draft Convention or Recommendation.

[49] Compare the above-quoted provisions with the corresponding provisions of the Regulations of the United Nations Conference on Food and Agriculture:

"ART. 16. A delegation not present at the session at which a vote is taken may deposit or transmit its vote in writing to the Secretary, which shall be counted provided it had been transmitted or deposited before the vote is declared closed. In this event, the delegation shall be considered as present and its vote counted.

"ART. 19. Attendance by a majority of the nations participating in the Conference shall constitute a quorum at plenary sessions. Similarly, the presence of a majority of the delegations participating in the Technical Sections shall constitute a quorum at the meetings of the respective Sections and the presence of the same proportion of members of general Committees shall constitute a quorum.

"ART. 21. Votes as a general rule shall be taken orally unless any delegate should request that they be taken in writing. In this case each delegate shall deposit in an urn a ballot containing the name of the nation which it represents and the sense in which the vote is cast. The secretary shall read aloud these ballots, count the votes, and record the results.

"ART. 22. The Conference shall not proceed to vote on any report, project, or proposal relating to any of the subjects included in the agenda unless at least two-thirds of the nations attending the Conference are represented by one or more delegates. The same proportion of the delegations participating in the Technical Sections shall be present before a vote is undertaken at Section meetings. The general Committees likewise shall proceed to vote only with the attendance of at least two-thirds of their respective members. In the event of written voting at any session or meeting, the count shall be taken of the votes deposited in writing as provided for in articles 16 and 21, the absent delegates being considered present, only for the purpose of the vote, when they have submitted their vote in the manner indicated.

"ART. 23. Except in cases expressly indicated in these regulations, proposals, reports and projects under consideration by the Conference or by any of the Committees or Technical Sections shall be considered approved when they have obtained the affirmative vote of an absolute majority of the delegations represented by one or more of their members at the meeting where the vote is taken. Any delegation which may have deposited its vote in the manner prescribed in article 16 shall be considered as present at the meeting."

Article X, paragraph 1, of the Rules of Procedure of the Council of the United Nations Relief and Rehabilitation Administration provides that "A majority of the members of the Council shall constitute a quorum for any formal action by the Council, except that for any proposal to amend the Agreement three-fourths of the members shall constitute a quorum."

The rule according to which representatives who abstained from voting at a League meeting were considered as not present led sometimes to strange results. For instance, in July, 1936, the Ethiopian delegation asked the Assembly for financial assistance in conformity with the Convention on Financial Assistance for states which are victims of aggression. A vote was taken by roll-call and the result of the voting was as follows:

Number of ballots cast.	49
Ballots valid.	49
Ballots indicating abstentions.	25
Number of votes in favor.	1
Number of votes against.	23

Thus, in accordance with the above-mentioned rule, the majority of the delegations was technically absent from the meeting room.[50]

In point of fact the problem of a quorum never arose at the meetings of the Assembly [51] and the Council of the League. It was also exceptional for standing committees in which the Rules of Procedure provided for a quorum, to postpone a meeting or a vote because a quorum was lacking.

METHODS OF VOTING

(a) *Assembly of the League.*

Rule 20 of the Rules of Procedure of the Assembly stated that:

The Assembly shall vote by "Appel Nominal," except when the Members of the League represented at the meeting agree that the method of voting shall be by

[50] L.N., *Official Journal*, Special Supplement No. 151, p. 69.
[51] At the Fourteenth Ordinary Session of the Assembly of the League of Nations, in 1933, during the discussion in the First Committee of the Assembly of a draft resolution proposing that the Finance Committee of the Assembly should be convened by the Secretary General of the League one week before the opening of the session, the Delegate of Chile, Mr. Valdes-Mendeville, made the following interesting remark concerning the quorum in the committees of the Assembly: ". . . That motion was particularly dangerous for distant countries, and would lead to the problem of a quorum at meetings of committees. *Up to the present, it had never been necessary to raise that question.* If the Finance Committee had to meet several days before the Assembly, what would its position be? How could it sit validly and reach decisions if only a small number of countries were represented and particularly if the responsible heads of the various delegations were absent?" See *ibid.*, Special Supplement No. 116, p. 20. (Italics by the author.)

heads of delegations rising in their seats, and except in the cases provided for in Rule 21.[52] The "Appel Nominal" shall be taken in one of the following manners, as the Assembly may decide:

(a) The name of each delegation shall be called, and one of its members shall reply "Yes", "No", or "Not Voting". The result of the vote shall be recorded and announced to the Assembly; or

(b) The delegation of each Member of the League represented at the meeting shall be provided with two voting tickets, on which the name of the country is written, one red and one blue, the former being "Aye" the latter "No". The voting tickets shall be deposited in an urn placed near the President's platform. When all the votes have been collected the President shall declare the ballot closed, and the General Committee [53] shall proceed to count the votes. The individual votes shall be communicated to the Assembly and the result shall be announced by the President.

Generally, there was not a vote by *appel nominal* or roll-call. The President simply consulted the Assembly, and if no one had any remarks to offer concerning a proposal submitted to the Assembly, he assumed that the delegates agreed to the proposal.

Votes in writing were a rare occurrence. As a matter of fact the author of this handbook has no recollection of a vote taken in writing except in the case of elections, for which such a procedure was compulsory.

Record votes were taken by calling upon each member of the League who was represented at the session. Each delegation voted in turn in the French alphabetical order of the names of the countries they represented.

(b) *Council of the League.*

Paragraph 3 of Article IX of the Rules of Procedure of the Council states: ". . . each Member of the Council shall be called upon separately to vote, if a Member of the Council so requires." On September 29, 1937, the Council decided:

4. It is recommended that the following procedure, which corresponds to the practice generally adopted hitherto, should be followed, unless the Council, in a given case, should decide otherwise:

When a vote by roll-call is required under Article IX, paragraph 3, of the Rules of Procedure, it shall be taken in French alphabetical order of the Members of the League represented at the meeting, the President voting last. In cases in which the vote concerns a dispute, the representatives of the parties to the dispute shall vote after the other members of the Council and the President. The vote of the parties shall also be taken in French alphabetical order.[54]

[52] This rule deals with elections.
[53] It seems that in this instance the French term "Bureau" would be more adequately translated by the term "Chair." The official English text quoted above seems to have been due to a faulty translation.
[54] Annex 1676, L.N. Document C.395.1937., in *Official Journal*, 1937, p. 1169.

Usually, there was not a vote by roll-call. The President simply asked the members of the Council whether they had any observations to make regarding a proposal. If there were none, the President declared the proposal adopted, the absence of objections having been taken to signify the tacit agreement of the members of the Council. The Council never voted by show of hands.

A secret ballot was obligatory if demanded by any member of the Council in the case of votes concerning persons. (Article X of the Rules of Procedure of the Council.) In point of fact, a secret vote was very rarely asked for.

(c) *"Ad hoc" Conferences Held under the Auspices of the League.*

Most of the *ad hoc* conferences held under the auspices of the League employed methods of voting similar to those employed by the Assembly. Except in cases where it was decided that a vote must be taken by nominal roll-call, the votes were taken in the following manner: at conferences the leaders of delegations rose from their seats or voted by show of hands; in committees delegates raised their hands. Delegations which declared that they wished to abstain from voting were regarded as absent.

(d) *International Labor Conferences.*[55]

The International Labor Conferences vote "by a show of hands or by a record vote." The general rule is that the Conference votes by a show of hands. In case of doubt as to the result, however, the President may cause a record vote to be taken. A record vote may also be taken on any question if a request to that effect has been made in writing by not less than twenty delegates and handed to the President. A record vote must be taken in all cases in which a majority of two thirds of the votes is required by the Constitution of the Organization.

(e) *Pan American Conferences.*

The Regulations of the Eighth International Conference of American States (Article 23, paragraph 2) provided that:

Votes as a general rule shall be taken orally, unless any delegate should request that they be taken in writing. In this case each delegation shall deposit in an urn a ballot containing the name of the nation which it represents and the sense in which the vote is cast. The Secretary shall read aloud these ballots and count the votes.

A practice noted above which is peculiar to the Pan American Conferences is that an absent delegation may deposit or transmit its vote in

[55] For the methods of voting in the committees of the International Labor Conference, see Appendix XI, *infra.* These peculiar methods of voting are a consequence of the tripartite character of the International Labor Office.

writing to the secretary. In that event, the delegation shall be considered as present and its vote counted.[56]

(f) *Council of the United Nations Relief and Rehabilitation Administration.*

Article X of the Rules of Procedure of the Council provides, *inter alia*, that:

5. Voting shall be by show of hands except as hereinafter provided.

6. In case of doubt as to the result of any vote by show of hands, the Chairman shall cause a record vote to be taken.

7. A record vote shall be taken in all cases where a special majority is required by the Agreement.

8. A record vote shall also be taken on any question if requested in writing by not less than five members of the Council and handed to the Chairman in advance of the vote or immediately after a show of hands.

9. Record votes shall be taken by calling upon members in the alphabetical order of the governments which they represent.

10. The vote of each member participating in any record vote shall be inserted in the verbatim report of the meeting.

11. On decisions relating to individuals, a secret ballot shall be taken whenever requested in writing by at least five members of the Council.

PROCEDURE FOR VOTING PROPOSALS AND AMENDMENTS

The practice of the Assembly of the League of Nations was to vote first on the proposal farthest removed in substance from the principal proposal whenever a number of proposals were before the Assembly.

Further, if an amendment aimed at striking out part of a proposal was moved, the Assembly pronounced itself on the question of whether or not the contested text was to stand as part of the proposal. If the decision was in the negative, the amendment was then put to a vote. Finally, when an amendment was considered as enlarging the scope of a proposal, it had to be voted on first; and if it was adopted the amended proposal had then to be voted on.

The rules provided that parts of proposals could be put to vote separately ("division of proposals") whenever a delegation requested that such be done. In this case, a vote had to be taken on the whole text after its various parts had been voted upon separately.[57]

[56] The United Nations Conference on Food and Agriculture adopted regulations concerning voting which were a mere copy of the methods in force in Pan American Conferences. See *supra*, p. 140, n. 49.

[57] Occasionally, the practice of submitting amendments and requesting the division of proposals was resorted to as a means of prolonging and obstructing the discussion in order to gain time and enable a delegate to get into touch by telephone, or by another means, with a superior national authority for further instructions or in order to bring pressure upon other delegations to vote in a certain way.

This practice of the Assembly was adopted by most of the *ad hoc* conferences held under the auspices of the League.

In the League practice governing the treatment of a proposal or an amendment by the chair it was unnecessary that the motion be seconded. The Anglo-Saxon practice to act upon a motion only after it has been seconded is, however, referred to in the Standing Orders of the International Labor Conference. Article 14, paragraph 6, of these Orders provides that "No motion, resolution or amendment shall be discussed unless and until it has been seconded." Similarly, at meetings of the Council and committees of the United Nations Relief and Rehabilitation Administration no vote is taken on a motion unless it has been formally moved and seconded in spite of the fact that the Rules of Procedure of the Council and its committees are silent on this subject.

For a layman the rules concerning amendments may seem complicated.[58] In point of fact they have considerable value. For the success or failure of a proposal sometimes depends on the order in which proposals are put to the vote. In this respect it is not always easy for the chair to decide which proposal is the farthest removed in substance from the principal. Usually, these problems of procedure must be solved immediately and the parliamentary skill of the president and of the officials of the secretariat who advise him is subjected to a severe test.

The following example is given as an illustration of such tactics. In 1937, the Assembly of the League of Nations had to act upon a resolution concerning the situation in Spain, which at that time was engulfed in the civil war. Italy, no longer represented at the Assembly but technically still a member of the League, was opposed to it. The delegates of Austria and Hungary were requested by the Italian observers in Geneva to vote against the resolution. It must be remembered that in the practice of the League one single vote cast against a resolution was sufficient to defeat it. The delegates of Austria and Hungary replied that they had received instructions to abstain when the vote would be taken by the Assembly. They were, however, willing to use dilatory tactics during the Assembly meeting at which the resolution had to be acted upon, in order to enable the delegate of Albania to receive instructions from Tirana where pressure was applied directly by the Italian Government to vote against the resolution. With this in mind the Austrian and Hungarian delegates submitted four amendments to the draft resolution. Moreover, the Hungarian delegate requested the division of two paragraphs of the draft resolution. The result was that the Assembly had to take seven separate votes by roll-call. The meeting lasted more than three hours, and in the meantime the Albanian delegate had received the expected instructions. As a matter of fact, all this complicated *mise en scène* had been needless since the delegate of Portugal declared during the discussion and before the votes were taken that he had been instructed to vote against the resolution. See L.N., *Official Journal*, Special Supplement No. 169, pp. 99-108.

[58] The Regulations of the Eighth International Conference of American States (Article 26) provided simply that "Amendments shall be submitted for discussion and put to a vote before the article or motion, the text of which they are intended to modify, is acted upon."

35. ELECTIONS

Number 21 of the Rules of Procedure of the Assembly of the League of Nations is based upon the general principle that "all decisions relating to individuals shall be taken by a secret ballot." However, as has been pointed out, the Assembly departed in certain cases from this general principle and elected some of its officers or committees by acclamation.[59] For instance, it was customary for the Assembly to elect the Credentials Committee by accepting a list of names submitted by the chair.[60]

A brief description of the manner in which elections were carried out by secret ballot in the League of Nations may be of interest.

The Chairman announced that the next item on the agenda of the meeting was the election of .... and that in conformity with the Rules of Procedure, voting would take place by secret ballot. He then called upon two delegates to act as tellers. The duties of tellers were considered an honor, and those who were called upon to perform them were selected by the Chairman in accordance with the nature of the election. Thus, for the election of the President of the Assembly, the custom was to appoint as tellers two former presidents of the Assembly. For an election of nonpermanent members of the Council, the tellers were the representatives of two states which were already on the Council, etc.

The tellers went to the rostrum and sat at a table facing the Assembly. An urn was placed in front of the rostrum in the middle, and one of the secretaries of the chair verified the fact that it was empty. The urn was then locked and the key handed to the Secretary General, who took his seat near the tellers.

As the roll of the members of the League was called in the French alphabetical order, the first delegate of each nation rose and proceeded to the rostrum. He dropped a card into the urn bearing the name of the individual or the country of his choice, according to the type of election which took place. After the last card had been deposited, the President pronounced the ballot closed. The urn was then brought to the tellers' table and the Secretary General unlocked it.

The contents of the ballot box was counted by the tellers with the assistance of the Secretary General. The results were recorded on a

[59] Similarly, at its second session, held in Montreal in September, 1944, the Council of the United Nations Relief and Rehabilitation Administration appointed the members of the Committee on Credentials, the Committee on Nominations, and the Committee on Observers by acclamation.

[60] Only once, in 1936, was the Credentials Committee elected by **secret ballot**.

special form containing headings and space for all the necessary information, such as: date of the meeting, kind of election, number of states voting, blank voting ballots, valid votes, absolute majority, etc. Both tellers signed the record, which was taken by the Secretary General to the President. The President thanked the tellers for their assistance and announced the results of the vote.

The League had special and elaborate rules for the election of non-permanent members of the Council and the members of the Permanent Court of International Justice. Lack of space prevents a detailed description of these rules. However, it might be useful to outline some practices which were in use in almost all bodies of the League.

When only one person was to be elected, and no one obtained an absolute majority of votes at the first ballot, a new ballot was taken; but on that occasion the voting had to be confined to the two candidates who had obtained the largest number of votes on the first ballot. If the two candidates received an equal number of votes at this second ballot, the elder candidate was automatically declared elected.

If a number of persons were to be elected by ballot simultaneously, a second balloting was statutory in all those cases where the number of persons to be elected was greater than the number of those who obtained an absolute majority of votes in the first ballot. The object of this subsequent (second) ballot was therefore to fill the remaining posts, and the choice of candidates was restricted to candidates figuring in the first ballot who had obtained the greatest number of votes immediately following the candidates who had obtained an absolute majority. The number of candidates figuring in the second ballot was restricted, however, to twice the number of the places to be filled. Those candidates for the number of places to be filled who received the greatest number of votes at the second ballot were declared elected independently of the fact whether the votes cast in their favor constituted a majority or not.

These rules served merely as a safeguard. Ordinarily the first ballot sufficed to complete elections. The special rules governing the elections of the Judges of the Permanent Court of International Justice have already been mentioned. Those elections often necessitated several ballots.

36. PROTOCOL AND ENTERTAINMENT

In the early days of the League, little attention was paid to questions of protocol. Meetings of the Council of the Assembly and *ad hoc* conferences were held on premises lacking both in space and decorum. Several years passed before a barrier was erected between the public and the Council table, and several more years went by before a dais was built to give to the members of the Council a prominent place in the meeting room. In 1929, the Assembly appointed a special committee "to make suggestions for the improvement of arrangements for sessions of the Assembly." This committee functioned until 1932 and made several reports, resulting in certain improvements of the conditions under which the meetings of the Assembly were held. The committee also gave some attention to measures aimed at enhancing the dignity of important international conferences.

For instance, in the early days of the League, the ushers wore only an armband bearing the letters S.D.N. in order to distinguish them from the conferees, the Secretariat, and the public. In 1930, the ushers were, on solemn occasions, appropriately uniformed in blue frock-coats with gold buttons.

The surroundings in which the Assembly sat were also improved, first, by holding meetings at the *Bâtiment Electoral*, and, later, by moving into the new building of the League.

The new Council room, with its black and gold mural frescoes painted by the Spanish painter Sert and its huge Council table, was especially impressive. However, the arrangement of the semicircular table on a dais, with the members of the Council facing the public, suggested that the group constituted a court rather than a political body. In this connection it is a little-known fact that in the early thirties an American admirer of the League sent to the Secretariat a complete wardrobe, consisting of elaborate robes and solemn caps for the members of the Council. The shipment, of course, was returned to the donor with a letter of thanks and polite regrets that the gift could not be accepted.

The new arrangements in the Council's meeting room gave the members of the Council direct access to the dais without compelling them to cross the space reserved for the audience. This arrangement contributed to the dignity of the meeting.

The declaration of loyalty which the high officials of the Secretariat were required to make before the Council in public session was performed in a ceremony which will be briefly described.

The Chairman called upon the high official who was to make the declaration. The latter proceeded to the Council table, ushered to his assigned place by a member of the Central Section who acted as *Chef du Protocole*. After reading aloud the text of the declaration, the official signed in a special register and was then ushered back to his seat by the *Chef du Protocole*.

A ceremony which should have been characterized by special dignity was the admission of new members into the League. Since, however, there was no organized *Service du Protocole*, as has been pointed out in Part I of this handbook, it fell to the lot of an official, who was designated only at the last moment to act as *Chef du Protocole*, to make the necessary arrangements. In 1934, when several new members were admitted into the League, the ceremonies were a dismal failure. The official who acted as *Chef du Protocole*, and who happened to be at that time the Chief of the Internal Services, ushered the delegates of a newly admitted great power into the meeting room at the wrong moment. Moreover, these delegates had to wait at the doorway until the President ordered their entrance. The whole impression was one of confusion and disorder.

On the other hand, three years later the admission of Egypt was surrounded with exceptional ceremonial pomp. All the Egyptian delegates were dressed in morning coats and fezes. The *Chef du Protocole* and the delegates were both preceded and followed by ushers in full dress.

At some time during the session, it was customary for the President of the Assembly to give a large reception to which all the members of the delegations and many officials of the Secretariat were invited.[61] Sometimes this reception was preceded by a dinner to which the heads of delegations and some high officials were invited. Moreover, the President of the Assembly gave a luncheon in honor of the members of the General Commission (Bureau). The Secretary General, the Deputy Secretaries General, the Under Secretaries General, and the secretaries of the Chair and of the main committees of the Assembly were also invited to this luncheon. Naturally, many other receptions were given in the course of the sessions of the Assembly.

It was also customary for the Secretary General to give a series of luncheons, dinners, and cocktail parties to which the members of the delegations and the officials of the Secretariat directly connected with the work of the Assembly were invited. Many delegations arranged their own receptions, since it is a political truism, well known to all those experienced in the ways of international conferences, that social activities are conducive to the settlement of controversial matters.

[61] The Aga Khan, as President of the Assembly in 1937, gave a brilliant reception at the new building of the League. The "Salle des Pas Perdus" and the adjacent committee rooms were a beautiful setting for the *rout*. This reception was the only one given in the new building of the League.

When a large *ad hoc* international conference was held under the auspices of the League at Geneva, the customs of the Assembly were generally followed as far as official entertainment was concerned.

Naturally, less time was devoted to official entertainment during the sessions of the Council. It was a prevailing custom for the President of the Council to give a luncheon to which the members of the Council and the high officials of the Secretariat above the rank of Director were invited. The Secretary General reciprocated by giving a return luncheon to which the same dignataries were invited. Frequently, the chairman of a standing committee of the League followed the practice of the Council and during the sessions of his committee gave a luncheon to which the members of the committee were invited along with the officials of the Secretariat who worked immediately for the committee.

When a meeting of an international organization is held outside the permanent seat of the organization or when a conference has been called upon the initiative of a single government, it is customary for the government which is host to the international gathering to assume special responsibilities for the social activities connected with the conference. Usually, a special committee of reception is appointed to take care of drawing up a program of entertainment. The head of the state, the minister of foreign affairs, the municipal authorities of the city in which the conference is held will generally give a series of receptions. The size and nature of the reception are determined by the traditions of hospitality of the country holding the affair.

Sometimes an effort is made to commemorate in a material form the meeting of an international conference. Special stamps are issued, and medals in remembrance of the gathering are coined.

The social side of international conferences must not be exaggerated, but obviously official receptions, dinners, and luncheons afford excellent opportunities to the delegates and the members of the secretariat to discuss matters in an atmosphere most propitious for reaching a common understanding of mutual problems.

PART IV

RECORDING AND REVIEWING

The documents in which the work and the results of international conferences are recorded have been dealt with in Parts I, II, and III of this treatise. To the preparatory documentation submitted to the conference at the beginning of its work a large number of memoranda originating from the secretariat of the conference or the delegations are added, as well as numerous proposals, amendments, and motions emanating from the delegates.

These documents are usually discussed first in committees, which after due consideration of the various questions submitted to them, draw up draft reports, resolutions, or recommendations. The conference, in plenary meeting, then takes cognizance of the findings of the committees and decides whether to amend, reject, or adopt them. Often the results of the work of a conference will be embodied in special documents which will be called, according to their form, a convention, agreement, general act, protocol, protocol of signature, or final act. In addition to these documents, records of the proceedings are established called minutes, verbatim reports, *procès-verbaux*, summary, communiqué to the press, etc., according to the form which is given to the records.

37. MEMORANDA, MOTIONS, RESOLUTIONS, AND AMENDMENTS

Space is lacking here for a detailed study of the form that may be given to memoranda, motions, resolutions, and amendments submitted to an international conference. As a general rule, they must emanate from a member of the conference or of the organization or from the secretariat.[1] In order to regulate and to limit the flow of these documents, provisions concerning their introduction, distribution, and discussion are usually included in the constitution of the organization or in the rules of procedure or "regulations" of international conferences.

In certain cases it is specifically provided that parties to a dispute must submit statements to international gatherings.[2] Upon receipt of

[1] A communication emanating from the government of a state which is not a member of the organization or the conference is usually communicated to the members.
[2] See, for example, the stipulations of Article XV of the Covenant concerning submission of disputes to the Council of the League.

these statements it becomes the duty of the secretary general to arrange for full investigation and consideration by the assembled body. Similar obligations may also be imposed by international conventions.

Delegations to international meetings are as a rule entitled to submit whatever documents they choose relative to the purpose of the gathering. In making use of its right a delegation must conform to the rules laid down by the organization or the conference. One of the more important provisions in the rules of procedure governing almost all conferences is that motions, amendments, and resolutions must be submitted beforehand to the chair, in writing.

The documents mentioned above are included in the records of the conference in one form or another. Statements or memoranda are generally annexed to the minutes of the conference. Resolutions, amendments, and motions are for the most part included *in extenso* in the text of the minutes, if referred to by the conference during the discussions.

Memoranda, proposals, suggestions emanating from organizations or persons who are not members of the conference are not as a rule included in the records of the conference. Nevertheless, the conference is always free, at the request of the chair or of a member of the conference who assumes responsibility for it, to include in the records of the conference any statement submitted for its consideration.

38. Reports of Commissions or of Special "Rapporteurs" of the Conference

These reports are almost always drafted in the course of committee or subcommittee meetings and are fully discussed by these bodies. They are sometimes supplemented by oral explanations in plenary meetings on the part of the rapporteur or of the chair. Reports of this kind are usually either included *in extenso* in the record of the discussion or annexed to it after the circumstances in which they were submitted to the conference have been explained.

The first method was the usual one for reports submitted to the Council of the League by a rapporteur. Even though the rapporteur has not always read the report to the Council it has invariably been printed verbatim in its appropriate place.[3]

[3] The usual procedure regarding reports of a technical kind was for the rapporteur to submit the full text to the Council but to read only the resolution concluding the report in question.

As for the method used by the Assembly of the League, only oral explanations given by the rapporteur for the purpose of supplementing reports were printed at the relevant place in the discussions of the conference. The report itself figured as an annex to the minutes. Short reports only, such as the reports of the Credentials Committee, of the Agenda Committee, and the General Committee, were included in the text of the discussion. For *ad hoc* conferences convoked under the auspices of the League, the latter method was usually employed.

39. MINUTES, VERBATIM REPORTS, ETC.

For the recording of discussions of meetings held under the auspices of the League of Nations and the International Labor Organization various methods were or are still used, according to the size and importance of the meetings. Brief information concerning the methods employed by the United Nations Relief and Rehabilitation Administration and the International Conferences of American States has been added.

ASSEMBLY OF THE LEAGUE OF NATIONS

The Rules of Procedure of the Assembly of the League of Nations (Rule 25) provided briefly that "The verbatim report of each meeting [of the Assembly] shall be drawn up by the Secretariat and submitted to the Assembly after approval by the President." However, in practice the League procedure was less restrictive and more complicated. A series of different records of the proceedings of the Assembly and of its committees were made and circulated by the Secretariat, as follows:

A stenographic record of the plenary meetings of the Assembly was established by the parliamentary stenographers. Stencils of this transcript were cut by specially trained typists under the direction of the stenographers. A carbon copy of this record was immediately posted in the Press room. Not more than fifteen or twenty minutes elapsed between the delivery of the speech and the posting of the carbon copy in the Press room. The stencil was immediately mimeographed, and in about half an hour after the plenary meeting of the Assembly the full mimeographed record, both in French and English, was available. It was immediately distributed to the delegates at their homes or hotels. This record was, of course, provisional, as the translation of speeches was simply the verbal transcript of the interpretation.

Delegates, as a rule, were not entitled to correct their speeches before the mimeographed text had been circulated. In certain cases, however, exceptions were made. A very eloquent delegate of one of the big powers sent his secretary to correct his speeches before they were mimeographed, for, though brilliant, they often contained grammatical mistakes!

The following morning the *Assembly Journal* printed a summary of the speeches made at the plenary meeting of the Assembly in the two official languages.[4]

The provision that verbatim reports must be approved by the President was not applied in practice. Delegates were asked to forward their corrections within twenty-four hours. After all corrections were received and incorporated, the Secretariat considered the verbatim report as correct. It rarely happened that a delegate tried to change his speech to the extent that the meaning was altered. When this did occur the Secretariat had to act with firmness and, if necessary, to resort to the authority of the President.

The next step was the printing of the verbatim report, the translations of the speeches having in the meantime been carefully checked by the translators. Usually one week elapsed between the day on which the speech had been delivered and the day on which the revised text was ready for distribution to the delegates to the Assembly and to the members of the League.

A few days after the termination of the session a book containing the resolutions adopted by the Assembly was circulated. The preparation of this publication was undertaken immediately upon adjournment of the Assembly. The resolutions were assembled and classified under the various committees at which they were discussed prior to

[4] The *Assembly Journal* was an official publication issued daily in French and English and circulated to the delegations, the Secretariat staff, and the press during the sessions of the Assembly. The first issue contained information concerning general arrangements for the Assembly session (see Annex V, *infra*). Subsequent numbers contained summaries of all speeches delivered at plenary meetings. Resolutions were reproduced in full. Résumés of the proceedings of Assembly committee meetings were also included. Each number of the *Journal* contained the program of the meetings of the day and a list of the Assembly documents distributed to the delegations. It also contained lists of the members of the Assembly committees and of telegraphic agencies and newspapers represented at the session, as well as varied information, such as notices concerning receptions by the President of the Assembly for representatives of non-official international organizations, extracts of resolutions adopted by important non-governmental international organizations (for instance, Interparliamentary Union, International Federation of the League of Nations Societies), and signature or ratification of, or accession to, international conventions concluded under the auspices of the League of Nations, which took place during the session. The last number enumerated all resolutions adopted by the Assembly during the session and contained an alphabetical index of these resolutions. Recent League of Nations publications were also advertised in the *Journal*.

their submission to the Assembly. The French and English texts were carefully drafted and checked (for discrepancies and printing errors). The distribution numbers of the documents to which the resolutions referred, were added and a Table of Contents prepared. The completed manuscript was sent to the Legal Section for final approval, and its attention was drawn to any discrepancies in the texts, as the Legal Section was responsible for deciding whether or not to remove them; if that Section did not feel competent to do so, it referred the points in doubt to the Central Section.

Three or four months after the close of the Assembly a final edition of the proceedings of the plenary meetings of the Assembly was printed and circulated as part of the *Official Journal*. (This tardiness was occasioned chiefly by the delay in the delivery of the corrections on the part of delegates from remote countries who had spoken during the last meetings of the Assembly and had been unable to forward their corrected speeches before leaving Europe.) This final edition contained also all of the reports submitted by the committees to the Assembly, as well as other relevant documents.

COMMITTEES OF THE ASSEMBLY OF THE LEAGUE

The practice of the large committees of the Assembly was very similar to that employed at the plenary meetings. Stenographic records were made of the discussions of most of the important committees, such as the Third Committee of the Assembly dealing with disarmament. A carbon copy of the stenographic transcript was posted in the Press room. No mimeographed copy of the transcript was circulated immediately in this case.

A text in the third person was set up as soon as possible by the minute-writers attached to the meeting and was distributed to the delegations in a mimeographed form in the two official languages.[5] Forty-eight hours usually elapsed between the meeting and the distribution of the mimeographed minutes. Delegates were requested to return their corrections to the Secretariat not later than twenty-four hours after the receipt of the minutes.

A summary of the discussion was drafted by a member of the section within whose province lay the work of the respective committee. This summary was translated and both texts, French and English, were included in the next issue of the *Assembly Journal*. As the space of the

[5] In later years the minutes of the committees of the Assembly tended to be more a summary than a verbatim report.

Journal was too restricted for the reproduction of full reports, the summary had to be concise and unimportant remarks eliminated. This sometimes created difficulties as delegates were occasionally offended by these condensations and omissions. The secretary in charge of the summary had to possess some skill in psychology in order to avoid diplomatic difficulties.

A second summary was prepared by a member of the Information Section for the use of the Press. This summary, mimeographed both in French and English, was available a few minutes after the end of the meeting. As its purpose was different, a comparison of the two summaries covering the same meeting often showed considerable divergencies.

Exactly as in the case of the plenary meetings of the Assembly, complete records of the deliberations of large committees of the Assembly were made available four or five months after the end of the session. This final edition embodied all draft reports submitted to the committee and all other relevant documents in the same manner as the minutes of the plenary meetings of the Assembly.

Minutes of such committees as the Credentials Committee, the Agenda Committee, etc., were not mimeographed and circulated. A simple summary of their decisions was published in the *Assembly Journal*. During many years no minutes were kept of the discussions of the General Committee (or Bureau) of the Assembly. When, however, this committee became a political committee instead of a body chiefly concerned with problems of procedure and coordination, minutes of the meetings of the Bureau were drafted. They were, however, not distributed, but a copy was kept in the archives of the League. A summary of the decisions of the Bureau was published in the *Assembly Journal*.

Similarly, it was not customary to supply minutes of the subcommittee meetings; ordinarily, a member of a section of the League Secretariat who was attached to the subcommittee drew up a brief summary of the proceedings. As for the discussions of the drafting committee, no minutes were, as a rule, set up.

COUNCIL OF THE LEAGUE

The technique of drafting and publishing the minutes of the Council of the League was similar to the methods used with regard to the Assembly. It must suffice here to list merely the different kinds of records established by the services of the Secretariat:

Verbatim records, made by parliamentary stenographers and posted in the Press room.

Summaries, drafted by a member of the Information Section and distributed immediately after the meeting to journalists.

Mimeographed provisional minutes, distributed to the members of the Council a few hours after the meeting. These minutes, drafted in the third person, were set up from the shorthand notes of the parliamentary reporters, but care was taken to correct minor mistakes of language and grammar frequently made by a speaker. Speeches delivered in French were carefully translated into English and vice-versa.[6]

When all the corrections of the provisional minutes by the members of the Council had been received, revised editions of the minutes were printed separately for each meeting. These minutes were distributed to all of the members of the League.

A few weeks after the end of the session, a final edition of the minutes was published. Like the final edition of the minutes of the Assembly, it was published as an issue of the *Official Journal* of the League. Reports of the standing committees which had been discussed during the Council session were annexed to this edition along with all other relevant documents.

"AD HOC" CONFERENCES

The arrangements for all large conferences held under the auspices of the League were similar to those used in the Assembly meetings. Shorthand notes of the debates in plenary meetings were taken, a provisional mimeographed record was distributed, and a final record printed to which were annexed the reports, resolutions, and recommendations adopted by the conference, as well as the final act, the protocol of signature, and the convention, which are the usual result of most of the international conferences. The text of the original draft of the convention, discussed by the conference, was as a rule also annexed.

A *Journal of the Conference* similar to the *Assembly Journal* was published during the sessions of important gatherings such as the Conference on Disarmament or the Economic Conference.

Press *communiqués* were published by the Information Section of

[6] The minutes of public meetings were in fact verbatim reports polished up and turned into the third-person form, while those of private meetings (as opposed to secret) were very brief summaries. Sometimes only a decision was reported even after a long discussion.

the League during all the conferences held under the auspices of the League. Moreover, the Information Section often published, immediately after the end of the conference, a pamphlet or a résumé summarizing in a form easily grasped by the public the results of the conference. Similar to those rules in force for the recording of the discussions of the committees and subcommittees of the Assembly were the regulations established for the committees and subcommittees of *ad hoc* conferences.

STANDING AND "AD HOC" COMMITTEES OF THE LEAGUE

Space is lacking for a comprehensive study of the practice of the League in recording the discussions of the committees of the League of Nations. The methods varied considerably, according to the importance and the size of the committee. Arrangements, almost as detailed as those for recording the sessions of the Council, were made in the case of the Preparatory Commission for the Disarmament Conference and the Commission of Enquiry for European Union. The deliberations of other committees, however, were simply recorded in a report which was subsequently submitted to the Assembly or the Council. Sometimes no minutes of the discussions were kept.

INTERNATIONAL LABOR CONFERENCE

Article 21 of the Standing Orders of the Conference provides:

1. A verbatim report shall be printed at the conclusion of each sitting by the secretariat. There shall be included in the report the list of Delegates present at the sitting, together with any texts adopted and the results of any votes taken.
2. Before the report is printed in its final form, any Delegate may demand the right to revise any part of the report containing a speech which he has made. Speeches or part of speeches that have not been delivered during the sitting shall not be published in the report.
3. In order that any proposed corrections may be inserted, they should be handed in to the secretariat during the evening following the sitting.
4. The verbatim reports shall be signed by the President of the Conference and the Secretary-General.

The verbatim report is published in the *Provisional Record* of the Conference. Delegates are requested to hand corrections of the text of their statements to the Chief Editor within forty-eight hours from the appearance of the *Provisional Record*, which is issued in French, English, and Spanish. During the last session of the International Labor

Conference, held in April–May, 1944, at Philadelphia, Pennsylvania, the English edition was printed and the French and Spanish editions were mimeographed. In addition to the verbatim report of the plenary meetings, the *Provisional Record* contains information concerning the general arrangements for the session, the reports submitted by the committees of the Conference, and the texts of the resolutions, recommendations, and conventions discussed by the Conference.

As far as the minutes of the committees of the Conference are concerned, Article 14 of the Standing Orders for the Committees of the Conference provides that:

1. No verbatim record will be made, but, as far as may be possible, after each sitting of a Committee the secretariat will draw up minutes which will be roneographed and circulated to the members. These minutes will only be a summarized record of the proceedings, their primary object being to record the decisions of a Committee.

2. Any corrections to the minutes should be communicated within twenty-four hours to the secretariat of the Committee, which will arrange for their distribution as early as possible to members of the Committee.

The following instructions were given to the secretaries of the committees of the Conference concerning the form to be given to the minutes of the committee meetings.

Minutes are intended to give a record of decisions rather than a record of debates.

The summaries of speeches should be as short as is compatible with making the resulting decision intelligible. Secretaries may make use of notes handed in by speakers for the purpose of making their summaries, but speakers who ask for their speeches to be recorded more or less in full should be told that this is not possible, having regard to the nature of the minutes. The same principle should be followed in regard to corrections, a distinction being made between corrections proper and amplifications.

In summarizing speeches, useless formulas, cliches, etc., should be avoided. So also should unnecessary underlinings, variations in type, etc. Discussions concerning procedure should be summarized in a very succinct form when they do not affect the substance of the proceedings. In many cases it may be sufficient to state "after an exchange of views on such and such a point of procedure, the Committee decided that. . . ." It is important that the minutes should constitute, as far as possible, a clear and self-explanatory record of the proceedings. An exact reference should be given as regards texts appearing in the reports under discussion, which need not be reproduced. The texts of amendments under discussion, however, should be quoted in full (single spacing) together with their reference number.

The heading of the minutes of each sitting should be as follows:

(Reference No.)   (Page No.)

INTERNATIONAL LABOUR CONFERENCE
XXVIth SESSION, PHILADELPHIA, 1944

Committee on. . . . .
. . . .
. . . . .Sitting (date), (Time at which the Sitting begins)
Chairman:. . . . .

The reference number in the top left-hand corner will give the initials of the Committee (as determined in agreement with the Distribution Service), the number of the sitting and its date and time, thus:

C P/ P V 1. for the minutes of the First Sitting of the Selection Committee, 20.4.1944
Afternoon   held in the afternoon of 20 April 1944.

The reference numbers will be the same for the English, French and Spanish minutes. The page number in the top right-hand corner indicates in Roman figures the number of the sitting and in Arabic figures the number of the page, thus I/1, I/2, I/3, etc., for the First Sitting; II/1, II/2, II/3, etc., for the Second Sitting.

The summaries of speeches should be as succinct and direct as possible, thus:

Sir J. FORBES WATSON: The proposal could not be given practical effect because . . . .

The following form should be avoided:

Sir J. FORBES WATSON (Employers' Member, Great Britain): I consider that the proposal cannot be given practical effect because. . . .

or:

Sir J. FORBES WATSON (representing British Employers) considers that the proposal. . . .

References to "groups" should be avoided; say instead "Government members", "Employers' members" or "Workers' members".

The results of votes on resolutions, amendments, etc., should be recorded uniformly as follows:

Vote on amendment D. 31: 37–7. Adopted.
Vote on amendment D. 32: 9–31. Rejected.

All decisions should be *underlined*, with a view to facilitating consultation of the minutes.

A complete list of the members of the Committee, of its Officers, and of the Committee secretariat should be given in the minutes of as early a sitting as possible. Lists of the members present at sittings should not be given.

Corrections to minutes, unless specially urgent or important, should not be roneoed separately for distribution, but should be reserved until several can be grouped together and given in an appendix to the minutes of a later sitting.

A set of the minutes in all three languages, incorporating any corrections, must be made for the Registry file and submitted to the Chairman for signature at, or immediately after, the last sitting. The file with these signed copies is to be sent to the Registry after the Conference.

UNITED NATIONS RELIEF AND REHABILITATION ADMINISTRATION

(a) *Minutes of Council Meetings.*

Article XII of the Rules of Procedure of the Council of the United Nations Relief and Rehabilitation Administration provides that:

1. A verbatim report of all plenary meetings held during each session of the Council shall be prepared by the secretariat and filed with the Director General. Such report shall be made available to any member government upon request. It shall not otherwise be distributed or published unless the Council shall decide to the contrary.

2. The secretariat shall prepare minutes of each session of the Council which shall be printed and circulated to member governments and which may be made public. The minutes of all private meetings shall be printed separately, distributed to member governments, and kept confidential.

So far the Council has held two sessions: the practice as set up at the second session held in Montreal, in September, 1944, is the following:

A printed *Journal* is published every day. It is circulated to the delegates, the staff, and the press and contains a "Hansard" of public plenary meetings of the Council and résumés of private meetings of the Council and Committee meetings.

1. Public Plenary Meetings.

A "Hansard" of the verbatims made by court reporters is prepared by the staff of the *Journal*. Speeches are included practically verbatim; no clearance is made with the speakers on their speeches before publication.

2. Private Plenary Meetings.

Résumés prepared by the office of the Assistant Chief of the Secretariat are published in the *Journal* for most private sessions. In certain instances a "Hansard" is prepared and published in lieu of the résumés; in these cases speeches are cleared before publication. At Montreal this was done in the case of the discussion on the Director General's Report.

3. Committee Meetings during the Council Session.

In some instances, the discussion of a certain item may be published in the *Journal*. In Montreal, the debate in the Committee on Policy on the question of aid to Italy was published in the *Journal*. The speeches were cleared with the speakers before publication. But, as a general rule, only résumés of proceedings of committee meetings are published in the *Journal*.

These résumés are drawn up by the secretaries of the committees who are instructed to make them "brief, informative and interesting." They must give an accurate and as complete a picture of what takes place at the meeting as is possible. All important actions taken by the committee, and the names of the members of any subcommittee which is appointed must be included in the résumé.

4. Additional information published in the *Journal*.

In addition to the minutes of the plenary meetings and the résumés of the committee meetings, the *Journal* contains the order of the day, a cumulative guide to the documents issued during the session, information concerning general arrangements for the session, receptions given by the Chairman, the Director General of the Administration, or the local authorities, and other miscellaneous items which might be of interest for the delegations and the staff.

After the session a revised edition of the *Journal* is published which contains the corrections made by the delegates in their speeches.

(b) *Minutes of the Standing Committees*.

Article VI of the Rules of the Standing Committees of the Council provides that:

The secretary of each Standing Committee shall prepare minutes of each meeting which shall contain a record of the conclusions reached by the Committee. When approved by the Chairman, the minutes shall be filed with the Director General, who shall distribute a copy thereof to each Member Government of the Administration.

A verbatim report of the meetings of any Standing Committee shall be kept if the Committee so decides, such report shall be filed with the Director General and made available to any Member Government of the Administration upon specific request, but shall not otherwise be distributed or published.

The practice in drawing up the minutes of the committee meetings is the following. The secretary of the committee on the day following the meeting obtains the stenographic transcript of the proceedings from the Secretariat, if such transcript has been made. The secretary then prepares the minutes, and these minutes are transmitted to the Chief of the Committee Division of the Secretariat not later than five days after the meeting is held. After the Chief of the Committee Division of the Secretariat has reviewed them and made any appropriate suggestions, he returns them to the committee secretary, who then promptly secures the approval of the committee chairman and returns them to the Secretariat. The minutes are mimeographed and distributed by the Secretariat to (1) committee members, (2) staff members concerned, and (3) all member governments. During Council sessions minutes of the Standing Committees are drawn up in accordance with the usual procedure. Owing, however, to the volume of work incumbent upon the Secretariat and the functional divisions, the mimeographing of the minutes suffer a certain delay. The same is true concerning the minutes of the *ad hoc* committees set up by the Council during its sessions.

(c) *Press Release.*

During the Council session the Office of Public Information of the Administration prepares statements concerning the work of the Council and its committees. These statements are distributed to the press. Similarly, between the sessions of the Council, except when in the opinion of the Secretariat, or the Office of Public Information, public announcement of discussions seems undesirable, the Secretariat prepares statements for radio and press release concerning the actions taken at the committee meetings. Such statements are transmitted to the Office of Public Information for issuance. The Secretariat distributes copies of these statements to the member governments.

INTERNATIONAL CONFERENCES OF AMERICAN STATES

A *Diario* of the Conference is published which corresponds to the *Assembly Journal* of the League. The *Diario* contains the minutes of the plenary sessions and of the committees, the projects submitted by the delegations, the reports of reporting delegates and of subcommittees, and other materials pertaining to the Conference. The minutes of plenary sessions are verbatim. As far as committees are concerned, the secretary of each committee prepares a brief minute of each session in which he summarizes the remarks of the delegates and in which he records in full the conclusions at which the committee has arrived.

The minutes are printed in the *Diario* of the Conference as soon as possible after the session to which they relate. They appear first in provisional form and a revised text is published later. The original minutes are preserved in the archives of the Pan American Union.

40. APPROVAL OF RECORDS

It was formerly customary in the diplomatic practice of international conferences to read at the beginning of each meeting the *procès-verbal* of the preceding one. The text was then formally approved and signed by all the first plenipotentiaries.

This custom was discontinued in the League of Nations, and minutes were generally neither formally approved nor signed. This development was chiefly due to the wish to expedite the work of international gatherings and also to the confidence which the governments and delegations placed in the work of the Secretariat. The minutes were considered as approved when the corrections requested by the delegations had been introduced by the Secretariat and the time allowed for sending in corrections had elapsed. Minutes of secret meetings of the Council, signed by the Secretary General, were an exception. Another exception was the minutes of the Advisory Committee on Traffic in Opium which were formally approved by the Committee after the corrections had been read in a private meeting.

An intermediate practice has been evolved by the International Labor Conferences: the minutes are signed by the President of the Conference and the Secretary General. This formality is required only for verbatim reports of the plenary meetings of the International Labor Conferences. The minutes of committee meetings are signed by the chairman of the respective committee.

Article 22 of the Regulations of the Eighth International Conference of American States provided that:

At the opening of the meeting the secretary general shall read the minutes of the preceding meeting unless such reading is dispensed with. Notes shall be taken of any remarks the president or any of the delegates may make thereon, and approval of the minutes shall be in order.

The Minutes of the plenary meetings of the Council of the United Nations Relief and Rehabilitation Administration are signed neither by the Chairman nor by the Secretary of the Council. The minutes of the *ad hoc* committees created during the sessions by the Council are signed both by the chairman and the secretary of the respective committees. As far as the standing committees of the Council are concerned the minutes are signed both by the chairman and the secretary of the committee and then formally approved by the committee at its next meeting.

If a conference is held under the auspices of an international organization the approved minutes must be kept in the archives of its secretariat. If a conference is sponsored by a particular state, the original minutes are generally preserved in the archives of the government of that state. The rules of procedure of this type of conference usually include a provision dealing with this matter.

41. THE LEAGUE OF NATIONS TECHNIQUE IN EDITING DOCUMENTS

The records of the proceedings published by the Secretariat of the League of Nations and the International Labor Organization were considered almost perfect. This was due in part to the very high qualifications of the personnel entrusted with the preparation of the documents of the League and in part to the organization of the respective services.

As a rule, interpreters, translators, and minute-writers were recruited by means of very difficult competitive examinations. The Secretariat probably had the cream of the personnel available for this work in all of Europe — and, indeed, in the world.[7] Verbatim reporters, stenographers, typists, and proofreaders were also hired after competitive examinations, and their standards of work were very high.

Owing to the organization of the *Document Service*, all of the operations relating to the duplication, translation, and printing of the documents were carefully checked and timed. It is impossible to describe here in detail the entire system. But it may be pointed out merely by way of example that the translation of a document was as a rule first checked once or twice in the translator's service, then scrutinized by an internal drafting committee composed of a member of the staff of the Document Service and a member of the section especially concerned with the problem treated in the document. The document then went to the Distribution Service which gave it a serial number. If the document was to be circulated in mimeographed form, a member of the interested section very often examined the carbon copies of the stencil before it was duplicated. If the document was to be circulated in printed form, proofreaders carefully checked the proofs, attentively comparing the French and English texts. Nevertheless, there almost always remained questions which the section especially concerned had to answer. In every section, one or more officials were in charge of

[7] In an article in the London *Times* of September 4, 1928, Professor Salvador de Madariaga, former Director of the Disarmament Section of the Secretariat, wrote: "The League has had to create a wholly original service, that of interpreters and translators, who along with the précis-writers are engaged in the almost superhuman task of keeping a steady sense of the King's English and of French Academy French in the bewildering cacophony of varieties of these two languages to be heard in Geneva. To anyone familiar with League meetings, the efficiency, swiftness, and accuracy of this central machinery is one of the wonders of the Secretariat."

maintaining the necessary liaison with the Document Service. As a rule no document was sent to the printer without proper authorization, a *bon à tirer*, of the section specially concerned.

In the early days of the League the French and English texts of the proceedings of the Assembly and its committees, as well as the final minutes of the Council, were published in the same volume, the French and English texts being arranged on pages facing each other in the document. This practice was discontinued as early as 1922, since it was found that this was more expensive than to have the French and English texts printed separately.

However, the *Assembly Journal* continued to be printed in French and English, the two corresponding texts being placed side by side on each page. The same practice is followed by the International Labor Organization for recommendations and draft conventions adopted by the International Labor Conference. The resolutions adopted by the Assembly of the League of Nations were printed in French and English in the same document; first the French text of all the resolutions and then the English text.

Apart from the careful recruiting and organizing of personnel, another factor contributed to the high standard of efficiency reached by these services, namely, the existence of a unique *esprit de corps* among the staffs of the Service of Documents and the Distribution Branch. Their officials were always willing to work far into the night and even until morning despite the fact that compensation for overtime was paid only to personnel below the rank of Member of Section and that shift-work was not always possible. The personnel, nevertheless, worked with enthusiasm, and discipline was maintained without effort. The bulk of the employees was genuinely eager to work for the promotion of peace, and they were unsparing in their efforts to serve the League.

42. FINAL INSTRUMENTS

The final results of a conference, as noted above, are often embodied in a formal compact which may be termed Treaty, Pact, Convention, Agreement, Protocol, Protocol of Signature, General Act, Final Act, etc. No detailed description of each of these compacts will be attempted here. There is no definite and generally valid terminology allowing for a clear differentiation between these various types of international instruments, though usage and practice make certain distinctions which are more or less accepted. In the following pages, however, an attempt will be made to delimitate and describe some of these compacts in view of the practice governing the League in this matter.

TREATY

A treaty is the most solemn form given to a diplomatic instrument embodying the results of the work of a conference, a congress, or diplomatic parleys. No compact concluded under the direct auspices of the League was termed a treaty. But the League formulated a series of draft treaties, chiefly in connection with the settlement of disputes and the subject of security. Thus, for instance, the Temporary Mixed Commission on Disarmament submitted to the Assembly in September, 1923, a draft Treaty of Mutual Assistance. Unfortunately, the Fifth Assembly in September, 1924, was unable to reach an agreement on the subject. The draft, which had been accepted in principle by eighteen states, had to be abandoned. This draft treaty specified means of determining the aggressor, defined obligations in the matter of assistance, and provided for agreements for assistance within continental limits. In 1928, the Assembly recommended to the attention of states a series of model bilateral or multilateral treaties concerning the pacific settlement of disputes, non-aggression, and mutual assistance. The provisions concerning non-aggression and mutual assistance were based on the Locarno Treaty of Mutual Guarantee of October 16, 1925.

Occasionally the Pan American Conferences draw up the text of a treaty for subsequent signature by American states. Thus, in 1929, at a conference specially convened for the purpose in Washington, a General Convention of Inter-American Conciliation and a General Treaty of Inter-American Arbitration were signed.

It is difficult to differentiate between a treaty and a convention. As a rule, the term "treaty" is always given to agreements relative to peace, alliance, or territorial cession.

PACT

A treaty is sometimes called a pact. No pact was drawn up by the League of Nations,[8] but several conferences held between the two World Wars framed instruments which were termed pacts. Thus on August 27, 1928, a treaty renouncing war as an instrument of national policy, known as the Paris Pact or Kellogg-Briand Pact, was signed in Paris.

[8] The case of the Covenant of the League — in French, *Pacte de la Société des Nations* — is naturally disregarded here.

Subsequently a Pact of Non-Aggression and Conciliation was signed at Rio de Janeiro on October 10, 1933.

CONVENTION

Most frequently a convention or a series of conventions embodies the results both of conferences held under League auspices and of the International Labor Conferences; the same has been true of the Pan American Conferences. Besides the convention, a protocol of signature and a final act are usually drawn up.[9]

Conventions framed by the International Labor Organization have a peculiar form. As has been pointed out, the conventions drawn up by the International Labor Conferences are not signed but are adopted by vote. A two-thirds majority vote of all delegates is required. Thus the draft conventions adopted by the International Labor Conference have rather the form of detailed resolutions, subject to ratification, than that of treaties signed by plenipotentiaries. For a draft convention adopted by an International Labor Conference to become binding it must be ratified by several states, a minimum of two ratifications being as a rule sufficient. Ratification is the only act required from a state which wishes to become a party to the compact.

In recent years the League of Nations developed the practice of drafting model conventions which can be adapted to national conditions and utilized in a series of similar but not identical bilateral treaties freely entered into by the various states. Among these model conventions those relating to double taxation have found the widest application. Model conventions of this type are in reality detailed reports or resolutions to which the form of a draft treaty has been given.

The great majority of international compacts concluded under the auspices of the League of Nations took the form of multilateral international conventions.[10] The essential parts of conventions adopted under League auspices were as a rule:

1. *List of the High Contracting Parties.* In the early days of the League this list enumerated the Heads of State of the High Contracting Parties. After the adoption of the Statute of Westminster, this practice was modified and the formula "The Governments of —" was employed. Sometimes an even simpler method was used, i.e., the enumeration of states which had designated plenipotentiaries, as for example: "Afghanistan, Union of South Africa, Albania, etc." The

---

[9] For details regarding these two types of diplomatic instruments, see *infra*.

[10] For a list of conventions adopted under the auspices of the League of Nations, see Appendix XIII, *infra*.

order in which the states appeared was the alphabetical order of the states in French.

2. *Preamble.* This part of the convention, which, incidentally, had no binding force, varied considerably in length according to the circumstances. The preamble states the purpose of the convention. The practice of the League of Nations was to abridge preambles as much as possible in order to prevent a contradictory interpretation of the text of the preamble as compared with the corresponding text of the articles contained in the body of the convention. For instance, the preamble of the "Convention for Limiting the Manufacture and Regulating the Distribution of Narcotic Drugs" of July 13, 1931, reads as follows:

Desiring to supplement the provisions of the International Opium Conventions, signed at The Hague on January 23rd, 1912, and at Geneva on February 19th, 1925, by rendering effective by international agreement the limitation of the manufacture of narcotic drugs to the world's legitimate requirements for medical and scientific purposes and by regulating their distribution. . . .

3. *Statement of Resolve.* The tenor of such statements was that the High Contracting Parties had resolved to conclude a convention for the purpose stated in the preamble and had appointed plenipotentiaries to this end, for instance: ". . . have resolved to conclude a Convention for that purpose and have appointed as their Plenipotentiaries. . . ."

4. *List of Plenipotentiaries.* The names of the plenipotentiaries were listed in accordance with the French alphabetical order of the names of the states represented in the conference, for instance:

Albania

M. Thomas Luarassi, Secretary of the Permanent Delegation to the League of Nations.

Argentine Republic

M. Carlos A. Pardo, Commercial Adviser to the Legation at Berne.

Austria

His Excellency Dr. Marcus Leitmaier, Envoy Extraordinary and Minister Plenipotentiary.

etc.

5. *Body of the Convention.* The text was usually divided into articles. When the convention was lengthy the text was divided into sections, chapters, etc. For instance the above-mentioned convention of July 13, 1931, concerning dangerous drugs is divided into seven chapters:

Definitions, Estimates, Limitation of Manufacture, Prohibitions and Restrictions, Control, Administrative Provisions, and General Provisions.

6. *General Provisions.*[11] The practice of the League of Nations in drafting the part of the convention known as general provisions or *clauses protocolaires* deserves special mention.[12] The clauses were usually drafted under the close supervision of the head of the Treaty Registration Branch of the Legal Section of the Secretariat. These provisions deal generally with the following matters:

(*a*) Languages in which the convention has been drafted.

This question is discussed in section 43 of this handbook;

(*b*) Date of the convention and period during which it will be open for signature.

The date of the convention is, as a rule, the date of its signature. In the conventions concluded under the auspices of the League, considerable time was usually allowed during which they were open for signature. A period of several months was not exceptional. Thus, Article 27 of the Convention for Limiting the Manufacture and Regulating the Distribution of Narcotic Drugs of July 13, 1931, provides:

> The present Convention, of which the French and English texts shall both be authoritative, shall bear this day's date, and shall, until December 31st, 1931, be open for signature on behalf of any Member of the League of Nations, or of any non-member State which was represented at the Conference which drew up this Convention, or to which the Council of the League of Nations shall have communicated a copy of the Convention for this purpose.

> The power thus customarily given to the Council in conventions concluded under the auspices of the League of Nations was always exercised so as to open the conventions for signature or accession to all states whose participation could be of interest to themselves and to the other parties, but it retains a certain permanent value as a means of admitting to the conventions any newly establish or any existing states which were not originally considered as suitable parties.[13]

[11] Most of the material studied below is discussed in detail in the excellent work of Wilcox, *op. cit.* See also Harold Nicolson, *Diplomacy* (London: Thornton Butterworth, Ltd., 1939), pp. 234–50, for a definition of several terms used in this section.

[12] An example of the general provisions of the International Convention concerning the Use of Broadcasting in the Cause of Peace will be found in Appendix XIV, *infra.* Compare them with the model of general provisions of treaties and conventions signed at International Conferences of American States as annexed to the Rules of Procedure of the Eighth Pan American Conference. See Appendix VII, *infra.*

[13] Memorandum of the Secretariat of the League of Nations, *Powers and Duties Attributed to the League of Nations by International Treaties,* L.N. Document C.3.M.3. 1944.V., p. 11.

(c) Ratification.

As a rule conventions concluded under the auspices of the League of Nations contained a special clause subjecting them specifically to ratification. The instruments of ratification had to be transmitted to the Secretary General of the League of Nations who was entrusted with the task of notifying their receipt to all members of the League and to the non-member states concerned. However, treaties and conventions are not always subject to ratification. Lacking a specific provision concerning ratification, the states are bound by their simple signature. Whether or not it is necessary to have parliamentary or other approval of signature depends on the constitution of the states concerned. Similarly, when a provision concerning ratification is included, parliamentary or other legislative approval may or may not be required for valid ratification. Ratification, which is an act of international law, and parliamentary approval (often wrongly called ratification), which is an act of municipal law, are frequently confused. Legally there is no connection between the existence or non-existence in a treaty or convention of a provision concerning ratification on the one hand and the constitutional requirements of particular countries on the other.

It is not because a treaty or convention contains a provision concerning ratification that it requires parliamentary approval and, conversely, the absence of a provision concerning ratification in a treaty or convention does not make such approval unnecessary. An illustration is afforded in the Agreement for the United Nations Relief and Rehabilitation Administration. Article IX of this agreement provides that it shall enter into force with respect to each signatory on the date it is signed by that signatory, unless otherwise specified by the latter. The agreement was signed on behalf of forty-four governments. Fourteen of them made a reservation or statement to the effect, in each case, that the agreement was signed subject to ratification or legislative approval. The following are examples of the reservations or statements that were made:

[For Chile:] This Agreement will enter into effect with respect to Chile, in conformity with the provisions of its Constitution, once it has been approved by the Congress and ratified by the appropriate constitutional agencies of the Republic.

[For Ethiopia:] Subject to the ratification of the Imperial Ethiopian Government.

[For Guatemala:] Pending the required approval by the National Assembly of Guatemala, the immediate application of this Agreement shall be considered provisional with regard to the Government of Guatemala.

(d) Accession.

Accession, according to Oppenheim, means "the formal entrance of a third state into an existing treaty, so that it becomes a party to the treaty, with all rights and duties arising therefrom." [14]

The clause concerning accession provided that on the day following the expiration of the period during which a convention could still be signed, it was open for accession. Instruments of accession had to be transmitted, exactly as instruments of ratification, to the Secretary General of the League of Nations, who was charged with notifying their receipt to all the members of the League and to the non-member states concerned.

Accessions normally do not require ratification. However, on September 23, 1927, the Assembly of the League adopted a resolution as follows:

> The procedure of accession to international agreements given subject to ratification is an admissible one which the League should neither discourage nor encourage.
> Nevertheless, if a State gives its accession, it should know that, if it does not expressly mention that this accession is subject to ratification, it shall be deemed to have undertaken a final obligation. If it desires to prevent this consequence, it must expressly declare at the time of accession that the accession is given subject to ratification.

(e) Registration.

Article 18 of the Covenant of the League of Nations provides that:

> Every treaty or international engagement entered into hereafter by any Member of the League shall be forthwith registered with the Secretariat and shall as soon as possible be published by it. No such treaty or international engagement shall be binding until so registered.

Conventions concluded under the auspices of the League of Nations contained therefore, as a rule, a clause providing for registration at the time of their entry into force.

---

[14] L. Oppenheim, *International Law*, 4th edition (London: Longmans, Green and Co., 1928, 1926, 2 vols.), Vol. I., p. 742.

Sir Ernest Satow points out that "the proper English equivalents of the French words *adhérer* and *adhésion* are 'accede' and 'accession.'" He adds that "certain writers have in the past drawn a distinction between *accession* and *adhésion* in the sense that *accession* placed a state under the same conditions as the states which originally negotiated and signed the treaty, whereas *adhésion* did not constitute a definite acceptance of those conditions. At the present time any such distinctions appear rather to rest on the degree to which a state may by reservations qualify its acceptance of the provisions of a treaty, either when signing it, acceding to it, or ratifying it." *A Guide to Diplomatic Practice*, 3d edition, *op. cit.*, p. 413.

(*f*) Date of entry into force of the convention.

Conventions drawn up under the auspices of the League of Nations usually provided that the instrument should come into force after the Secretary General of the League had received a certain number of ratifications or accessions.[15] Sometimes the ratification or accession of certain states mentioned *nominatim* in the convention was made a condition of the entry into force of the compact. Thus, for instance, Article 30 of the Convention for Limiting the Manufacture and Regulating the Distribution of Narcotic Drugs of July 13, 1931, provides:

The present Convention shall come into force ninety days after the Secretary-General of the League of Nations has received the ratifications or accessions of twenty-five Members of the League of Nations or non-member States, including any four of the following: France, Germany, United Kingdom of Great Britain and Northern Ireland, Japan, Netherlands, Switzerland, Turkey, and the United States of America.

It was generally provided that the ratifications or accessions received after the coming into force of the convention would take effect as from the expiration of a period equal to the period fixed for the entry into force of the convention itself (in the case of the above-mentioned Convention of July 13, 1931, ninety days).

(*g*) Denunciation.

A provision concerning denunciation was included in most of the conventions concluded under the auspices of the League of Nations. If such a provision was lacking it was assumed that the instrument could not be unilaterally denounced. The tenor of this provision was generally that the compact may be denounced by a notification addressed to the Secretary General of the League of Nations. The Secretary General was under the obligation to notify the receipt of any such denunciation to all members of the League and to non-member states concerned. A period of time was generally fixed after the expiration of which the denunciation should take effect; for instance, one year. Sometimes the convention provided that the instrument could not be denounced until the expiration of a certain period of time after its entry into force. Thus, Article 32 of the Convention for Limiting the Manufacture and Regulating the Distribution of Narcotic Drugs provides formally that: "After the expiration of five years from the

---

[15] In 1930, the Assembly proposed that at the time of the signing of conventions concluded under the auspices of the League of Nations, protocols of signature be signed for expediting the entry into force of those conventions. The model draft protocols proposed by the Assembly have been appended to this handbook as Appendix XVII, *infra*.

date of the coming into force of this Convention, the Convention may be denounced by an instrument in writing, deposited with the Secretary-General of the League of Nations."

It was also often provided that if, as a result of denunciations, the number of parties to the convention should fall under a certain minimum, the convention should cease to apply.

(h) Application to colonies, protectorates, overseas territories, etc.

This clause provided that any of the High Contracting Parties had the right on signing, ratifying, or acceding to the convention, or at any subsequent date, to declare, by a document addressed to the Secretary General, that the convention should apply to all or any of its colonies, protectorates, etc. The clause often added that, failing such a declaration, the convention should not apply to any such territories. This was a simplification of the practice followed in the twenties and the early thirties. Thus, the clause concerning the application of the convention to colonies and protectorates, in the Convention for Limiting the Manufacture and Regulating the Distribution of Narcotic Drugs of July 13, 1931 (Article 26), still read as follows:

Any High Contracting Party may, at the time of signature, ratification or accession, declare that, in accepting the present Convention, he does not assume any obligation in respect of all or any of his colonies, protectorates and overseas territories or territories under suzerainty or mandate, and the present Convention shall not apply to any territories named in such declaration.

Any High Contracting Party may give notice to the Secretary-General of the League of Nations at any time subsequently that he desires that the Convention shall apply to all or any of his territories which have been made the subject of a declaration under the preceding paragraph, and the Convention shall apply to all the territories named in such notice in the same manner as in the case of a country ratifying or acceding to the Convention.

(i) Revision.

A provision permitting revision was generally inserted in League conventions. The request for revision, which could emanate from any party to the convention, had to be addressed to the Secretary General. Such notices were immediately communicated by the Secretary General to the other members of the League and to the non-member states bound by the convention. If the proposal was endorsed by a certain number of the parties to the convention (for instance one third) a conference had to be convoked for the revision of the convention.

(j) Interpretation.

In addition to the above-studied general provisions, conventions concluded under the auspices of the League of Nations often contained a clause for the settlement of disputes regarding the interpretation or application of the convention. The following means of settlement were generally indicated:

(i) settlement through diplomatic channels;
(ii) settlement in conformity with the provisions in force between the parties concerning the settlement of international disputes;
(iii) submission of the dispute to arbitration or judicial settlement;
(iv) failing agreement concerning the choice of a tribunal, submission of the dispute to the Permanent Court of International Justice, or,
(v) submission of the dispute to an arbitral tribunal, constituted in conformity with the Hague Convention of October 18, 1907, for the Pacific Settlement of International Disputes;
(vi) it was often provided that before having recourse to the procedure listed above the parties may, by common consent, appeal to the good offices of a technical committee of the League.

7. *In-faith-whereof Statement.* This was a formal statement to the following effect: "In Faith Whereof the above-mentioned Plenipotentiaries have signed the present Convention." In recent years this clause was often omitted.

8. *Place and Date.* Here particulars were given concerning where and when the convention had been signed, in what archives the original was to be deposited, and to whom copies were to be delivered, for instance: "Done at Geneva the thirteenth day of July, one thousand nine hundred and thirty-one, in a single copy, which shall remain deposited in the archives of the Secretariat of the League of Nations, and certified true copies[16] of which shall be delivered to all the Members of the League and to the non-member States referred to in Article . . . ."

9. *Signatures.* Then followed the signatures of the plenipotentiaries in the French alphabetical order of the names of countries.

Sometimes a plenipotentiary signs the compact *ad referendum*. Daniel Antokoletz gives the following explanation concerning this mention: "The mention *ad referendum* is employed when the plenipotentiary lacks necessary instructions and has no time to consult his government. In this case, if the instrument seems advantageous, he accepts it *ad referendum*, i.e., with the understanding that he will report to his government."[17] The mention *ad referendum* can be employed even when the treaty or convention contains a provision concerning ratification.

[16] The certified true copies were signed for the Secretary General by the Legal Adviser of the Secretariat.
[17] *Tratado de derecho internacional publico en tiempo de paz*, 2d édición (Buenos Aires: La Facultad, 1928, 3 vols.), Vol. III, p. 454.

Thus, Article 28 of the 1931 Convention for Limiting the Manufacture and Regulating the Distribution of Narcotic Drugs provides that "The present Convention shall be ratified . . ." Nevertheless, the plenipotentiaries of Argentina and Venezuela signed the convention *ad referendum*.

Reservations of a specific character were, as a rule, in the practice of the League, embodied in a Protocol of Signature, but it was not exceptional for such reservations to be recorded alongside the signature of the plenipotentiary. Thus, for instance, the plenipotentiary for Siam signed the 1931 Convention for Limiting the Manufacture and Regulating the Distribution of Narcotic Drugs with the following mention below his signature: "As our Harmful Habit-forming Drugs Law goes beyond the provision of the Geneva Convention and the present Convention on certain points, my Government reserves the right to apply our existing law." [18]

RULES CONCERNING THE MATERIAL PREPARATION OF THE TEXT OF CONVENTIONS

Special care was taken by the Secretariat of the League in the preparation of the text of conventions. In order to facilitate the work of the officials entrusted with this task, a series of rules was set up.[19] These rules read as follows:

1. PREPARATION OF TEXT

(*a*) A single official should be designated by the responsible Section to take general responsibility for the completeness of the text. If there is a drafting committee of delegates, he might well be the secretary of that committee. If an agreement is drawn up in committees working separately, he will receive the clauses drafted by the committees and be responsible for their being included in the final text of the agreement. He will be responsible for certifying, when the final text is ready, that the rules made to insure its completeness and accuracy have in all essentials been complied with. The initials of the members of Section who collaborated in the work should be obtained to those parts of the work in which they have assisted.

(*b*) A translator familiar with both official languages should be attached to the conference with the special duty of being responsible for the translation, or provisional translation, of clauses adopted in one language only.

(*c*) The Section generally responsible for the conference should at an early stage ask the Legal Section to delegate a member of the latter to co-operate in the preparation of the draft, with special reference to the decision of any legal questions arising in the draft and the security of accuracy in the drafting.

[18] L.N. Document C.509.M.214.1931.XI, p. 389.
[19] See Annex II to League of Nations, *Secretariat Office Rules* (Geneva, 1936).

(*d*) Care should be taken to avoid having to transcribe corrections and amendments from one copy of a document to another. As soon as possible, a single copy of the text in each official language should be taken as the basis of work.

2. INDEPENDENT VERIFICATION OF FINAL TEXT

If possible, a member of the Secretariat who has not been engaged in the preparation of the draft should give his assistance in reading through, in both languages, the final text of the document. Such an independent study will often detect mistakes which are not noticed by persons too familiar with the text in question.

3. PREPARATION OF COPY FOR SIGNATURE

(*a*) When the material provisions of an international agreement have been settled, a special copy for signature should be printed on good paper and delegates should be induced to realise that sufficient time for this purpose must be allowed. In cases which should be altogether exceptional, as the practice has many disadvantages, the copy prepared for signature may be typed.

(*b*) The precedents which have been established with regard to the description of parties to an agreement, the order in which they are to be named, the form to be given to agreements which are concluded in both official languages (so that both languages are authoritative), and, generally to all formal parts of an agreement, should be carefully followed. On these points, assistance should be obtained from the Legal Section, which will give the assistance of their Treaty Registration Branch and orders for printing should be given in consultation with this Branch. The Legal Section should, of course, be warned a sufficient time in advance of the assistance required from it. They should also be consulted as to any necessary formalities in regard to signature.

4. ERRORS APPEARING IN SIGNATURE COPY

However careful the proof-reading, misprints may creep into the document at the last moment. Consequently, the actual document which is to be signed must be carefully read through before signature. If mistakes are detected and a reprint is not possible or is not considered necessary, the necessary corrections should be made in the text before any signatures are given and should be authenticated as follows:

(*a*) Where the correction is a correction of an obvious misprint and where the parties to the agreement are not too numerous, it is sufficient that the corrections should be initialed in the margin by the person signing.

(*b*) Where the corrections are not corrections of obvious mistakes, or where the parties are too numerous for initialing in the margin to be possible, a statement should be drawn up and attached to the copy of the agreement which is signed stating, with reference to page and line throughout, that the corrections in question were made before signature. This statement should be signed by all the parties to the agreement at the same time as they sign the agreement itself. The following formula may be used according to the nature of the corrections made:

"Statement of corrections made in the text of.........before signature.
"The following corrections were introduced into the text of the above-mentioned instrument in........ink before its signature:
       "Page........; line........; the following words....................
                                   ⎧ were struck out
...........................⎨ were inserted after the words............
                                   ⎨ and before the words..................
                                   ⎩ were replaced by the words.............
....

                              Date..............
                              Signed.............."

No modifications should be made in documents after their signature.

5. Preparation of Copies for Certification

Almost invariably, certified true copies of agreements with which the Secretariat is connected have to be sent to parties or Members of the League. These are to be prepared on the responsibility of the Legal Section, which will consult the Section concerned.

These copies must be an entirely faithful and complete duplicate of the text which has been signed. No part of the text may be omitted or abbreviated. The copies must have annexed to them any documents which are incorporated by reference in their text, so as to be essential to the proper interpretation of its provisions. The only changes in the copy printed for certification will be:

(a) Possibly the addition of distribution reference headings and, in certain cases, a title. The title should always be chosen very carefully, so as to offer no matter for possible discussion if questions of interpretation subsequently arise.

(b) The addition at the end of the formula of certification.

Wherever possible, copies for certification should be printed off at the earliest possible opportunity from the type which was set up to print the signature copy; any corrections made in that copy before signature will, of course, be effected. Where the copies for certification cannot be printed off until after, for example, the agreement has come into force, or the period during which signatures are allowable is at the end, the type can, of course, be used for the *Official Journal* or other purposes; but it must be realised that the fact that the type has to some extent been re-set for such purposes cannot interfere with the necessity for making the copies which are to be certified entirely faithful and complete duplicates of the agreement as signed.

6. Reprints

No international agreement which is in the custody of the Secretariat should be reprinted in the *Official Journal*, or in any other form, without reference being made to the Legal Section, whose Treaty Registration Branch will assure that the correct text is being used and that any signatures included are up to date, etc.

PROTOCOL OF SIGNATURE

A protocol of signature is an instrument which is signed as a rule simultaneously with the main agreement and which contains statements supplementing or clarifying the provisions of the main body of the instrument. It is a convenient method for recording reservations that are made by plenipotentiaries when signing the treaty or convention and for establishing the agreement or acquiescence of the other signers with these reservations.[20] The beginning of a protocol of signature may be drafted, for example, as follows:

When signing the Convention of 1936 for the Suppression of the Illicit Traffic in Dangerous Drugs dated this day, the undersigned Plenipotentiaries, in the name of their Governments, declare to have agreed:

Then follows the text of the reservation or reservations, as, for instance:

That India makes its acceptance of the Convention subject to the reservation that the said Convention does not apply to the Indian States or to the Shan States (which are part of British India).

The protocol concludes with a statement similar to that ending the convention:

IN FAITH WHEREOF the undersigned have affixed their signatures to the present Protocol.
DONE at Geneva [etc.]

The signatures follow in the same order as for the convention.

FINAL ACT

The Final Act is a very concise record of the composition and the objects and circumstances of the conference. It lists the delegates who attended the conference and the agreements which have been concluded. It may also contain the resolutions, declarations, and recommendations adopted by the conference,[21] as, for instance:

THE GOVERNMENTS OF ALBANIA, THE ARGENTINE REPUBLIC [etc.].
Having accepted the invitation addressed to them in pursuance of the resolution of the Council of the League of Nations dated January 20th, 1936, with a

[20] Extracts of the Protocol of Signature adopted by the Conference for the Suppression of the Illicit Traffic in Dangerous Drugs, Geneva, 1936, are given as an example in Appendix XV, *infra*.
[21] For a discussion of the binding force of the Final Act, see Paul Fauchille, *Traité de droit international public*, 8th edition (Paris: Rousseau et Cie, Editeurs, 1921-1926), Vol. 1, Part 3, pp. 245-48. In the practice of the International Conferences of American States, the Final Act "shall contain the resolutions, recommendations, votes and agreements, approved by the Conference, and in an appendix the treaties and conventions that may be negotiated." (Article 36 of the Regulations of the Eighth Conference of American States.)

view to the conclusion of an International Convention for the use of broadcasting in the cause of peace,

Appointed the following delegates:

ALBANIA

Delegate:

M. Thomas LUARASSI, Secretary of the Permanent Delegation to the League of Nations.

[etc.]

Attended the Conference in the capacity of observers:

ESTONIA

His Excellency M. Auguste SCHMIDT, Permanent Delegate to the League of Nations, Envoy Extraordinary and Minister Plenipotentiary to the Court of St. James and to the Swiss Federal Council.

[etc.]

Who assembled at Geneva.

The Council of the League of Nations appointed as President of the Conference:

M. Arnold RAESTAD, former Minister for Foreign Affairs of Norway.

The Conference appointed as Vice-Presidents:

[Names.]

The functions of Secretary-General of the Conference were assumed by:

[Name.]

The functions of Legal Adviser to the Conference were assumed by:

[Names.]

In the course of a series of meetings held between September 17th and 23rd, 1936, an

INTERNATIONAL CONVENTION CONCERNING THE USE OF BROADCASTING IN THE CAUSE OF PEACE was adopted.

The Conference also adopted the following

RECOMMENDATIONS.

[Text of the recommendations]

IN FAITH WHEREOF the Delegates have signed the present Act.

DONE at Geneva [etc.]

Then follow the signatures, the President and the Secretary General of the conference signing first. The signatures of the delegates follow by countries in the French alphabetical order.[22]

[22] As an example, extracts from the Final Act of the Conference for the Suppression of the Illicit Traffic in Dangerous Drugs are given in Appendix XVI, *infra.*

OTHER INSTRUMENTS: AGREEMENT, PROTOCOL, GENERAL ACT, PROCÈS-
VERBAL, DECLARATION

Other instruments were sometimes adopted by the League as the
result of a session of the Assembly or of an *ad hoc* conference. *Agreements* are less formal instruments than conventions. This term was
often given to conventions of a more limited scope and participation
than the usual general conventions adopted under the auspices of the
League.[23] Thus, for instance, in February, 1925, an Agreement concerning the Suppression of the Manufacture of, International Trade in,
and Use of, Prepared Opium, and in November, 1931, an Agreement
for the Suppression of Opium Smoking, were adopted. Both the aim and
the participation in the conferences which framed these agreements
were limited.

Protocol. The word Protocol suggests merely minutes or a record
but it has also the meaning of treaty or agreement. In the practice of
the League of Nations the term has only once been applied to an
important treaty; i.e., the Geneva Protocol of 1924 which attempted
a general solution of the problems of the pacific settlement of disputes,
of security, and of disarmament. The circumstances in which this ill-
fated treaty was abandoned are well known. More often the term has
been used for agreements paralleling, supplementing, or modifying a
more important convention or a previous agreement.

General Act. This designation sometimes has a meaning similar to
that attached to the term Final Act. The League of Nations used it
once, but in a different sense. In September, 1928, the Assembly
adopted a General Act of Arbitration for the Pacific Settlement of
International Disputes. In its various chapters the General Act provides for separate procedures: a procedure of conciliation for all
disputes (Chapter I); a procedure of judicial settlement or arbitration
for disputes of a legal nature (Chapter II); and a procedure of arbitration for other disputes (Chapter III). States may accede to the General
Act in whole or in part. In reality this General Act is the combination,

---

[23] Sometimes agreements are not subject to ratification. Section VI of a resolution
adopted by the Assembly of the League of Nations on October 3, 1930, reads: "That
the Council will investigate to what extent, in the case of general conventions dealing
with particular matters, it is possible — in view of the constitutional law and practices of different states — to adopt the procedure of signing instruments in the form
of governmental agreements which are not subject to ratification, and that, to the
extent that it is possible to do so, this procedure should be followed in regard to minor
and technical matters."

in a single compact, of three general treaties of conciliation and arbitration.[24]

Procès-verbal. This term usually means what the words imply — minutes or record. Sometimes, however, it indicates an agreement of minor importance. Thus, for instance, in the League a *procès-verbal* was drawn up in June, 1936, "to alter the latest date of issue of the annual statement of the estimated world requirements of dangerous drugs."

Declaration. This term is used in many ways. It may relate to a statement of policy made by a government; or to such communications as declarations of war, or of neutrality, etc. It may apply to instruments aimed at the definition of international law (Declaration of Paris, 1856, Declaration of St. Petersburg, 1868, etc.). Declarations are often appended to a treaty or convention to form a subsidiary compact, or to place on record some understanding reached or some explanation given. The term "declaration" is also frequently applied to agreements between governments regarding some minor matter. Declarations may or may not provide for ratification.

The only declaration drawn up under the auspices of the League of Nations is the "Declaration regarding the Territory of Ifni" appended to the Convention on Supervision of International Trade in Arms and Ammunition and in Implements of War of 1925.[25] No provision was made for the ratification of the declaration.

At its twenty-sixth session, held in Philadelphia in April–May, 1944, the International Labor Conference adopted a "Declaration concerning the Aim and Purposes of the International Labour Organisation." The preamble of this declaration reads as follows:

[24] Note the exceptional system adopted by the League as far as the entry into force of the General Act was concerned.
(1) The Assembly adopted a resolution on September 26, 1928, inviting "all States whether Members of the League or not, and in so far as their existing agreements do not already achieve this end, to accept obligations . . . by becoming parties to the annexed General Act. . . ."
(2) The General Act did not require the signatures of the delegates at the Assembly but only that of the President of the Assembly and the Secretary General (Article 116).
(3) The General Act was declared open to accession by all the heads of state or other competent authorities of the members of the League and the non-member states to which the Council of the League of Nations had communicated a copy of the Act for this purpose (Article 43).
(4) The General Act was to come into force on the ninetieth day following the receipt by the Secretary General of the League of Nations of the accession of not less than two contracting parties (Article 44).
Compare this system with the usual system as exemplified by the General Provisions of the International Convention concerning the Use of Broadcasting in the Cause of Peace. Appendix XIV, *infra*.
[25] L.N., *Official Journal*, 1925, p. 1154.

The General Conference of the International Labour Organisation, meeting in its Twenty-Sixth Session in Philadelphia, hereby adopts, this tenth day of May in the year nineteen hundred and forty-four, the present Declaration of the aims and purposes of the International Labour Organisation and of the principles which should inspire the policy of its Members.

The last paragraph reads as follows:

The Conference affirms that the principles set forth in this Declaration are fully applicable to all peoples everywhere and that, while the manner of their application must be determined with due regard to the stage of social and economic development reached by each people, their progressive application to peoples who are still dependent, as well as those who have already achieved self-government, is a matter of concern to the whole civilised world.

Declarations of this latter type have obviously an important moral value but, as a matter of fact, have no legal binding force.

43. Language of Treaties and Conventions

As a rule treaties are drawn up in the language selected by the signatories. Most of the time they are drawn up in the language of the contracting powers or of some of them, or in the language which is considered as the recognized diplomatic language. Latin was for centuries the language used in Europe for drawing up multilateral or even bilateral treaties until, in the middle of the seventeenth century, French gradually took its place.

It was in French that the Congress of Vienna pursued its labors and it was in French that the Final Act of the Congress was drawn up. It is true, however, that the following article of reservation regarding the use of the French language was inserted in the treaty signed on June 19, 1815:

The French language having been exclusively employed in all the Copies of the present Treaty, it is recognised by the Powers which have acceded to this Act, that the use of that language shall have no consequence for the future: so that each Power reserves for itself to adopt in future Negotiations and Conventions the language which it has hitherto employed in its diplomatic relations, without the present Treaty being cited as an example contrary to established usage.[26]

Notwithstanding this reservation, the use of French for drawing up international multilateral treaties or engagements was universally

[26] Stephen Gaselee, *The Language of Diplomacy* (Cambridge: Bowes & Bowes, 1939), p. 71.

recognized during the nineteenth and the beginning of the twentieth centuries. Thus in a circular dispatch from the British Foreign Office to Her Majesty's representatives abroad it was stated:

Foreign Office, June 7, 1895

SIR,

I have to inform you that Her Majesty's Government attach much importance to the strict observance of the rule that Treaties, Conventions, and other international engagements, between Great Britain and foreign Powers should, in all cases, be drawn up in the English language. This text may be accompanied by another version, either in French, or in the language of the foreign State which is a party to the Treaty; but in no case should an international engagement between this country and a foreign Power be concluded in a foreign language only.

It should, of course, be clearly understood that this rule does not apply to international Treaties or engagements to which three or more Powers are parties. Such instruments may, as heretofore, if so desired, be drawn up in the French language only.

I am, etc.

KIMBERLEY [27]

The international position in this matter was in some degree changed in 1919. The treaty of peace with Germany (Treaty of Versailles, Article 440) provided that "The Present Treaty, of which the French and English texts are both authentic, shall be ratified."

The treaty with Austria (Treaty of St. Germain-en-Laye, Article 381) provided that "The present Treaty, in French, in English, and in Italian, shall be ratified. In case of divergence the French text shall prevail, except in Parts I (Covenant of the League of Nations) and XIII (Labour), when the French and English texts shall be of equal force." Identical provisions were inserted in the treaties with Hungary (Treaty of Trianon), with Bulgaria (Treaty of Neuilly), and in the never ratified treaty with Turkey (Treaty of Sèvres).

French and English having been adopted as the languages of the League, all compacts concluded under the auspices of the League were drawn up in these two languages and a clause similar to the following inserted in them: "The present Convention, of which the French and English texts are both authentic. . . ."

Similarly, all the treaties, conventions, agreements, etc. sent for registration to the League, in accordance with Article 18 of the Covenant, were translated into French and English (if not already drawn up in one or both of these languages), and the French and English

[27] Stephen Gaselee, op. cit., p. 63.

texts published in the *Treaty Series* of the League of Nations besides the original text of the compact, whatever the language employed.

Conventions and recommendations adopted by the International Labor Conferences are drawn up in French and English, a translation in Spanish being simultaneously provided.

The International Conferences of American States adopt their final instruments in Spanish, English, Portuguese, and French. Article 27 of the Regulations of the Seventh International Conference of American States held in Montevideo in 1933 provided that:

> The final act shall be prepared as the work of the Conference develops. After each plenary session there shall be inserted in the draft of the final act, with a number and a title indicating the subject matter, the treaties, conventions, resolutions, agreements, votes and recommendations approved at the session and the date of the session on which they were approved. The day before the closing of the Conference the secretary general shall submit to the delegates for examination copies of the final act in Spanish, English, Portuguese and French.

It must be pointed out that for instruments adopted by governmental conferences, other than those held under the aegis of the League, the International Labor Organization, and the Pan American Union, French has been used most of the time, during the period between World War I and World War II, as the only official language.

For instance, French was the official language used during the Lausanne Conference in 1923, and the treaty of peace with Turkey which resulted was drawn up in French. Similarly, only French was spoken during the Conference of Locarno in 1925 and French was the official language of the Red Cross Conference held in Geneva in 1929, French being the authentic language of the instruments adopted on both occasions.

World War II has brought new changes in the situation. The declaration of the United Nations signed in Washington on January 1, 1942, was drawn up only in English. The text of the agreement setting up the United Nations Relief and Rehabilitation Administration is likewise only in the English language.

It is doubtful, however, that in the future English will be the only language employed for international multilateral compacts. This applies particularly to all treaties, conventions, or agreements modifying previous compacts which were drawn up only in French. During the Second Session of the Council of the United Nations Relief and Rehabilitation Administration, held in Montreal, in September, 1944, the following interesting case occurred. It had been proposed to the

Council to approve in principle two draft Sanitary Conventions modifying the International Maritime Sanitary Convention signed in Paris in 1926 and the International Sanitary Convention for Aerial Navigation signed in Paris in 1933. The authentic texts of these two conventions are in the French language. Notwithstanding the fact that English is the official language of the United Nations Relief and Rehabilitation Administration, it was agreed that the following clause was to be inserted in the preamble of the two draft conventions: "Whereas the authentic text of the 1926 (respectively 1933) Convention is in the French language, the present Convention shall be in English and French, both texts being equally authentic." It was further decided that the Director General be requested "to submit copies of the French and English texts of these drafts to member Governments for their early consideration." The procedure so adopted was a compromise between the new practice and the established tradition, since it seems that, in accordance with established precedents, modifications to a text previously drawn up in French should be made only in French.[28]

Those in favor of the use of English only for drawing up international multilateral agreements accepted a new compromise at the recent International Civil Aviation Conference, held at Chicago in November–December, 1944. The Interim Agreement on International Civil Aviation framed at the Conference provides *in fine*:

IN WITNESS WHEREOF, the undersigned, having been duly authorized, sign this Agreement on behalf of their respective governments on the date appearing opposite their signatures.

DONE at Chicago the seventh day of December 1944, in the English language. A text drawn up in the English, French, and Spanish languages, each of which shall be of equal authenticity, shall be opened for signature at Washington, D. C. Both texts shall be deposited in the archives of the Government of the United States of America, and certified copies shall be transmitted by that Government to the governments of all the States which may sign and accept this Agreement.

---

[28] Fauchille, *op. cit.*, Vol. I, Part III, p. 310, referring to the three conventions which were signed in Saint-Germain, by all the states which had signed the Covenant of the League, relating to the trade in arms and ammunition and to the liquor traffic in Africa, as well as the revision of the General Act of Berlin and the Declaration of Brussels, points out that they were drawn up only in French. He adds that when the French diplomat, M. de Peretti, on behalf of the committee which had drawn them up, presented them to the Supreme Council on which Lord Balfour represented the British Government, somebody observed that there was no English text. M. de Peretti answered that what had to be done was to make modifications or additions to acts drawn up only in French, and that, consequently, there was no need to change the custom. Lord Balfour, after listening to him, answered immediately "He is right," proving, so says Fauchille, his good faith and his generosity of mind.

A similar provision was inserted in the Convention on Civil Aviation and in the International Air Transport Agreement set up by the same Conference.

44. FOLLOW-UP

The purpose of a conference is not always entirely accomplished with the adoption of reports, resolutions, and recommendations, and with the drawing up of diplomatic instruments of acceptance and the recording of the results of the conference.

The secretariat of the conference, or a secretariat specially set up for the purpose, is responsible for the printing of all the final documents and their distribution to the delegates who attended the conference and to their governments. The secretariat may also be entrusted with special tasks in conformity with the decisions of the conference. Moreover, it is often necessary to set up special bodies for supervising the application of the conference decisions, for continuing investigations, or for preparing new meetings. A few examples taken from the practice of the League will serve as illustrations. Thus, in February, 1933, the Assembly, meeting in extraordinary session, decided to appoint an advisory committee to follow the situation in the Far East and to assist the Assembly in performing its duties under Article 3, paragraph 3, of the Covenant. During the dispute between Ethiopia and Italy, the Assembly created a Committee of Coordination which had the task of considering and facilitating the coordination of the measures taken under Article 16 and, if necessary, drawing the attention of the Assembly or Council to situations requiring examination. The Second Opium Conference of the League of Nations, Geneva, 1925, created a Permanent Central Opium Board entrusted with watching the application of certain provisions of the 1925 Drug Convention. Furthermore, under Article 5 of the 1931 Convention for the Limitation of the Manufacture and Regulation of the Distribution of Narcotic Drugs, the Drug Supervisory Body was set up. It was entrusted with special duties in relation to the operation of the above-mentioned convention.

In the practice of the League of Nations, permanent or *ad hoc* bodies most frequently relied upon the Secretary General to give proper effect to their decisions.

First of all the Secretary General had to provide for the duplication and distribution of all final documents of the conference. The Rules of Procedure of the Assembly (Rule 26), for instance, provided that

"The resolutions adopted by the Assembly shall be circulated by the Secretary General to the Members of the League within fifteen days after the termination of the session."

The rôle of the Secretariat in the final editing of the records of the meetings of the League has already been described. This work was performed with extraordinary care. All corrections sent by the delegates were transcribed on a master copy of the minutes by the Editor of the *Official Journal* or a responsible member of the section especially interested in the contents of the minutes. Next came a minute comparison of the French and English texts by a Drafting Committee composed of the Editor of the *Official Journal* or of a member of the competent section, and of a translator having special experience in this type of work and, if possible, a particular knowledge of the subject or subjects discussed. References were added to all annexes or important documents mentioned in the minutes. Ambiguities or misunderstandings which might have arisen as a result of corrections made by delegates were clarified by correspondence.

Even before the records of League meetings were completed the Secretary General sent a *Circular Letter* to the governments, drawing their attention to those decisions of League bodies which required special action on their part.

With very few exceptions, all the international League conventions, concluded at conferences held under the auspices of the League of Nations, provide for the deposit of the instrument with the Secretariat of the League and make the Secretary General responsible for its custody and registration, for providing certified copies, and for receiving ratifications, accessions, notifications regarding its applicability to overseas possessions and mandated territories, and denunciations.

The means of expediting the ratification of conventions concluded under the auspices of the League of Nations were studied several times by the League, and here again an Assembly resolution, dated October 3, 1930, entrusted special duties to the Secretary General.

The relevant provisions of this resolution read as follows:

I. That each year the Secretary-General should request any Member of the League or non-Member State which has signed any general convention concluded under the auspices of the League of Nations, but has not ratified it before the expiry of one year from the date at which the protocol of signature is closed, to inform him what are its intentions with regard to the ratification of the convention. Such requests of the Secretary-General to Governments should be sent at such a date in each year as to allow time for the replies of Governments to be received before the date of the Assembly, and information as to the requests so made and replies received should be communicated to the Assembly for its consideration.

II. That, at such times and at such intervals as seem suitable in the circumstances, the Secretary-General should, in the case of each general convention concluded under the auspices of the League of Nations, request the Government of any Member of the League of Nations which has neither signed nor acceded to a convention within a period of five years from the date on which the convention became open for signature, to state its views with regard to the convention — in particular, whether such Government considers there is any possibility of its accession to the convention or whether it has objections to the substance of the convention which prevent it from accepting the convention. Information of all such requests made by the Secretary-General and of all replies received should be communicated to the Assembly.

III. That the Council of the League should, with regard to each existing general convention negotiated under the auspices of the League of Nations, consider, after consultation with any appropriate organ or committee of the League, and in the light of such information as may be available as to the result of the enquiries recommended in resolutions Nos. I and II, and any other enquiries that the Council may think fit, whether it would be desirable and expedient that a second conference should be summoned for the purpose of determining whether amendments should be introduced into the convention, or other means adopted, to facilitate the acceptance of the convention by a greater number of countries.[29]

In compliance with this resolution of the Assembly the Secretary General sent circular letters every year to the member states requesting them to state their intentions concerning the conventions. Apart from this official action the Secretariat seized every opportunity to expedite the ratification of or accession to League conventions. Officials of the Secretariat on missions in their own country or touring capitals of the members of the League or of non-member states in an official or semi-official capacity, were often instructed to approach governments semi-officially in order to accelerate, if possible, the ratification of or the accession to League conventions. Sometimes very good results were obtained by this method.[30]

Special rules based on the *sui generis* constitution of the International Labor Organization govern the supervision of the application of conventions adopted by International Labor Conferences.

[29] Moreover, the Assembly recommended that special protocols of signature should be drawn up on the general lines of two alternative drafts appended as Annexes I and II to this resolution. These two annexes are given in Appendix XVII, *infra*.

[30] In compliance with an Assembly resolution adopted in 1926, the Secretary General of the League distributed each year to the members of the League a complete and up-to-date list showing the status of the ratifications, reservations, adhesions, and denunciations of the conventions and agreements concluded under the auspices of the League.

It will be remembered that the only act required of the states to put into force the conventions voted by an International Labor Conference is that of ratification; but states assume no obligation to ratify draft conventions even after their delegates have voted for them.

Under the Constitution of the International Labor Organization the various states are required, however, to bring draft conventions or recommendations voted by International Labor Conferences before competent national authorities within one year (or, in exceptional cases, eighteen months) after the end of the session of the conference at which they were adopted.

States undertake the obligation to bring their laws into harmony with the provisions of conventions which they have ratified. Article 22 of the Constitution of the International Labor Organization obliges each member state to make an annual report to the Labor Office on the measures it has taken to put into effect the provisions of conventions to which it is a party.

Any industrial association of employers or of workers is entitled to make *representations* to the International Labor Office if it has good reason to believe that a member state has failed to secure the effective observance of a convention to which it is a party. The Governing Body may then get into touch with the government against which an allegation of default or neglect has been made. It may publish both the representations and the government's reply.

All member states are entitled to file with the International Labor Office a *complaint* regarding the manner of execution of a convention by another member state. The same procedure can be adopted by the Governing Body either on its own motion or on receipt of a complaint from any delegate representing a government, the employers, or the workers. Complaints are more effective than representations. In the case of a complaint, a Commission of Enquiry, and even the Permanent Court of International Justice, may be called upon to intervene. Should the accused state fail to comply with the report of the Commission of Enquiry or the decision of the Court within the specified time, the other members may take action against it by applying economic measures appropriate to the case.

This technique of supervision of the application of the International Labor Convention is very advanced and it would probably not be possible to extend its application to other fields of international legislation without important changes in the present practice of concluding and applying international conventions.

In an attempt to expedite the ratification of treaties and conventions, and in order to stimulate the fulfilment of the resolutions and recommendations of the Pan American Conferences, the Seventh International Conference of American States, held at Montevideo in 1933, adopted two resolutions by which a follow-up technique very similar to the League practice has been created. The first resolution reads as follows:

RESOLUTION LVI. — *Ratification of Conventions*

The Seventh International Conference of American States Resolves:

1. To expedite the study, approval and ratification of inter-American treaties and conventions, and to stimulate the fulfilment of the resolutions and recommendations of inter-American conferences of every character, the Pan American Union, at the suggestion of the respective Governments, shall designate a representative ad-honorem, in each country, who shall not be a public official, and who shall fulfill his duty in agreement with the local Pan American Committee.

2. For the same purposes and with the object of maintaining interest in all continental matters, the Governments shall be requested to convoke periodic meetings of the Pan American Committees.

3. The Pan American Union may send one or more representatives to the American countries, with the object of promoting the examination, approval, ratifications and deposit of ratifications of treaties and conventions.

The second resolution reads as follows:

RESOLUTION LVII. — *Measures for the Ratification of Conventions*

The Seventh International Conference of American States Recommends:

1. That in the interval between two Inter-American Conferences, the Pan American Union may communicate with the Governments, inquiring whether they are willing to explain the objections they may have to the conventions open to their signature, with the sole object of studying the possibility of finding solutions in which the majority of the States, members of the Union, may concur.

2. That the Pan American Union shall report to each International Conference the result of this inquiry and, based thereon, the International Conferences shall designate, upon convening, a special Committee charged to study the modifications that it may be necessary to introduce in the conventions already signed, to obtain the ratification of a considerable majority, or to indicate the conventions which by reason of not being ratified by a majority of states, should only be considered as limited agreements.

3. That the Pan American Union shall transmit, every six months, through the representatives on the Governing Board, a chart showing the status of the ratifications, reservations, accessions and denunciations of the treaties and conventions signed at Conferences held by countries members of the Union.

In order to implement this last resolution the Governing Board of the Pan American Union adopted the following measures at its session of May 2, 1934:

1. Once treaties or conventions have been signed, the Government of the country in which the conference is held should remit to each of the signatory states as soon as possible after the adjournment of the conference, a certified copy of each of the treaties and conventions signed at the conference.

2. The signatory governments should be urged, in so far as constitutional provisions may permit, to submit the treaties and conventions to their respective Congresses at the first opportunity following the receipt of the certified copies mentioned in the preceding paragraph.

3. The Pan American Union shall transmit, every six months, through the members of the Governing Board, a chart showing the status of the ratifications, reservations, adherences, accessions and denunciations of treaties and conventions signed at conferences held by countries members of the Union.

4. The Pan American Union shall address a communication to each of the American governments requesting that, in accordance with resolution LVII of December 23, 1933, of the Seventh International Conference of American States, and with the sole purpose of studying the possibility of finding a formula acceptable to the majority of the countries members of the Union, the respective government is requested to make known the objections which it may have to the conventions open to its signature or awaiting ratification by its National Congress.

The communication while recognizing the right of each state to decide in accordance with its interests the question of ratification of treaties and conventions signed at the International Conferences of American States, shall furthermore request each Government to communicate to the Pan American Union the modifications which in its judgment will make ratification possible.

5. The communication addressed to the American Governments in accordance with the preceding paragraphs, shall be sent once a year, an endeavor being made to send it at the time of the regular session of the respective Congress.

These regulations were approved by the Eighth International Conference of American States, held at Lima in December, 1938.

If a conference is summoned at the initiative of a particular state or of a group of states, either a special body for following the application of the results of the conference is created, or this task is entrusted to the government of the country in which the meeting takes place. Thus, as an example of the first method it may be noted that the United Nations Conference on Food and Agriculture, held at Hot Springs in 1943, provided for the creation of a permanent organization in the field of food and agriculture. It entrusted the task of carrying out the recommendations of the Conference, up to the moment of actual operation of that permanent organization, to an Interim Commission.

An example of the other method can be found in the decision of the Opium Conference of The Hague to entrust the Dutch Government with the supervision of the opium traffic agreements.[31] The Hague Opium Convention affords an interesting example of a successful attempt to expedite the ratification of an international agreement. An article of the Treaty of Versailles provided that states ratifying the treaty became automatically parties to the Opium Convention. Through this ingenious provision, the number of the parties to the Hague Convention increased considerably within a very short time.

The fate of the conventions and agreements embodying the efforts of many League of Nations conferences to promote international cooperation will inevitably be discussed on the occasion of the future peace settlement. Numerous international conventions concluded under the auspices of the League confer special tasks upon the Secretary General of the League, upon the Council of the League, or upon special bodies affiliated with the League.[32] Methods must be evolved to preserve the results of these achievements of the League, and to incorporate the machinery created by the League conferences in the new international system which will emerge from the present war.

[31] This task was later entrusted to the League of Nations.
[32] See Memorandum of the Secretariat of the League of Nations, *Powers and Duties Attributed to the League of Nations by International Treaties*, L.N. Document C.3.M.3. 1944.V.

APPENDICES

I

PROCEDURE OF INTERNATIONAL CONFERENCES AND PROCEDURE FOR THE CONCLUSION AND DRAFTING OF TREATIES

CONDENSED VERSION OF A REPORT OF THE SUB-COMMITTEE OF THE COMMITTEE OF EXPERTS FOR THE PROGRESSIVE CODIFICATION OF INTERNATIONAL LAW [1]

M. MASTNY, Rapporteur
M. RUNDSTEIN, Member of the Sub-Committee

The two members of the Sub-Committee — the doubts and objections of various writers on international law on the possibility of the formulation of rules of procedure for international conferences notwithstanding — have come to the conclusion that systematically regulated procedures are possible and that rules for the organization of international conferences can be laid down "provided that these rules are sufficiently general to allow States and their representatives the requisite freedom in settling the details in each case according to circumstances and with due regard to the special requirements which may arise in practice."

"The technique of the organisation and procedure of international conferences has developed gradually since the seventeenth century (the first foundations were laid by the Congress of Westphalia and the Congress of Vienna).

"The procedure of present-day conferences has been based, in the case of political conferences, on the Berlin Congress of 1878; in the case of conferences relating to the codification of law, on the two Hague Conferences of 1899 and 1907; and in the case of administrative conferences, on the conferences of the International Unions (postal, telegraphic, etc.) and their international bureaux.

"As regards more especially the preparatory procedure (preliminaries, preparation of the subject, invitations and convocation), it is the London Maritime Conference of 1908–9 which serves as model.

"A certain number of practices have grown up and these reappear at each conference and are handed on from one to the other.

"Sometimes the rules *in concreto* are supplemented as to detail to meet special requirements which arise in practice, and sometimes the rules of procedure, particularly those of the meetings themselves, are simplified.

---

[1] Committee of Experts for the Progressive Codification of International Law, *Report to the Council of the League of Nations on the Questions which Appear Ripe for International Regulation*, L.N. Document C.196.M.70.1927.V. [C.P.D.I.95(2).], pp. 106–13.

"The process of evolution reached its culminating point in the Proceedings of the Peace Conferences at Paris and in the activities of the League of Nations and its Secretariat. The latter has rendered immense services in connection with the problem with which we are dealing by working out all the details involved by the complexity of the international life of to-day.

"The process of evolution has not yet ceased, however. To realise this, it is sufficient to study the history of recent conferences and to observe that the procedure, while in general following established precedent, has been modified in detail by the application of special provisions *in concreto.*"

.   .   .   .   .

"The rules which usually govern the procedure of international conferences may be divided into two categories.

"1. The first category includes a series of rules which are left to the free choice of the States and their representatives taking part in the conference.

"As regards this category it is impossible to say that a custom exists in the legal sense of the term, as the rules are purely formal and can constantly be changed at the discretion of the participating States.

"This category of rules is based on usage followed without "*opinio necessitatis.*"

"2. The second category, on the other hand, includes certain rules which from the legal point of view are merely the application of certain fundamental principles generally recognised as forming part of existing international law (customary law, "*opinio necessitatis*").

"It is in particular the questions coming within this second category which, having their origin in international customary law (substantive law), are not always interpreted and applied in the same way and offer difficulties which often hamper the smooth running of international conferences.

.   .   .   .   .

"Clearly, the codification of rules the terms of which depend on the previous solution of a controversial question would in principle present greater difficulties than a simple codification of customs and practices which are universally admitted and uniformly interpreted.

"The utility of codification is therefore not always in proportion to its practicability.

"The Rapporteur, for his part, has no hesitation, however, in pronouncing in favour of a codification extending even to controversial questions, and he believes that a codification of this kind in the wide sense of the term would render the greatest service to international relations in connection with conferences.

.   .   .   .   .

". . . the discussion of questions of substantive law should be limited to problems which are directly connected with questions of form.

"Apart from this, codification must necessarily avoid trespassing on the domain of politics, which nevertheless often has an influence on the provisions *in concreto.*

"At the same time it should adopt formulas sufficiently wide to allow of any special measures being taken which may be required in particular cases.

* * *

"To answer the question 'what such rules should be,' it is necessary first of all to decide on what basis regulation should be established.

"Three solutions suggest themselves:

"(1) Regulation of procedure containing only rules common to all types of conferences;

"(2) Detailed regulation of the procedure of a certain type of conference;

"(3) Adoption in a convention of certain general principles which should be observed by States when conferences are held, irrespective of the special nature of such conferences."

The Rapporteur considers solutions (1) and (2) as impracticable, the first necessitating such generality as would render it unfit for codification, and the second because it would not permit any uniform or universal type of rules of procedure. The third alternative appears capable of adoption.

The scope of codification to be undertaken is exemplified by the following list:

"LIST OF SUBJECTS TO BE EXAMINED

PROCEDURE OF INTERNATIONAL CONFERENCES

General principles.
Definition of International Conferences.
Classification of International Conferences.

A. *Organisation.*

Qualifications for membership.
    Independent States.
    Composite States.
    States not enjoying complete independence and other formations.
Right of representation.
    States concerned.
    Admission of third Powers.
Rights of members taking part.
System of representation.
Delegations.
Questions of competence.
    (a) Plenipotentiary delegates. Principal representatives.
        Assistant delegates.
      Substitute representatives.
      Secretaries of delegations.
      Experts.
      Technical assistants.
      Auxiliary staff.
    (b) Observers.
Diplomatic privileges and immunities.

B. *Preparatory Procedure.*

Preliminary conventions.
Initiative, invitation, convocation.
Previous agreement on the subjects of the conference.
Choice of place and date.
Preparation of the subject-matter and drafting of agenda (method and form).
Proposals and preliminary drafts (priority).
Reservations.

C. *Procedure of the Conference* (Rules of Procedure).

Rank and precedence.
Language employed (translation, interpreters).
Chairmanship (provisional chairmanship).
The Bureau: its competence.
Powers of the Chairman.
Verification (exchange, deposit) of full powers.
    Unlimited powers. Full powers.
    Limited powers.
    Authorization.
    Instructions.
    Credentials of diplomatic agents.
Committees and sub-committees.
Their members.
Drafting committee.
Rapporteurs; co-rapporteurs.
Debates.
Rules to be followed during the debates.
Agenda.
Proposals. Manner, initiative, priority. Placing of new questions on the agenda.
Draft resolutions, amendments and motions.
Previous question: motion for suspension.
Voting: method and form.
    Unanimity. Absolute majority. Specified majority.
    Plurality of votes.
    Voice in the decision.
    Voice in the discussion.
Right of a minority to withdraw.
Right of protest.
Declarations. Reservations.
Minutes (records).
    Intrinsic value. Form. Adoption.
Publicity. Public and Private Meetings.
    Press report.
Final Act.
Protocol of Closure."

In the second part of the Report the Rapporteur and the member of the Sub-Committee enter into a detailed examination of the list of subjects to be taken into account for the conclusion and drafting of treaties.

"The different classifications of international treaties are as numerous as the writers who have dealt with them, and vary with the individual point of view. Most of them are of little practical value.

"Nevertheless, it is the duty of the Rapporteur to call the attention of the Committee to the prevailing anarchy as regards terminology (treaty, convention, pact, agreement, arrangement, protocol, declaration, etc.). Up to the present, all attempts to obtain a uniform classification based on principles which take due account of the need of co-ordinating nomenclature, form and contents, have failed. In practice, little attention is paid to the exact meaning which should be given to terms customarily used.

"The choice of nomenclature and form is governed by arbitrary considerations and depends upon the nature of the relations between States, the custom of the respective chancelleries, and sometimes even upon the carelessness of those who draft diplomatic instruments.

"The Rapporteur sees no need to propose that these questions, which indeed are of no legal importance, should be regulated by treaty agreement, since in his opinion the remedy lies in the regular practice of registration as provided in Article 18 of the Covenant of the League of Nations, which is bound sooner or later to lead more or less automatically to the desired standardisation of nomenclature. At the same time, a certain elasticity in terminology is both inevitable and necessary in order that States may be left the freedom they require."

In this connection codification, therefore, is not considered feasible. As a remedy, apart from the practice of the registration of treaties, the Rapporteur recommends simplification of existing forms and elimination of certain antiquated formulas which are no longer in complete accord with contemporary legal ideas and which act as obstacles to the establishment of rules of procedure.

"Quite recent practice appears to be in favour of first ensuring the internal validity of treaties, but this treatment of the question can obviously only apply to particular cases and can provide no answer to disputed points of theory.

"Settlement by codification being excluded, would it not at least be possible to seek means of solving the problem in order to safeguard the legal relations between States?

"The various kinds of constitutional clauses referring to these questions and the different interpretations given of them — interpretations which may in the future differ still further — make the legal position in the matter very vague. The Rapporteur thinks that legal relations between States would greatly gain both in security and clearness if Governments decided to notify such clauses to one another together with the authentic interpretation which they give to them in practice.

"This idea is not entirely new and is akin to the proposal formulated by the League Secretariat in Article 10 of its memorandum of May 19, 1920.

"The Rapporteur has no doubt that such a list of the constitutional clauses of all countries, accompanied by their authentic interpretation, would greatly help in clarifying international relations."

II

DRAFT AGENDA OF THE CONFERENCE ON FOOD AND AGRICULTURE [1]

(*Hot Springs, Virginia, May 18 – June 3, 1943*)

AGENDA FOR THE CONFERENCE

The agenda is organized around the following conception of the problem with which the Conference should deal:

The agenda begins with an effort to ascertain the facts as to what are the needs of the various peoples of the world for food and other essential agricultural products, with due regard to differing conditions and possibilities among countries. It recognizes that in the past excessive accumulations of certain agricultural products were in fact not surpluses at all when measured by the world's minimum needs of food and clothing; that these so-called surpluses were usually the result of maldistribution and underconsumption. It then seeks to ascertain the prospects for so organizing world agricultural production as to enable the satisfaction of these needs and to explore the measures, both domestic and international, by which production can be enhanced and better directed in terms of consumption. Finally it examines the measures and conditions which are necessary to assure that what can be produced moves into consumption.

I. Consumption levels and requirements

    A. Food

        1. Character and extent of consumption deficiencies in each country
        2. Causes and consequences of malnutrition
        3. Measures for improving standards of consumption (education, etc.)
        4. Reasonable national and international goals for improved food consumption

    B. Other essential agricultural products

        1. Pre-war consumption levels in various countries as influenced by prosperity or depression and by buying power of the population
        2. Reasonable national and international goals for improved consumption with sustained employment and expanded industrial activity

II. Expansion of production and adaptation to consumption needs

    A. Measures for direction of production toward commodities, the supply of which should be increased

    B. Measures for shifting production out of commodities in chronic surplus

[1] "Agenda for the United Nations Conference on Food and Agriculture," U. S. Department of State, *Bulletin*, May 1, 1943, Vol. VIII, No. 201, pp. 388–89.

    C. Measures for improving agricultural productivity and efficiency

    D. Measures for development and conservation of agricultural resources

    E. Opportunities for occupational adjustments in agricultural populations

III. Facilitation and improvement of distribution

    A. Relation of national and international economic policies to agricultural problems, with special reference to the facilitation of the movement of agricultural products in commerce

        1. Expansion of international trade

        2. Broad policies for assuring increased production and consumption in general

    B. Improvement of agricultural marketing, processing, and distribution

    C. Special measures for wider food distribution

        1. Improvement of consumption of low-income groups

        2. International disposition of commodities in oversupply

    D. Buffer stocks and commodity arrangements to assure equitable prices and adequate supplies

IV. Recommendations for continuing and carrying forward the work of the Conference

III

INVITATION, SEVENTH INTERNATIONAL CONFERENCE OF AMERICAN STATES [1]

(*Montevideo, 1933*)

TEXT OF THE INVITATION SENT BY THE GOVERNMENT OF THE
REPUBLIC OF URUGUAY TO THE MINISTERS OF FOREIGN
AFFAIRS OF ALL THE AMERICAN REPUBLICS

MINISTRY OF FOREIGN AFFAIRS
Montevideo, August, 1933.

MR. MINISTER:

By decision of the Sixth International Conference of American States met at La Habana, the next convention of the American Nations shall take place in the City of Montevideo.

The date of the inaugural session of the Seventh International Conference having been definitely fixed for the 3rd of December by the Pan American Union in accord with the Government of Uruguay, — my Government has the high honor of transmitting to Your Excellency the respective invitation, in the hope that no American country shall be absent from the future assembly of American nations.

The order of the day of the Seventh International Conference of American States, has been duly remitted to Your Excellency by the Pan American Union together with the Regulations of the convention.

It would be superfluous to point out on this occasion the capital importance of the topics to be examined, since the exceptional gravity of the hour confess to [*confers on*] the future Assembly of American countries a transcendency unequalled until the present.

The deep preoccupation created by the economic, financial, political and social difficulties in the midst of which are struggling, beside the other countries, the States of the New World, shall envelop the Conference in an atmosphere of anxious hope and expectant serenity.

An acute sense of reality must inevitably open its way through what, until today, has constituted an ideal plan which has gradually been taking concrete form for several decades.

Economic interdependence must be examined with a sincere deep realization of the reciprocal fraternal interest of all the peoples of the Continent.

[1] Seventh International Conference of American States, *Plenary Sessions, Minutes and Antecedents*, Montevideo, 1933, p. 10.

America, in its creative vocation, may, and must discover the new way leading to pacific external and internal stability and to work, which is productive only when justly and normally remunerated.

It is necessary that there be faith between men and nations; that political and economic peace go forth together, since they are both aspects of the loyal understanding of nations; that eyes may not be closed to the hard and unfortunate reality; in a word, that Pan Americanism and fraternity be what they should be, — the maintenance of incessant energy towards collective superiority.

Because of these reasons the Government of Uruguay trusts that Your Excellency's Government shall grant us the honor of attending the future assembly of American Nations to be convened at Montevideo, where the Delegates of your country shall be received by their Uruguayan brothers, with the loyal affection and cordial welcome peculiar to fraternal meetings.

I reiterate to Your Excellency the assurances of my highest consideration.

ALBERTO MAÑÉ

To his Excellency,
    Minister of Foreign Affairs of.....

IV

OFFICE RULES OF THE LEAGUE OF NATIONS CONCERNING ARRANGEMENTS FOR MEETINGS [1]

The relevant passages of the Office Rules read as follows:

Preliminary Consultation

246 (*a*) The convocation of a meeting may in certain circumstances raise questions of a political rather than an administrative character. In such cases, Sections shall submit the matter to the Secretary-General before proposing the necessary administrative arrangements.

(*b*) As a preliminary to the fixing of the date of a meeting and before a formal request for administrative assistance is submitted in accordance with Rule 247 below, the action Section shall consult the Chief of the Document Service in order to ascertain whether at the date proposed the necessary staff and accommodation may be expected to be available. When the Council or the Assembly is in session, other meetings will, in principle, not be authorised.

Authorisation

247. The definitive request for the necessary administrative assistance for a meeting shall be made on the prescribed form (Form 22).

In accordance with the directions on the form, the action Section shall give particulars regarding the nature, place, date, and probable duration of the meeting; the kind of records which it is proposed to issue; the staff and accommodation required; and the item of the budget under which it is proposed to meet the expense. Moreover, in order that the final decision may be based on knowledge of the entire administrative and financial charge involved, the action Section shall attach to the form:

(*a*) a list of the names and places of residence of committee members or any persons, other than officials of the Secretariat, who may be expected to attend the meeting at the expense of the League;

(*b*) (in the case of meetings held away from the seat of the League) a list of the names of *all* officials of the Secretariat, other than those of the internal administrative services, whose presence at the meeting it considers desirable. In compiling this list, the action Section shall consult the Head of any other Section concerned.

Printing

248. When printing is required, authorisation shall be sought independently.

[1] League of Nations, *Secretariat Office Rules* (Geneva, 1936), Rules 246–249, pp. 94–95.

Minutes

249. Except when the necessity is clearly demonstrated, Minutes of the sub-committees shall not be made and Minute-writers will therefore not be provided. A short record of the meetings of sub-committees drafted by a member of the action Section should usually suffice.

V

JOURNAL OF THE NINETEENTH SESSION OF THE ASSEMBLY OF THE LEAGUE OF NATIONS [1,2]

(*First Issue*)

No. 1.—Geneva, Saturday, September 10th, 1938

COMMUNICATIONS TO THE EDITOR OF THE *JOURNAL*

[Material for inclusion in the *Journal* should be addressed to the Editor, Mr. ....
Room ..., Tel. ...]

NOTICE

For the benefit of delegations and the public, various improvements will be made in the *Assembly Journal* this year.

1. In future, the *Journal* will contain summaries of all speeches delivered at plenary meetings of the Assembly.

2. All resolutions will be reproduced in full.

[The last number of the *Journal* will contain a special index to the resolutions, for the use of readers and subscribers, pending their publication in book form.]

[3. Following the suggestion of several delegates, the reports of committee meetings will appear in the *Journal* in a (more) condensed form.

Full minutes will be circulated with the least possible delay.]

I. OPENING OF THE SESSION

The nineteenth ordinary session of the Assembly opens the day after to-morrow, Monday, September 12th, 1938, at 11 a.m.

Pending the election of the President of the Assembly, Mr. W. J. Jordan, Delegate of New Zealand and President of the Council, will take the chair.

II. PLACES OF MEETING OF THE ASSEMBLY, COUNCIL, AND COMMITTEES

Meetings of the Assembly, Committees, and the Council will be held in the League of Nations Building.

---

[1] League of Nations, *Journal of the Nineteenth Session of the Assembly*, pp. 1–9.
[2] Condensations of paragraphs are marked by brackets.

The Assembly Committees will sit as follows:

[First Committee in Committee-room XI. Second to Sixth Committee and General Committee of the Assembly in.....]

[Room numbers of additional Committees set up by the Assembly will be announced in the *Assembly Journal*.]

III. PROGRAMME OF MEETINGS[3]

[Note by the Secretary-General stating that the following programme must be considered provisional, the Assembly being sole judge of its procedure.]

FIRST PLENARY MEETING OF THE ASSEMBLY [4]

Monday, September 12th, 1938, at 11 a.m.

1. Constitution of the Credentials Committee.
2. Opening Speech by the President of the Council, as temporary President of the Assembly.
3. Report of the Credentials Committee.
4. Constitution of the Nomination Committee.

IV. SECRETARIAT OF THE ASSEMBLY

The Secretary-General, in his capacity of Secretary to the Assembly, will have the assistance of the Central Section (Head of Section: Mr....)

The following officials will act as secretaries to the President (also to the General Committee[5]) and to the Committees:

President:[5]

    Mr....
    Mr....

Committees:

    [First Committee: Mr. ...
    Second to
    Sixth Committee: Mr. ...]

---

[3] The agenda of the nineteenth session of the Assembly has been circulated to delegates as L.N. Document A.2(I).1938. — *Note in original.*

[4] At the opening of the first meeting, the Secretariat will distribute forms to the delegations, so that the latter can fill in the names of the delegates who will take part in the work of the various committees. These forms will be collected without delay, so that a list of members of committees may be compiled by the Secretariat and supplied to delegations at the opening of the afternoon meeting of the Assembly. — *Note in original.*

[5] All communications for the President's Secretariat should be addressed to: President's Secretariat, Room ... (Telephone ...). — *Note in original.*

In addition, a member of the Legal Section will be attached to the Secretariat of each of the main Committees.

Agenda Committee: Mr. ...
Credentials Committee: Mr. ...

V. ORDER OF MEETINGS OF COMMITTEES

[It is customary for three Committees to meet in the morning and for the remaining three to meet in the afternoon.
Suggested modifications for this practice are to be found in document C.169. 1938.II.B. and, in abbreviated form, in document A.31.1938.]

VI. VERBATIM RECORD OF PLENARY MEETINGS AND MINUTES OF COMMITTEES

(a) PLENARY MEETINGS

[A mimeographed provisional copy of the speeches delivered at the meetings of the Assembly will be handed to each delegate soon after the meeting. No additional copies will be available.

Delegates desiring to make corrections in their speeches are requested to address their communications to ... (Room ...; Tel. ...), *within twenty-four hours after the meeting.*]

The final text of the Verbatim Record will be distributed to the delegations as soon as possible.

(b) COMMITTEES OF THE ASSEMBLY

The usual Provisional Minutes, which are summaries and not stenographic records, of the meetings of Committees, will be distributed to the delegates as soon as possible after each meeting.

Delegates are requested to forward to the Secretary of the Committee within twenty-four hours after the distribution of the provisional text any corrections which they desire to have included in the final summary.

There will also be verbatim records for certain meetings of Committees.

VII. CREDENTIALS OF DELEGATES

[In accordance with the Rules of Procedure of the Assembly, "the full powers of the representatives shall be delivered to the Secretary-General, if possible, one week before the date fixed for the opening of the session."

It is requested that Delegates' credentials not previously sent to the Secretariat be forwarded to . . ., or handed to . . . .]

VIII. CHANGES IN THE MEMBERSHIP OF DELEGATIONS

[Secretaries of delegations are asked to notify changes in the membership of delegations to Miss . . ., Room . . ., Tel. . . . .]

IX. RECEIPT AND DISTRIBUTION OF DOCUMENTS

Delegates desiring to have documents duplicated, translated and distributed to the Assembly or its Committees should hand them — in duplicate if possible — to the Secretary of the President if they are for circulation to the Assembly, or, if they are for circulation to one of the Committees, to the Secretary of the Committee in question.

Assembly documents will be distributed individually to principal delegates.

Committee documents (roneoed). — One copy will be distributed to each delegate and substitute delegate sitting on any Committee.

Supplementary copies of documents for the use of secretariats of delegations will, on special request only, be sent to their offices.

A form for the request of supplementary copies has been sent to each delegation.

The Distribution Service in the Assembly building will work during plenary meetings only. At other times, members of delegations should apply to the Distribution Service (first floor of the Council Building).

X. SPECIAL ARRANGEMENTS FOR MEETINGS OF THE ASSEMBLY, COUNCIL AND COMMITTEES

[*Note.* — The Secretary-General has the honor to inform the members of delegations of the rules in force with reference to admittance to meetings and the maintenance of order.

These rules provide in particular for a strict scrutiny of admission tickets. Having been established in the interest of the delegations themselves, the Secretary-General feels sure that the latter will be good enough to facilitate their application by showing their tickets to the doorkeepers of their own accord.

The Secretary-General himself has made the necessary arrangements to obviate as far as possible any inconvenience that might be caused to delegates by the enforcement of the rules in question.]

I. Maintenance of Order

1. Order will be maintained inside the Assembly Hall, the Council Room, and the Committee Rooms by uniformed attendants of the Secretariat, who may be re-inforced, on the authority of the Secretary-General, by plainclothes policemen. Uniformed policemen (*gendarmes*) may not take action inside the meeting-rooms without the permission of the President of the Assembly, the President of the Council, or the Secretary-General.

2. Smoking is forbidden in the Assembly Hall and the Council Room.

3. Members of delegations and officials are asked to refrain as far as possible from leaving or entering the Assembly Hall or the Council Room during speeches or their interpretations.

4. Two minutes will always be allowed to elapse between the end of a speech and its interpretation, and only during this period will members of the public be allowed to enter or leave. At other times, the doors will be kept closed.

5. Demonstrations of any kind, including applause, are prohibited on the diplomatic benches and in the seats reserved for the Press and public. The President of the Assembly, the President of the Council, or the Secretary-General may order demonstrators to be removed and the galleries cleared.

[6. Uniformed attendants will be instructed to insure complete quiet during speeches and their interpretations.]

7. A bell will be rung to indicate the opening, adjournment, resumption, and closing of meetings, and the beginning and end of interpretations.

8. A representative of the Internal Services will remain permanently on the presidential platform. He will be stationed on the left-hand side of the rostrum in the Assembly Hall and on the right-hand in the Council Room, facing the audience.

II. Admittance to Meetings

1. *General Arrangements*

Only holders of tickets issued by the competent department of the Secretariat may enter meeting-rooms. All tickets are strictly personal and non-transferable. They must be presented at the doors and whenever requested by the officials in charge. The doorkeepers will refuse to admit anyone on a ticket issued in another person's name, and will confiscate the ticket.

2. *Admittance of Secretariat Officials*

(a) To obtain admittance to the meeting-rooms, an official must show his identity-card, or, failing this, a "Service" Card.

(b) "Service" Cards with a vertical stripe may be given to temporary officials of the Secretariat on duty in the Assembly Hall or the Council Room.

(c) *Assembly*

(i) *Only* members of the Secretariat on duty at *Assembly* meetings may enter the ground floor of the hall.

[The front row of seats facing the presidential platform is reserved for directors. A restricted number of seats is furthermore reserved for experts and secretaries who are at the disposal of officials on duty during meetings.

(ii) Other officials may sit in the front row of one of the side galleries reserved for the public.]

(d) *Council*

(i) At Council meetings, the seats near the Council table are reserved for members of the delegations to the Council and for officials on duty.

[(ii) Members of the Secretariat who have permission to attend meetings will sit in the public gallery where seats are reserved for them.]

3. *Issue of Admission Tickets*

(a) *To Members of Delegations*

[Admission tickets for meetings of the Assembly, the Council and Committees will be issued to members of delegations by the Ticket Office on the basis of the official lists sent by Governments to the Secretariat.]

Should the names of members of delegations not be shown on the official lists, delegations may obtain tickets by making a *written* and signed application to the Ticket Office, Door ....

Should admission tickets be left behind or lost, members of delegations are requested to inform the Ticket Office.

(b) *To Relatives of Members of Delegations and Persons sponsored by the Latter.*

[Relatives of members of delegations and persons sponsored by them may obtain tickets for public meetings. Application should be made through delegations to the Ticket Office.]

As a general rule, such tickets will be valid for one meeting only.

The accommodation in the public gallery of the *Council Room* being very limited (fifty seats for all the delegations), the Secretary-General is obliged to confine the number of "permanent reserved" tickets to one for each delegation. When there is room, however, an additional day ticket, giving access to the diplomatic gallery, will be placed at the disposal of each delegation. Delegations are requested to supply the Ticket Office in writing with all necessary information (rank, profession, nationality, etc.) relating to persons for whom a card is requested.

(c) *To Relatives of Members of the Secretariat and Persons sponsored by the Latter*

Assembly. — Officials can obtain for relations or friends day tickets for the public gallery.

Council. — As a large proportion of the seats in the public gallery has to be reserved for the families of members of delegations, the Press, and organisations, the number of places available for the public is very limited. Officials of the Secretariat are therefore asked to confine their applications to the strict minimum.

(d) *To Members of International Organisations*

International organisations wishing to secure for their members admission tickets to public meetings of the Assembly and Committees should apply to ....

(e) *To Journalists, Cinema-operators, Cartoonists, and Photographers*

Journalists, cinema-operators, cartoonists, and photographers wishing for admission tickets should apply to the Information Section as laid down in the special regulations.

Three special galleries are reserved for journalists at public meetings in the Assembly Hall.

Journalists, and if necessary their secretaries, cinema-operators, cartoonists, and photographers must show their tickets at the door and whenever requested by the responsible officials.

On the recommendation of the Information Section, which will consult the Internal Administration in each case, the Secretary-General will decide before each meeting the number of cinema-operators, cartoonists, and photographers to be admitted to the Assembly Hall. They must conform strictly to the regulations and perform their work solely at the places reserved for them.

No cinema-operators, cartoonists, or photographers will be admitetd to Committee meetings.

(f) *To the Public*

Members of the public may obtain admission tickets for public meetings of the Assembly and the Council by applying to the Ticket Office and submitting identity-papers and a recommendation signed by a member of a delegation, an official of the Secretariat or International Labour Office, a public authority, or a person known to the Secretariat. Tickets will only be issued for the number of seats available.

[The Ticket Office is situated. . . . A branch office for the issue of tickets for public meetings of the Assembly will be open in . . . half-an-hour before and half-an-hour after the opening of each meeting.]

Note. — Applications by telephone cannot be considered.

4. *Supervision of Entry to and Presence at Meetings*

(*a*) The official doorkeepers are instructed to insist on admission tickets being shown, and to see that persons entering the meeting-room or Assembly Hall do so by the proper door.

(*b*) It will be the constant duty of ushers to see that the doors and their approaches are kept clear.

(*c*) Members of the public, journalists, and the families of members of delegations and members of the Secretariat are not admitted to the accommodation reserved for delegates.

5. *Admission of Visitors to the Secretariat*

[Persons wishing to see members of the Secretariat are requested to wait in Room ....] The messenger on duty will telephone to the official concerned, who will inform him whether he can receive them. If he can, the visitors will be accompanied to and from the official's office by a messenger.

XI. MOTOR-CARS

(*a*) LABELS FOR CARS

[To facilitate the parking of cars, the following labels will be issued:
Circular labels "S.D.N.1938" to delegates and members of delegations;
A *green star* to officials of the Secretariat;
A *green disk* to journalists.
Applications for the various labels may be made to the Internal Services, Room....]

(*b*) CAR PARKS

[Cars are not allowed to park near the entrances.
Allocation of car parks (see plan included in the present number of the *Journal*):

(*a*) Members of Delegations to the Assembly: Park...
(*b*) Members of the Council and Senior Officials: Park...
(*c*) Officials of the Secretariat: Park...
(*d*) Journalists: Park...
(*e*) Public: Parks...

Taxis ....]

[Section (*c*) states that a Room (...) is available for Delegates' chauffeurs.]

XII. MISCELLANEOUS INFORMATION OF PRACTICAL VALUE

I. INFORMATION OFFICE

There will be an Information Office (Telephone ...) in the lobby, near ... to which members of delegations may apply for admission tickets in the event of last-minute changes in the membership of delegations. The Information Office will transmit to members of delegations correspondence or parcels received for them.
Lost property may be claimed at the same office.

II. Offices for the Use of Delegations

Offices in the Assembly Building will be available for delegations on request.

III. Rooms for Members of Delegations

(a) *Waiting-room*

A waiting-room near the Information Office is available for members of delegations wishing to comply with requests for interviews from representatives of international organisations or private persons.

(b) *Private Rooms and Writing-rooms*

Rooms . . . are available for members of delegations for private conversations. The rooms . . . have been set aside as writing-rooms.

IV. Postal, Telegraph, and Telephone Facilities

The Swiss postal authorities will have a sub-post-office open near the Entrance Hall of the Assembly building . . . for members of delegations.

Telephone and telegraph facilities for journalists will be found *on the 1st floor.*

V. Newspaper and Bookstalls, etc.

Newspapers, cigars, and cigarettes will be on sale in the lobby near. . . . The room for the sale of Secretariat publications will be found. . . .

VI. Restaurant and Snack Bar

Members of delegations, journalists, and officials may use the restaurant and snack bar on the upper floor of the Assembly building.

VII. First-aid Post

A first-aid post in charge of a nurse will be set up in . . . and supplied with equipment as recommended by the Medical Adviser. Two attendants will be responsible for the transport of sick or injured persons.

In emergency, apply to the doorkeepers, to the Information Office (Telephone ...), to the representative of the Internal Services on duty near the platform or direct to the hospital (Telephone ...).

VIII. Plan of Meeting-Rooms and Car Parks

A plan showing how to reach the meeting-rooms and car parks is included in the present number of the *Journal*. Members of delegations can obtain copies of the plan on application to the Information Office in the lobby near Door No. . . . .

Note. — A special note should be made of the following telephone and office numbers:

Secretariat of the President and Bureau of the Assembly:

[*Information Office:*

Ticket Office:
     (*a*) Principal office:
     (*b*) Branch office:

First-aid Post:
     Information Office, Telephone ...
     Hospital, Telephone ....]

XIII. LOCAL MOTOR-OMNIBUS SERVICE

[Contains description of various bus routes to places of meeting; time tables can be consulted at Information Office and bus termini. Prices of fares are given.]

VI

REPORT ON THE ARRANGEMENTS FOR THE SEVENTH INTERNATIONAL CONFERENCE OF AMERICAN STATES [1]

REPORT OF THE SECRETARY GENERAL OF THE CONFERENCE [2]

MONTEVIDEO, *January 4, 1934.*

To Mr. ALBERTO MAÑÉ,
    Minister of Foreign Affairs,
      Montevideo.

Mr. Minister:

I am pleased to submit for your consideration, and within the period designated, the detailed report regarding the organization of the Seventh International Conference of American States, which took place in our capital from the 3rd to the 26th of December.

Upon being named Secretary General by decree of the Executive Powers on May 19th, and charged with directing the preparatory work of organization, my first concern was to choose a place where the Conference might be held.

At first it seemed that the Ateneo of Montevideo met the conditions necessary for the ends sought. For this reason I requested the authorities to grant the use of the building, which request met with the most favorable response on the part of the authorities.

Later, however, it proved impossible to house all the sessions of the Conference in the Ateneo building, except by making many costly improvements and essential alterations.

The Legislative Palace was then solicited immediately, because of its special adaptability to the purposes of the Conference, a judgment which has been vindicated in the celebration of the Conference.

Meanwhile the Secretary General was working toward the best organization for the gathering. Therefore he kept in constant touch with Mr. Leo S. Rowe, Director General of the Pan American Union, from whom he received very valuable suggestions accredited by his vast experience in this type of conferences.

[The Report then goes on enumerating the names and functions of various interpreters, supervisors and persons responsible for translation and interpretation, altogether numbering eighteen persons.]

From the United States also, was secured the two-fold telephone system for simultaneous translation which worked very satisfactorily in the Chamber of the House of Representatives.

---

[1] "Report of the Secretary General of the Conference," in Seventh International Conference of American States, *Plenary Sessions, Minutes and Antecedents*, Montevideo, 1933, pp. 242–46.
[2] Condensations or omissions of paragraphs are indicated by brackets.

The alterations necessary for the numerous meetings demanded by an International Conference were made in the Legislative Palace. Whereupon, the lower floor of the Palace was put at the disposition of the press and communication service, with their respective agencies.

Ample space was allotted to the several telegraph agencies for the installation of their booths, so that all telegraphic and telephonic communications might be attended from the Palace itself.

The "All American Cables," the "Western," the "T. T." and the "Transradio" hastened to accept this offer, consequently it was possible to guarantee a rapid communication service without leaving the Palace. Cables were opportunely laid and the necessary connections made with no expense to the State.

The telephone service is worthy of special mention. It must be remembered that many delegates were located in hotels, such as Hotel Carrasco and Parque Hotel, with which there was no automatic telephone service. Eng. Bernardo Kayel, President of the Electric Power Plant and Telephones of the State, afforded a solution for this problem, installing special cables with these hotels so that on the day of the inauguration of the Conference the automatic telephone service with the various hotel apartments occupied by foreign delegates was a reality.

In the Palace also an automatic network was installed so that the offices of the personnel and those of the several delegations had at their service an autonomous, automatic system of communication, without the necessity of being tributaries of the central switchboard of the Palace.

Adjacent to the journalists' headquarters twelve telephone booths were placed, constructed especially by the Administration of the Electric Power-Plant of the State. These proved to be of great usefulness.

Finally, the Uruguayan Postal Department installed a booth on the lower floor of the Palace. Under the direction of Mr. Duthut this model organization rendered invaluable services.

The Hall of "Pasos Perdidos" was adequately improved, having been complemented with work which it was indispensable to realize. Over the archways leading to the waiting rooms of the Senate and the House of Representatives were placed the plaster models which were to serve for the carrying out of the marble and bronze bas relief which Architect Moretti had sketched.

[Paragraph referring to the artistic aspect of the alterations mentioned above omitted.]

The Reception Hall, also, was subjected to necessary alterations. In fact, it may be said that the Reception Hall is only now usable, since its former presentation and unfinished aspect made it unfit for any function. The Reception Hall was used, during the Conference, as the seat of several committees which held their sessions there. Space was provided there for the public and galleries for the journalists.

Finally, certain alterations were introduced in the Chamber of the House of Representatives, in order to offer better accommodation to press agents, the great number of which agents made it necessary to provide adequate space.

A work room for reporters and journalists was installed on the lower floor of the Palace, agencies such as the United Press and La Nación having put in special installations for the greater convenience of their editors.

Given the fact that Montevideo, in spite of its great importance, lacks hotels in sufficient numbers and that, in these, there are not the conveniences for numerous meetings, the Secretary General proposed that rooms within the Legislative Palace itself be put at the disposal of each delegation, these rooms to serve as the seat of the delegations' respective headquarters.

For this reason all the delegations gathered in Montevideo had the accommodation of comfortable meeting places where they were able to file their documents, hold their meetings and, in many instances, these rooms served as the seat of sub-committees of the Conference itself.

As concerns the material organization, the disposal of the Legislative Palace in its totality, was an essential factor in the success of the Conference. On certain days, as many as seventeen committees and sub-committees were in session at the same time. The spaciousness of the Palace permitting so many meetings at one and the same time greatly expedited the work, avoiding annoyances which might otherwise have been experienced.

The organization by the Secretary General was made on the following bases:

In addition to the Secretary General's cabinet, the departments of "Protocol," "Press," "Conference Bulletin," "Distribution of Documents," "Secretaries of Committees," "Information," "Calligraphists, Editing, and Preparation of Treaties," "Supplies and Internal Matters," "Stenography," "Interpreters and Translators," were created.

[The Protocol Department had to do with preparations for the reception and entertainment of the delegates, the regulation of entrance to the Palace, etc.]

The Press Department, has had the mission of establishing a link with the journalists; its labor has been so intense that it has merited the most favorable comments on the part of all who have been served by this organ.

A daily Bulletin was published giving reports of all the work of the day. The Bulletin appeared regularly before 9:00 P.M. so that its contents might be utilized by all the newspapers of the Capital as well as by foreign news service.

The editing of a radio message was also a part of this department's work. Daily at 3:00 P.M. these messages were broadcast via Transradio in English and in Spanish and thus reached the farthest limits of the world. Furthermore this department superintended the motion-picture photography which lent valuable services to the Conference.

[Paragraph referring to a detailed report of the Press Department omitted.]

The Conference Bulletin under the direction of Mr. Héctor Gómez Guillot, appeared punctually each morning, and contained information, stenographic reports, minutes of committees, projects and initiatives related to the work of the Conference. Twenty-three numbers were published with a total of 764 pages containing documents corresponding to the Conference.

The Department of Distribution of Documents, under the direction of Mr. Abelardo Torres Mendoza, carried out the delicate task of duplicating and distributing all documents of the Conference. Ninety-seven articles, treatises, etc., and 63 committee publications were printed, 215,556 sheets of paper and 1,977 mimeograph stencils having been used. Printed works reach 328 in number. These data give an idea of the enormous task accomplished by this department.

A general organization of Secretaries of Committees, under the direction of Mr. A. Carbonell Debali, coordinated the efforts of the Secretaries of each of the committees into which the Conference was divided.

Heading said committees was a select group of young lawyers who dedicated their efforts integrally in a patriotic and wholly unselfish manner, abandoning temporarily their habitual occupation in order to dedicate themselves wholeheartedly to this exacting task.

[The Report enumerates the names of the holders of these positions. Assistant secretaries for these committees were selected from the personnel of the Deliberating Assembly.]

The Information Department with Mr. Enrique Blixen in charge, gave very satisfactory results. The matter of the entertainment of the delegations was opportunely solved, this being a particularly arduous task, due to the scarcity of hotels adequate to satisfy the extraordinary demands placed upon them.

Even though, following the tradition of international conferences meeting periodically, the State was not meeting the cost of entertaining our illustrious guests, it was absolutely necessary to establish a control of prices, in order to avoid abuses, and a discreet supervision for the securing of an equitable distribution of available space among the various delegations.

The Information Department was not only in charge of this phase of work but also that of preparing and organizing entertainments and receptions, such as the banquet offered by the President of the Republic in the Hall of "Pasos Perdidos" of the Legislative Palace, the official balls offered by the Minister of Foreign Affairs in the Club Uruguay on December 2nd and in Hotel Carrasco on December 24th, the Christmas Eve Ball, the Luncheon in Maroñas on the 10th of December, and the Tea in the Punta Carretas Golf Club, which demanded the greatest attention, competence and good will.

[The Department of Editing and Preparation of Treaties has been entrusted with the preparation of documents; original documents which were presented to the delegations for signature were prepared by the head of the Department of Calligraphists.]

The Department of Supplies and Internal Matters undertook the preparation of halls and committee rooms, vigilance and supervision of the personnel in general, control of supplies and provisions and the internal police vigilance of the Palace. Mr. Ricardo Paysée, distinguished official of the Deliberating Assembly, and his assistant, Mr. Rodolfo Henestrosa, fulfilled the obligations of this department of difficult and exacting labor.

The Stenographic Personnel was under the supervision of Messrs. Carlos Otero and Servando Suarez. The entire staff of stenographers of the Deliberating Assembly was put at the disposal of the Conference. The service of this staff, which has been a real honor to the Uruguayan Administration, has already received my recognition, in a note of thanks to the Deliberating Assembly, sent at the close of the sessions of the Conference.

[The Department of Interpreters and Translators is still functioning in view of the necessity of publishing, in the four official languages, the Final Act and the minutes of the sessions of the Conference and its Committees.]

In order to give an adequate idea of the intensity of the Secretary General's tasks, it will be sufficient to record that 486 letters have been sent. Furthermore, the correspondence of the "Pan American Union" Section of the Ministry of Foreign Affairs, was left to the care of the Secretary General from the beginning of last August, 180 communications having been dispatched.

These tasks have been carried out by personnel of the Department of Foreign Affairs who were transferred to the Secretary General's staff without extra remuneration of any sort.

[The efficient organization made it possible to conduct the Conference in the most economical manner.]

For example, expenses for telegrams have been insignificant, due to the fact that all questions related to organization have been treated by correspondence and the use of telegrams assiduously avoided.

The efficiency of technical experts also has been an essential factor in the smooth running of the Conference. It should be mentioned, in this connection, that in employing this personnel, the competence of the candidates was the exclusive consideration; they were selected in accordance to their degree of efficiency, and exemplary dedication being required of each.

A special hand-book for the use of the delegates, the press and the public in general was issued, appearing the very day of the inauguration of the Conference.

The List of Delegates, later corrected and amplified, was also published before the initiation of the Conference.

[Paragraph relative to the preparation of a commemorative medal omitted.]

The Department of Communications, in its turn, issued a special series of stamps, which were also given to the members of the foreign delegations.

This report would not be complete if I did not mention the phase of the Conference related to the expenses occasioned by the Seventh International Conference of American States.

At the beginning, and upon the initiative accepted by your Ministry, incorporating it into the text of the respective proposed law, a permanent intervention of the General Accounting Department was organized in the Secretary General's office.

In this way, we may say that the control was meticulously observed, payments being made by personal checks prepared by the Auditor General, Mr. Goyret Gard, and signed by the Minister of Foreign Affairs and the Secretary General of the Conference.

Against the funds provided by law for Conference expenses (50.000 Uruguayan pesos), orders were drawn, proceeds of which were deposited integrally in a special Sub-account in the National Treasury, designated as "VII Conferencia Internacional Americana."

Checks issued by the Minister of Foreign Affairs and the Secretary General of the Conference were cashed with the funds of this account, obligations for supplies and to the personnel being met punctually.

Expenses occasioned by the Conference are as follows:

1) Personnel of technicians and experts under special contract. (Interpreters, translators, calligraphists and stenographers, — English, French and Portuguese) . . . . $16.882.—
2) Secretarial Staff. (Extra employees who have lent their services since last August, and who do not form part of the Administrative Staff) . . . . $ 7.057.—
3) Alterations in the Legislative Palace. (General carpentry and masonry) . . . . $ 3.696.—
4) Supplies and printing of the Conference Bulletin, List of Delegates, Official Handbook, etc. . . . . $ 9.524.—
5) Entertainment of Foreign Delegations. (Details already published) . . . . $19.258.—
6) Apparatus for simultaneous translation, films for talking photography, motion-picture photography, preparation of medals . . . . $10.200.—
7) Restaurant of the personnel and subvention of same . . . . . . $ 1.500.—
8) Installation of telephones in Carrasco, Parque Hotel and Palacio Legislativo, and Telephone Booths. (Contribution to the Electric Power-Plan) . . . . $ 2.000.—
9) Locomotion during the time and the organization of the Conference . . . . $ 745.19
10) Other expenses . . . . $ 4.600.—

[The Report adds that a total of approximately $76,000 Uruguayan pesos had been spent on the Conference, including the cost of entertaining the delegates. An audited account will state in detail the expenditure incurred. As only $50,000 had been appropriated it will be necessary to request an additional sum to cover pending obligations and meet costs of printing the Final Act, the Minutes and stenographic version of the Conference and Committee Sessions in Spanish and English. The amount of this expenditure being difficult to determine beforehand, the matter might well be brought before Parliament at a later date.]

In order to give an idea of the care with which these monies have been invested in the Conference held in Montevideo, it might be well to call to mind that in the Habana Conference the Cuban Government appropriated 750.000 dollars; even so the minutes and stenographic versions of that Conference have not yet been published. The only documents published up to the present time are the Final Act, in Spanish only, and the Conference Bulletin.

The Delegation which represented Uruguay in Habana cost the public exchequer the sum of 20.000 pesos.

For the organization and preparation of the Fifth Conference, held in Santiago, Chile, the Chilean Government appropriated one million Chilean pesos, according to information opportunely communicated to us by our Legation in that neighboring country.

As an additional datum, it is well to keep in mind that for the reception of foreign Embassies on the occasion of our Centenary Celebrations, the sum of 94.000 pesos was appropriated.

[These data clearly show the economical utilization of the public funds set aside for the Conference.]

The Conference was solemnly inaugurated on the 3rd of December, its sessions being adjourned the 26th of the same month. In the time of its duration six plenary sessions were held, and the ten Committees into which the Conference was divided held 63 plenary sessions, in addition to the sub-committees.

The entire program which was formulated was strictly carried out, 97 resolutions having been passed. The resolutions are incorporated in the Final Act, the printed form of which, in Spanish and English, was distributed the day in which the Conference adjourned.

It does not correspond to me to comment on the political accomplishments and rapprochement of the Americas which the Conference has realized. My duty has been adequately to prepare the celebration of the Conference with a view to avoiding the chance event that an unforeseen failure of the same might be attributed to its faulty technical organization.

[The Report concludes with an expression of satisfaction regarding the flattering judgments expressed by the delegations on the successful outcome of the Conference, considered as one of the most important gatherings held on the American Continent.]

ENRIQUE E. BUERO

VII

REGULATIONS OF THE EIGHTH INTERNATIONAL CONFERENCE OF AMERICAN STATES [1]

CHAPTER I

PERSONNEL OF THE CONFERENCE

SECTION I. — *Temporary President*

ARTICLE 1. The President of the Republic of Peru shall designate the temporary president who shall preside at the opening session and shall continue to preside until the Conference elects a permanent president.

SECTION II. — *Permanent President*

ARTICLE 2. The permanent president of the Conference shall be elected by an absolute majority of the States represented at the Conference.

ARTICLE 3. The duties of the permanent president shall be:

First. To preside at the meetings of the Conference and to submit for consideration in their regular order the subjects contained in the order of the day.

Second. To concede the floor to the delegates in the order in which they may have requested it.

Third. To decide all questions of order raised during the debates of the Conference. Nevertheless, if any delegate shall so request, the ruling made by the chair shall be submitted to the Conference for decision.

Fourth. To call for votes and to announce the result of the vote to the Conference, as provided for by Article 23.

Fifth. To transmit to the delegates in advance, through the secretary general, the order of business of each plenary session.

Sixth. To direct the secretary, after the approval of the minutes, to lay before the Conference such matters as may have been presented since the last meeting.

Seventh. To prescribe all necessary measures for the maintenance of order and strict compliance with the regulations.

SECTION III. — *Vice Presidents*

ARTICLE 4. The presidents of delegations shall be ex officio vice presidents of the Conference. In the first session there shall be settled by lot the numerical order of the delegations for the purpose of establishing the order of precedence of

---

[1] Eighth International Conference of American States, Lima, Peru, December 9, 1938, *Special Handbook for the Use of Delegates*, pp. 5-10.

their location. In this order the presidents of the delegations shall be called to occupy the chair in the absence of the president, as provided by these regulations.

Section IV. — *Secretary General*

Article 5. The secretary general of the Conference shall be appointed by the President of the Republic of Peru.

Article 6. The duties of the secretary general are:

First. To organize, direct, and coordinate the work of the assistant secretaries, secretaries of committees, interpreters, clerks and other employees which the Government of Peru may appoint for service with the secretariat of the Conference.

Second. To receive, distribute, and answer the official correspondence of the Conference in conformity with the resolutions of that body.

Third. To prepare, or cause to be prepared under his supervision, the minutes of the meeting in conformity with the notes the secretaries shall furnish him; and to distribute among the delegates, before each session, printed or mimeographed copies of the minutes of the previous session, for the consideration of the Conference.

Fourth. To revise the translations made by the interpreters of the Conference.

Fifth. To distribute among the committees the matters on which they are required to present reports, and place at the disposal of the committees everything that may be necessary for the discharge of their duties.

Sixth. To prepare the order of the day in conformity with the instructions of the president.

Seventh. To be the intermediary between the delegations or their respective members in matters relating to the Conference, and between the delegates and the Peruvian authorities.

Eighth. To transmit the original minutes of the Conference and of the committees to the Director General of the Pan American Union for preservation in the archives of the Union.

Ninth. To perform such other functions as may be assigned to him by the regulations, by the Conference, or by the president.

CHAPTER II

Committees of the Conference

Article 7. There shall be a Committee on Initiatives, composed of the Presidents of delegations and presided over by the President of the Conference; a Committee on Credentials, to be appointed at the first plenary session; and a Drafting Committee consisting of one representative for each of the official languages of the Conference.

Article 8. Prior to the first plenary session a meeting of the Committee on Initiatives shall be held, at which the organization of the Conference shall be considered and recommendations formulated for submission to the Conference in plenary session.

ARTICLE 9. There shall also be organized committees for each chapter into which the program of the Conference is divided, to study, report, and formulate projects on the topics of the agenda. Each delegation shall be entitled to be represented by one or more of its members on each committee, the names of such members to be transmitted by each delegation to the secretary general as soon as possible and in any event before the first meetings of the committees.

ARTICLE 10. Each committee shall elect from among its members a chairman and a vice chairman.

ARTICLE 11. For each topic or group of related topics, the chairman of each committee shall appoint a reporting delegate and, if the committee considers it advisable, a subcommittee to consist of as many members as the committee may decide. The reporting delegates shall serve as chairmen of the respective subcommittees.

ARTICLE 12. The functions of the reporting delegates or subcommittees shall be:

1. To examine the projects and other documents in order to formulate a report which shall contain the antecedents, an analysis of the question, and a project based on the opinions presented by the various delegations.

2. The reporting delegate or chairman of the subcommittee shall present the report to the secretary of the committee, who shall distribute it among the delegations informing them, in advance, of the date on which the project will be discussed.

3. Said project shall serve as a basis for the general discussion. Once this has been concluded, the reporting delegate in accordance with the opinion of the majority shall formulate the definitive project which, after approval by the committee, shall be presented to the plenary session of the Conference.

ARTICLE 13. Each committee shall appoint a general reporting delegate to present the conclusions of the committee to the plenary session of the Conference.

ARTICLE 14. Following approval by the committee, and before submission to the plenary session, all treaties, conventions, resolutions and other conclusions shall be referred to the Drafting Committee for the addition of the Protocolary clauses indicated in the Annex to these Regulations, and for coordination of the text in the several languages of the Conference.

ARTICLE 15. All projects submitted by delegations on the various topics of the program shall be presented to the secretary general as soon as possible and in any event within one week after the opening of the Conference, thereby affording the respective committees adequate time in which to consider all subjects on the agenda. The secretary general shall refer the projects to the corresponding committee.

ARTICLE 16. All projects submitted by delegations shall have indicated thereon the topic of the program to which they relate, in order that they may be referred by the secretary general to the corresponding committee. Projects not so indicated, or which, in the opinion of the secretary general, do not relate to any of the topics assigned to it, shall be referred to the Committee on Initiatives and follow the procedure indicated for new topics.

CHAPTER III

THE DELEGATIONS

ARTICLE 17. Delegates may speak in their own languages from manuscript or otherwise. The interpreters shall render a summary of the speech in the other official languages of the conference, unless the speaker or any delegate may request a complete translation of his remarks.

The interpreters shall also render in the other official languages the remarks of the president and the secretary general of the Conference.

ARTICLE 18. Any delegate may submit to the conference his written opinion upon the matter under discussion, and may request that it be spread upon the minutes of the meeting in which it has been submitted.

A delegation not present at the session may deposit or transmit its vote in writing to the secretary, which shall be counted provided it has been transmitted or deposited before the vote is declared closed. In this event, the delegation shall be considered as present and its vote counted.

ARTICLE 19. The Director General of the Pan American Union shall be considered as a member ex officio of the Conference, but without a right to vote.

CHAPTER IV

MEETINGS OF THE CONFERENCE AND THE COMMITTEES

ARTICLE 20. The first meeting shall be held at the time and place designated by the Government of Peru, and the further sessions on such days as the Conference may determine.

ARTICLE 21. To hold a meeting it is necessary that a majority of the nations attending the Conference be represented by at least one of their delegates.

ARTICLE 22. At the opening of the meeting the secretary general shall read the minutes of the preceding meeting, unless such reading is dispensed with. Notes shall be taken of any remarks the president or any of the delegates may make thereon, and approval of the minutes shall be in order.

ARTICLE 23. In the deliberations in the plenary sessions as well as in the committees, the delegation of each Republic represented at the Conference shall have but one vote, and the votes shall be taken separately by countries and shall be recorded in the minutes.

Votes as a general rule shall be taken orally, unless any delegate should request that they be taken in writing. In this case each delegation shall deposit in an urn a ballot containing the name of the nation which it represents and the sense in which the vote is cast. The secretary shall read aloud these ballots and count the votes.

ARTICLE 24. The Conference shall not proceed to vote on any report, project, or proposal relating to any of the subjects included in the program, except when at least two thirds of the nations attending the Conference are represented by one or more delegates. In the voting account shall be taken of the votes sent in writing as provided for in articles 18 and 28, the absent delegations being considered present, only for the purposes of the vote, when they have submitted their vote in the manner indicated.

ARTICLE 25. All proposals amending the motion, project, or resolution under consideration shall be referred to the respective committee, unless the Conference shall by a two-thirds vote decide otherwise.

ARTICLE 26. Amendments shall be submitted for discussion and put to a vote before the article or motion the text of which they are intended to modify is acted upon.

ARTICLE 27. The Conference may, by a two-thirds vote of the delegations present, suspend the rules and proceed to the consideration of a motion, provided, however, that in all cases the procedure with respect to new topics as set forth in article 31 shall be followed.

ARTICLE 28. Except in cases expressly indicated in these regulations, proposals, reports, and projects under consideration by the Conference shall be considered approved when they have obtained the affirmative vote of an absolute majority of the delegations represented by one or more of their members at the meeting where the vote is taken. The delegation which may have sent its vote to the secretary shall be considered as present at the meeting.

ARTICLE 29. The following may attend the sessions of the Conference and of the committees: The delegates with their respective secretaries and attachés; the Director General and other accredited representatives of the Pan American Union; the secretaries and members of the secretariat of the Conference; duly accredited representatives of the press; and any others to whom the Conference may by a majority vote extend this privilege.

At the request of any delegation the Conference may agree to go into secret session. A motion to this effect shall immediately be put and voted upon without discussion.

At the close of the session the secretary general shall issue to the press a statement summarizing the results of the session, except in the event set forth in the preceding paragraph, in which case the Conference shall decide as to the publication of the results of the session.

ARTICLE 30. The official languages of the Conference shall be Spanish, English, Portuguese, and French. The reports, projects, and other documents shall be printed and submitted to the consideration of the Conference and of the committees at least in Spanish and English.

The reports and projects shall be submitted for discussion at a meeting subsequent to that at which they were distributed.

CHAPTER V

New Topics

ARTICLE 31. If any delegation should propose for the consideration of the Conference a topic not included in the program, the topic shall be referred to the Committee on Initiatives and, if accepted by a two-thirds vote of the delegations represented at the Conference, shall be referred to the respective committee, or, if the topic warrants, a new committee shall be named.

All proposals for the inclusion of additional topics in the program shall be presented to the Committee on Initiatives as soon as possible, and in any event within one week after the opening of the Conference, thereby affording adequate time for the consideration of all subjects presented to the Conference.

CHAPTER VI

Minutes of the Sessions and Publications of the Conference

Section I. — *Minutes of Plenary Sessions and of Committees*

ARTICLE 32. Minutes shall be kept of the plenary sessions as well as of the committees of the Conference.

The minutes of the plenary sessions shall be verbatim. Of the committees, the secretary of each committee shall prepare a brief minute of each session, in which shall be briefly summarized the remarks of the delegates and in which shall be recorded in full the conclusions at which the committee may have arrived.

ARTICLE 33. The minutes shall be printed in the "Diario" of the Conference as soon as possible after the session to which they relate. They shall appear first in provisional form, and in the event of any modification in the minute by any delegate, a revised, definitive text shall be published.

ARTICLE 34. The original minutes shall be preserved in the archives of the Pan American Union, to which they shall be sent by the secretary general.

Section II. — *"Diario" of the Conference*

ARTICLE 35. The secretary general shall publish a "Diario" of the Conference in which shall appear the minutes of the plenary sessions and of the committees, the projects submitted by the delegations, the reports of reporting delegates and of subcommittees, and other material pertaining to the Conference.

Section III. — *Final Act*

ARTICLE 36. The final act shall contain the resolutions, recommendations, votes and agreements, approved by the Conference, and in an appendix the treaties and conventions that may be negotiated. The final act shall be prepared as the work of the Conference develops.

ARTICLE 37. After approval by the respective committees and before presentation to the plenary session, the treaties, conventions, resolutions, recommendations, votes and agreements shall be submitted to the Drafting Committee for purposes of coordination in the several official languages.

ARTICLE 38. After each plenary session there shall be inserted in the draft of the final act, with a number and title indicating the subject matter, the resolutions, agreements, votes, and recommendations approved at the session and the date of the session on which they were approved. The day before the closing of the Conference the secretary general shall submit copies of the final act to the delegates for examination. The delegates shall communicate to the secretary general whatever comments they may have to make with respect to the drafting of the final act.

ARTICLE 39. The original of the final act shall be signed by the delegations at the closing session of the Conference and transmitted by the secretary general to the Minister of Foreign Affairs of Peru in order that certified copies may be sent to the Governments of the American Republics, to the delegates, and to the Pan American Union within ninety days following the close of the Conference.

SECTION IV. — *Diplomatic Instruments*

ARTICLE 40. Treaties and conventions approved by the Conference shall be drafted in Spanish, English, Portuguese, and French and submitted to the delegations for examination, and shall be signed at the final session. After signature, the instruments shall be transmitted by the secretary general of the Conference to the Minister of Foreign Affairs of Peru, who shall transmit certified copies to the Governments of the American Republics represented at the Conference, to the delegates and to the Pan American Union.

ARTICLE 41. The signatory states shall deposit in the Pan American Union the instruments of ratification of the treaties and conventions signed at the Eighth International Conference of American States, and the Pan American Union shall notify the other signatory States of the deposit.

ARTICLE 42. The protocolary articles that shall be used in the treaties and conventions signed at the Conference are appended to these regulations. The Conference may, if it deems it advisable, modify the wording of these protocolary articles.

SECTION V. — *Proceedings of the Conference*

ARTICLE 43. As soon as possible after adjournment, the proceedings of the Conference shall be published in Spanish, English, Portuguese and French.

The proceedings shall consist of the minutes of the plenary sessions and of the committees, and copies shall be sent by the Government of Peru to the Governments represented at the Conference, the delegates attending the sessions, and the Pan American Union.

CHAPTER VII

AMENDMENTS TO THE REGULATIONS

ARTICLE 44. These regulations, after approval by the Governing Board, shall be transmitted to the Eighth International Conference, through the intermediary of the Government of the Republic of Peru. The regulations shall be subject to such modifications as may be determined by a vote of two-thirds of the delegations at the Conference.

ANNEX

PROTOCOLARY ARTICLES

The preamble to treaties and conventions signed at the Conference shall be as follows:

The Governments represented at the Eighth International Conference of American States:

Wishing to conclude a Treaty (Convention) on.........................,
have appointed the following Plenipotentiaries:

(Here shall follow the names of the Plenipotentiaries)

Who, after having deposited their Full Powers, found to be in good and due form, have agreed as follows:

ARTICLE I, ETC.

The concluding articles of treaties and conventions shall be as follows:

ARTICLE......

The present Treaty (Convention) shall be ratified by the High Contracting Parties in conformity with their respective constitutional procedures. The original instrument shall be deposited in the Ministry of Foreign Affairs of the Republic of Peru, which shall transmit authentic certified copies to the Governments for the aforementioned purpose of ratification. The instruments of ratification shall be deposited in the archives of the Pan American Union in Washington, which shall notify the signatory governments of said deposit. Such notification shall be considered as an exchange of ratifications.

ARTICLE......

The present Treaty (Convention) will come into effect between the High Contracting Parties in the order in which they deposit their respective ratifications.

ARTICLE......

The present Treaty (Convention) shall remain in effect indefinitely, but may be denounced by means of one year's notice given to the Pan American Union, which shall transmit it to the other signatory governments. After the expiration of this period the Treaty (Convention) shall cease in its effects as regards the party which denounces it, but shall remain in effect for the remaining High Contracting Parties.

ARTICLE......

The present Treaty (Convention) shall be open to the adherence and accession of American States which may not have signed. The corresponding instruments shall be deposited in the archives of the Pan American Union, which shall communicate them to the other High Contracting Parties.

In witness whereof, the above-mentioned Plenipotentiaries sign the present Treaty (Convention), and hereunto affix their respective seals, at the City of Lima, Capital of the Republic of Peru, on the......day of the month of......

VIII

RULES OF PROCEDURE OF THE ASSEMBLY OF THE LEAGUE OF NATIONS [1]

Sessions

Ordinary

RULE 1

1. The Assembly shall meet in general session every year at the seat of the League of Nations, commencing on the Monday which falls in the period September 10th to September 16th inclusive.

Extraordinary

2. Sessions may also be held at such times as the Assembly at a previous meeting decides, and at such times as the Council, by a majority vote, decides.

3. If a Member of the League considers a session to be desirable, it may request the Secretary-General to summon a special session of the Assembly. The Secretary-General shall thereupon inform the other Members of the League of the request, and enquire whether they concur in it. If within a period of one month from the date of the communication of the Secretary-General, a majority of the Members concur in the request, a special session of the Assembly shall be summoned.

Place of Meeting

RULE 2

The sessions of the Assembly shall be held at the seat of the League, or, in exceptional circumstances, at such other place as is designated by the Assembly or by a majority of the Council, or approved by a majority of the Members of the League.

Summons

RULE 3

1. The sessions of the Assembly shall be summoned by the President of the Council, acting through the Secretary-General.

2. The summons shall be addressed to the Members of the League not less than four months before the date fixed for the opening of the session. In exceptional circumstances, however, the Council, by a majority vote, may sanction a shorter period.

3. Nothing contained in paragraph 2 of this Rule shall affect the provisions, concerning special cases, contained in the Covenant.

[1] Revised Edition — April, 1937, L.N. Document C.144.M.92.1937.
The footnotes to these Rules of Procedure, with the exception of the present note, are in the original. The Annexes attached to the Rules have not been reproduced. — ED.

RULE 4   Agenda

1. The agenda shall be drawn up by the Secretary-General with the approval of the President of the Council. The complete agenda shall be circulated as nearly as possible four months before the date fixed for the opening of the session.

2. The agenda of a general session shall include:

    (a) A report on the work of the Council since the last session of the Assembly, on the work of the Secretariat, and on the measures taken to execute the decisions of the Assembly;

    (b) All items whose inclusion has been ordered by the Assembly at a previous session;

    (c) All items proposed by the Council;

    (d) All items proposed by a Member of the League; and

    (e) The Budget for the next fiscal period, and the report on the accounts of the last fiscal period.

3. Any Member of the League may, at least one month before *Inclusion of* the date fixed for the opening of the session, request the inclusion *Additional Items* of additional items in the agenda. Such items shall be placed on a supplementary list, which shall be circulated to the Members of the League at least three weeks before the date fixed for the opening of the session. The Assembly shall decide whether items on the supplementary list shall be included in the agenda of the session.

4. The Assembly may in exceptional circumstances place additional items on the agenda; but all consideration of such items shall, unless otherwise ordered by a two-thirds majority of the Assembly, be postponed until four days after they have been placed on the agenda, and until a committee has reported upon them.

4a. No proposal for the placing of a new question on the agenda of the Assembly may be signed by more than fifteen Members of the League.

5. No proposal for a modification of the allocation of expenses for the time being in force shall be inserted in the agenda, unless it has been communicated to the Members of the League at least four months before the date fixed for the opening of the session.

RULE 5   Communication
                                            of Names of
1. Each Member shall communicate to the Secretary-General, Representatives.
if possible one week before the date fixed for the opening of the Full Powers
session, the names of its representatives, of whom there shall be not more than three. The names of substitute-representatives may be added.

2. The full powers of the representatives shall be delivered to the Secretary-General, if possible, one week before the date fixed for the opening of the session. They shall be issued either by the Head of the State or by the Minister for Foreign Affairs.[2]

3. A Committee of nine members for the examination of the full powers shall be elected by the Assembly on the proposal of the President. The Committee shall appoint its own Chairman and Vice-Chairman. It shall report without delay.

4. Any representative to whose admission objection has been made shall sit provisionally with the same rights as other representatives, unless the Assembly decides otherwise.

Substitute Representatives and Substitutes

RULE 6

1. In addition to the substitute-representatives mentioned in paragraph 1 of Rule 5, the representatives of a Member of the League attending the Assembly, acting together as a delegation, may appoint substitutes. Any such appointment shall be communicated in writing to the President.

2. A substitute-representative appointed by a Member of the League may take the place of a representative without nomination by the representatives.

3. A substitute-representative or substitute may take the place of a representative who is absent from a meeting of the Assembly, or is temporarily prevented from taking part in its deliberations, but, if the representative is present at the meeting, the substitute-representative or substitute is only entitled to assist him.

Deputies and Technical Advisers

4. A delegation may appoint for service on a committee a deputy or technical adviser other than those referred to in the above paragraphs of this Rule; but a deputy or adviser so appointed shall not be eligible for appointment as Chairman or Rapporteur, or for a seat in the Assembly.

President, Vice-Presidents and General Committee

RULE 7[3]

1. The General Committee of the Assembly shall consist of the President of the Assembly, eight Vice-Presidents and the Chairmen of the main Committees of the Assembly, the Agenda Committee and the Committee for the examination of the full powers.

The Assembly may decide to add to the General Committee

---

[2] It is obvious that, in the case of countries which do not possess a Minister for Foreign Affairs, the full powers may be issued by an authority possessing similar or equivalent powers.

[3] On September 30th, 1933, the Assembly approved the following recommendation, which was made to it by the General Committee:

"When proceeding to the election of the Vice-Presidents of the Assembly, in application of Rule 7, paragraphs 1 and 4, of the Rules of Procedure, the voting-papers should not bear the names of individuals, but should be marked 'The First Delegate' of such and such a country."

the Chairmen of other Assembly Committees and, in exceptional cases, other members.

2. The President shall be elected at the beginning of each session.

3. Until the election of the President, the President of the Council shall act as President of the Assembly.

4. The election of the Vice-Presidents shall take place at one of the early meetings of the session.

RULE 7 (a)

Agenda Committee

1. An Agenda Committee shall be set up at the beginning of each session. It shall consist of seven members, who shall be appointed by the Assembly on the nomination of the President.

2. The Committee shall elect its own Chairman and Vice-Chairman.

3. The Committee shall consider applications for the inclusion of new questions in the agenda of the Assembly, and shall report to the Assembly thereon.

4. Proposals for the mere reference to one of the main Committees of portions of the Report on the Work of the League shall be decided upon by the Assembly without previous reference to the Agenda Committee.

RULE 7 (b) ⁴

Nomination Committee

1. *At the commencement of each session, the Assembly shall appoint a committee of eleven members whose duty shall be to nominate candidates for functions which carry with them a seat on the General Committee.*

2. *The provisional President of the Assembly shall submit proposals to it regarding the composition of this Committee.*

3. *The Members of the Assembly and the Committees shall retain the right to vote for persons other than those proposed by the above-mentioned Committee.*

RULE 8

Functions of President and General Committee

1. The President shall announce the opening, suspension and adjournment of the meetings of the Assembly, direct the work of the Assembly, ensure the observance of the Rules of Procedure, accord the right to address the Assembly, declare the debates to be closed, put questions to the vote, and announce the result of the voting.

⁴ On October 10th, 1936, the Assembly adopted as an experiment the procedure laid down in this rule, which, unless otherwise decided in the interval, is to have effect down to the termination of the ordinary session of 1939.

2. In the general direction of the work of the Assembly, in the constitution of such committees as the Assembly decides to create, in deciding on the communications to be made to the Assembly, in the framing of the agenda for each meeting, and in the determination of the order of priority for its various items, the President shall be assisted by the General Committee.

Secretariat

RULE 9

1. The Secretary-General shall be responsible for the organisation of the Secretariat of the Assembly and of the secretariat of any committees set up by the Assembly.

2. The Secretary-General may be assisted or replaced at the meetings of the Assembly by a deputy or deputies. The Secretary-General, or one of his deputies, may at any time, on the invitation of the President, bring before the Assembly reports concerning any question which is being considered by the Assembly, and may be invited by the President to make verbal communications concerning any question under consideration.

Documents

RULE 10

1. It shall be the duty of the Secretariat, *inter alia*, to receive, print, circulate and translate documents, reports and resolutions; to translate speeches made at the meetings; to draft, print and circulate the Minutes of the session; to have the custody and proper preservation of the documents in the archives of the Assembly; to publish the reports of the meetings, and, generally, to perform all other work which the Assembly thinks fit to entrust to it.

2. All documents emanating from the Assembly shall be circulated to the Governments of the Members of the League.

Publicity of Plenary Meetings

RULE 11

1. The public shall be admitted to the plenary meetings of the Assembly, by cards distributed by the Secretary-General.

2. The Assembly may decide that particular meetings shall be private.

3. All decisions of the Assembly upon items on the agenda, which have been taken at a private meeting, shall be announced at a public meeting of the Assembly.

RULE 12

(Deleted.)

RULE 13

At the beginning of each meeting the President shall present to the Assembly all communications addressed to the Assembly or to the League, the importance of which appears to him to warrant such action.

RULE 14[5]

1. The Assembly shall establish such committees as it thinks fit, for the consideration of the items on the agenda. Items of the same nature will be referred to the same committee. *Constitution*

2. The Assembly shall not decide items on the agenda in full meeting until the report of a committee upon them has been presented and circulated, unless the Assembly itself, by a two-thirds majority, determines otherwise. *Reports of Committees, particularly Reports involving Expenditure*

Decisions involving expenditure shall be subject to the rules laid down in the Regulations for the Financial Administration of the League of Nations.[6]

Reports by a committee involving the expenditure of money must indicate whether the expenditure will constitute part of the general expenses of the League or whether it will be recovered from the Members of the League particularly concerned.

No resolution involving expenditure shall in any case be voted by the Assembly before the Finance Committee shall have expressed its opinion on the advisability of the proposed expenditure from the point of view of general budgetary resources.[7]

3. Each delegation may designate one member, and may nominate technical advisers, for each committee. *Membership*

4. Each committee shall appoint its Chairman and Rapporteurs. *Officers*

5. Each committee may appoint sub-committees, which shall elect their own officers. *Sub-committees*

6. Each committee shall meet in private unless it decides otherwise. It shall keep a register of its discussions, and Minutes, which shall be published at the earliest possible date, but not until they *Publicity of Meetings. Minutes*

[5] On October 10th, 1936, the Assembly decided that the following rule, established as an experiment by the Assembly's resolution of October 11th, 1933, should be maintained for the session of 1937:
The President of the Council, after consulting the Chairman of the Supervisory Commission, may convene the Finance Committee for a date preceding by not more than one week the first meeting of the ordinary session of the Assembly. The Committee shall be composed of the representatives accredited for the purpose by the Members of the League. It shall appoint its Chairman, who shall thereby become a member of the General Committee of the Assembly under the terms of Rule 7 of the Rules of Procedure. The establishment of the Committee shall be reported to the Assembly at the first plenary meeting of the Assembly.
[6] See Annex III.   [7] See Annex II.

have been approved by the committee. They may at any time be consulted by any Member of the Assembly.

7. Every representative shall have the right to place before any committee any communication which he considers should be made to it, but no representative may, without special leave from the Chairman, speak at a meeting of any committee of which he is not a member.

8. The Secretary-General or his deputies may make to any committee or sub-committee any report or verbal communication which he or they may consider desirable.

**Procedure for
Presentation and
Adoption of
Reports of
Committees in
Plenary Session**

RULE 14 (*a*)

1. When the reports and resolutions submitted by the various Committees of the Assembly are brought up for adoption in plenary session, the President, in the cases indicated below, shall read the titles of the reports and put forthwith to the vote the resolutions which are proposed.

2. The procedure provided for in paragraph 1 shall only apply in cases where the Committee has unanimously declared that it does not consider a discussion of the report in plenary session to be necessary and where no delegation has subsequently asked the President to open a discussion on the report. The report must be circulated to the delegations twenty-four hours before it is brought up in plenary session.

RULE 15

1. No representative may address the Assembly without having previously obtained the permission of the President.

2. Speakers shall be called upon in the order in which they have signified their desire to speak. The Chairman and the Rapporteur of a committee may be accorded precedence for the purpose of defending or explaining the conclusions arrived at by their committee. The same principle shall apply to any Member of the Council.

3. The President may call a speaker to order if his remarks are not relevant to the subject under discussion. If necessary, he may direct the speaker to resume his seat.

4. When a motion is under discussion, a representative may rise to a point of order, and such point of order shall be immediately decided by the President in accordance with the Rules of Procedure.

5. The Assembly may limit the time allowed to each speaker.

RULE 16

1. Speeches in French shall be summarised in English, and *vice versa*, by an interpreter belonging to the Secretariat.

2. A representative speaking in another language shall provide for the translation of his speech into one of these two languages.

3. All documents, resolutions and reports circulated by the President or the Secretariat shall be rendered in both French and English.

4. Any representative may have documents circulated in a language other than French or English, but the Secretariat will not be responsible for their translation or printing.

5. Any Member of the League, or any group of Members, may require that all documents and publications of the League shall be regularly translated into, and printed and circulated in, a language other than French and English, but shall in such case defray all the necessary expenses.

Translation of Speeches and Documents

RULE 17

1. Resolutions, amendments and motions must be introduced in writing and handed to the President. The President shall cause copies to be distributed to the representatives.

1*a*. No resolution, amendment or motion may be signed by more than fifteen Members of the League.

2. As a general rule, no proposal shall be discussed or put to the vote at any meeting of the Assembly unless copies of it have been circulated to all representatives not later than the day preceding the meeting.

3. The President may, however, permit the discussion and consideration of amendments, or of motions as to procedure, without previous circulation of copies.

Resolutions, Amendments and Motions

RULE 18

1. During the discussion of any question, any representative may move the previous question or the adjournment. Any such motion shall have priority in the debate. In addition to the proposer of the motion, two representatives may speak in favour of, and two against, the motion.

2. Parts of a proposal shall be voted on separately, if a representative request that the proposal be divided.

3. A representative may at any time move the closure of the debate, whether any other representative has signified his wish to speak or not. If application is made for permission to speak against the closure, it may be accorded to not more than two speakers.

4. The President shall take the sense of the Assembly on a

Previous Question or Adjournment

Division of Proposals

Closure

motion for closure. If the Assembly decides in favour of the
closure, the President shall declare the closure of the debate.

Procedure for voting Proposals and Amendments

5. When a number of proposals are before the Assembly, the
proposal furthest removed in substance from the principal one
shall be voted on first.

6. If an amendment striking out part of a proposal is moved,
the Assembly shall first vote on whether the words in question
shall stand part of the proposal. If the decision is in the negative,
the amendment shall then be put to the vote.

7. When an amendment adds to a proposal it shall be voted on
first, and if it is adopted the amended proposal shall then be voted
on.

Majority

RULE 19

1. Except where otherwise expressly provided in the Covenant
or by the terms of a treaty, decisions of the Assembly shall be
taken by a unanimous vote of the Members of the League represented at the meeting.

2. All matters of procedure at a meeting of the Assembly, including the appointment of committees to investigate particular
matters, shall be decided by a majority of the Members of the
League represented at the meeting.

3. All decisions taken in virtue of these Rules shall be considered as matters of procedure.

4. A majority decision requires the affirmative votes of more
than half of the Members of the League represented at the
meeting.

5. For the purposes of this Rule, representatives who abstain
from voting shall be considered as not present.

"Appel Nominal"

RULE 20

The Assembly shall vote by "Appel Nominal", except when
the Members of the League represented at the meeting agree that
the method of voting shall be by heads of delegations rising in
their seats, and except in the cases provided for in Rule 21. The
"Appel Nominal" shall be taken in one of the following manners,
as the Assembly may decide:

(a) The name of each delegation shall be called, and one of its
members shall reply "Yes", "No", or "Not voting". The result
of the vote shall be recorded and announced to the Assembly;
or

(b) The delegation of each Member of the League represented
at the meeting shall be provided with two voting tickets, on which
the name of the country is written, one red and one blue, the
former being "Aye" the latter "No". The voting tickets shall be

deposited in an urn placed near the President's platform. When all the votes have been collected the President shall declare the ballot closed, and the General Committee shall proceed to count the votes. The individual votes shall be communicated to the Assembly and the result shall be announced by the President.

RULE 21

Elections

1. All decisions relating to individuals shall be taken by a secret ballot.

2. If, when one person only is to be elected, no one person obtains at the first ballot an absolute majority of votes, an entirely new ballot shall be taken; but on this occasion the voting shall be confined to the two candidates who obtained the largest number of votes at the first ballot. If there is at this ballot an equality of votes for the two candidates, the elder candidate shall be declared elected.

3. When a number of elective places of the same nature are to be filled at one time, those persons who obtain an absolute majority at the first ballot shall be elected. If the number of persons obtaining such majority is less than the number of persons to be elected, there shall be a second ballot to fill the remaining places, the voting being restricted to the unsuccessful candidates who obtained the greatest number of votes at the first ballot, not more than double in number the places remaining to be filled. Those candidates, to the number required to be elected, who receive the greatest number of votes at the second ballot shall be declared elected.[8]

RULE 22

Equality in Voting. Second Vote

In case of equality in any voting other than that referred to in Rule 21, in which a majority is required, a second vote shall be taken in the course of the next meeting; this meeting shall be held within 48 hours from the date on which the first vote was taken, and it shall be expressly mentioned on the agenda that a second vote will be taken on the matter in question. Unless there is at this subsequent meeting a majority in favour of the proposal, it shall be considered as lost.

RULE 22a

Election of Non-permanent Members of the Council

1. The Members whose representatives are to sit on the Council as non-permanent Members of that body shall be selected by the Assembly by secret ballot.

[8] For the rules concerning the election of members of the Permanent Court of International Justice, see Annex VI.

2. Where several seats are to be filled, the election shall be made by voting a list of names. Any ballot-paper containing more names than there are seats to be filled shall be null and void.

3. No Member shall be elected at the first or at the second ballot unless it has obtained at least the absolute majority of the votes. If, after two ballots, there still remain seats to be filled, a third ballot shall be held upon a list consisting of the candidates which obtained most votes at the second ballot, up to a number double that of the seats still to be filled, and those Members shall be elected which obtain the greatest number of votes.

4. If two or more Members obtain the same number of votes and there is not a seat available for each, a special ballot shall be held between them; if they again obtain an equal number of votes, the President shall decide between them by drawing lots.

RULE 23

Adjournment or Suspension of Meetings

1. The President may declare a meeting to be adjourned or suspended if a proposal for adjournment or suspension made by him does not meet with objection from the Assembly.

2. The President shall declare an adjournment or suspension of the meeting upon a vote to this effect by the Assembly.

RULE 24

Revision of Resolutions

The General Committee, in cases where it deems it necessary, may revise the resolutions adopted by the Assembly, changing their form but not their substance. Any such changes shall be reported to the Assembly.

RULE 25

Verbatim Reports

The verbatim report of each meeting shall be drawn up by the Secretariat and submitted to the Assembly after approval by the President.

RULE 26

Circulation of Assembly Resolutions

The resolutions adopted by the Assembly shall be circulated by the Secretary-General to the Members of the League within fifteen days after the termination of the session.

RULE 27

Application of Rules to Committee Proceedings

These Rules of Procedure shall apply to the proceedings of committees of the Assembly.[9]

[9] As regards the adoption of decisions by committees by a majority vote, and the question of minority reports, see the report adopted by the Assembly in 1924 (Annex V).

RULE 28

These Rules of Procedure may be altered by a decision of the Assembly; but no such alteration shall be made except upon a majority vote of the Assembly, taken after a committee has reported on the proposed alteration.

IX

SCOPE OF THE WORK OF AN INTERNATIONAL CONFERENCE

EXTRACT FROM THE MINUTES OF THE CONFERENCE FOR THE SUPPRESSION OF THE ILLICIT TRAFFIC IN DANGEROUS DRUGS [1]

(*Geneva, June 8–26, 1936*)

· · · · ·

Mr. FULLER (United States of America) made the following statement:

I wish to express appreciation of the kindness and courtesy of our President in quoting, at the close of last evening's meeting, certain statements made by the American Government in regard to the first two drafts of the proposed Convention which we have at various times had sent us for consideration, drafts which were totally different from the one before us at present and which, having been found unsatisfactory, had been referred to a Committee of Experts. I only regret that he did not quote our complete replies and that he did not quote what we had to say in regard to the present draft, the one drawn up by the Committee of Experts. On the question of this proposed Convention for the Suppression of the Illicit Traffic, and I refer to the draft now before us, I should like to supplement what the Chairman had to say last evening by quoting from the statement on that draft which was made by my Government as follows:

The Government of the United States of America considers it important that the Conference consider prevention and punishment of illicit cultivation, gathering and production of poppy, coca and cannabis.

For over two years past, my Government has been saying that, in its opinion, the provisions of the existing treaties for the suppression of illicit activities connected with the traffic in narcotic drugs, if given proper effect by all the interested Governments, are adequate to accomplish the purpose of the treaties, and that the American Government would not, therefore, feel disposed to participate in this proposed Convention. Eventually, however, we received an invitation to participate in the present Conference.

Before replying to that invitation, my Government stated to the Secretary-General, from whom the invitation had emanated, that the terms of reference of the proposed Conference and the scope of the proposed Convention appeared to be so indefinite that my Government found difficulty in ascertaining what limits, if any, would be imposed upon the work of the Conference.

---

[1] *Records of the Conference for the Suppression of the Illicit Traffic in Dangerous Drugs* (*Geneva, June 8th to 26th, 1936*), *Text of the Debates*, L.N. Document C.341.M.216.1936.XI., p. 23.

Accordingly, we asked him the following questions:

(1) Whether the Preamble of the first and second draft substantially describes the scope of the work;

(2) Whether subjects which have not already been presented to Governments for observations but which are nevertheless connected with the prevention of, and punishment for, illicit operations may be considered by the Conference;

(3) Whether the work of the Conference is to be limited to the subjects included in the draft submitted by the Committee of Experts and printed as an annex to document S.T.D.2 or whether additional subjects connected with the prevention of and punishment for illicit traffic may be introduced;

(4) Whether the competence of the Conference will extend to questions involving (a) cannabis, (b) illicit trade in raw materials, (c) illicit manufacture of derivatives.

In reply to these enquiries, we were informed by the Secretary-General that:

The draft Convention to be submitted to the Conference will constitute only a basis of discussion, and that, as stated by the Rapporteur to the Council, its acceptance as a basis of discussion does not commit any Government.

We were further informed that:

According to the procedure followed at all conferences held under the auspices of the League of Nations, the Conference alone has sovereign powers; it may take whatever decisions it thinks fit, and is therefore fully entitled to modify any draft submitted to it as a basis of discussion.

We were further informed by him that:

Any delegation at the Conference may propose any matter for inclusion in the Convention, and the Conference itself will have complete liberty to accept or disregard such proposals.

With regard to the question whether the Preamble to the first and second drafts substantially describes the scope of the work of the Conference, we were informed by him that:

The existing draft Preamble cannot in any way be regarded as a final description of the objects of the Convention to be concluded, and still less serve as a limitation to the scope of the work of the Conference itself.

This was the basis on which my Government accepted the invitation to participate in these discussions.

X

RECOMMENDATIONS AS TO THE ARRANGEMENTS FOR THE DEBATES IN THE ASSEMBLY ON THE ANNUAL REPORT BY THE COUNCIL [1]

COMMUNICATED BY THE GENERAL COMMITTEE TO THE DELEGATES TO THE THIRD ORDINARY SESSION OF THE ASSEMBLY ON SEPTEMBER 29TH, 1922

The General Committee, in accordance with the desire expressed by the Assembly, has carefully investigated the proposals made by the President with regard to the arrangements for the debates in the Assembly on the report by the Council. The General Committee unanimously recognises the utility of these proposals and has adopted the following recommendations, which may perhaps serve for guidance in the procedure of future Assemblies and help their Presidents in the exercise of the powers conferred upon them in pursuance of Articles 8 and 15 of the Rules of Procedure:

1. The report by the Council on its work of the year shall be communicated to the Assembly at the beginning of the session, and as a general rule it shall constitute the first subject on the agenda after the organisation of the Assembly has been completed.

2. The report by the Council shall be submitted for debate in the Assembly, to be opened with a general discussion, which may be followed by consideration of particular subjects dealt with in the report or arising out of it.

3. The delegates shall be invited to inform the President before the beginning of the debate, or as soon thereafter as possible, whether they desire to participate, indicating at the same time their wishes as to engaging in the general debate, or more particularly in the discussion of specific matters covered by the Council's report; they should be invited to state also the subjects with which they wish to deal specially in the specific discussion.

4. The President will propose to the Assembly, as early as possible, the subjects to be covered in the specific discussion following the general debate, arranging to have speakers on the same topic heard in succession. The delegates will be invited to limit their speeches in the special debates, as far as possible, to the special topics under discussion at the time. It is in no sense inconsistent with the present Recommendations that delegates taking part in the general discussion should on that occasion refer to subjects on which a specific discussion will take place.

[1] Annex I of League of Nations, *Rules of Procedure of the Assembly* (Revised Edition — April, 1937), pp. 17–18.

XI

NOTE ON THE PROCEDURE OF THE INTERNATIONAL LABOR CONFERENCES

EXTRACT FROM NO. 1 OF THE PROVISIONAL RECORD OF THE TWENTY-SIXTH SESSION OF THE INTERNATIONAL LABOR CONFERENCE, HELD IN PHILADELPHIA IN APRIL–MAY, 1944 [1]

The procedure of the Conference is regulated by the Constitution of the Organisation and by the Standing Orders, which are reproduced in the booklet *Constitution and Rules of the International Labour Organisation* (obtainable from the Distribution Service). The following brief outline of the procedure may be helpful to members of delegations who are attending the Conference for the first time.

On the first day the Conference meets in plenary sitting. It is formally opened by the Chairman of the Governing Body and proceeds to the election of its President. After this plenary sitting the Government, Employers' and Workers' groups meet separately to elect their own Officers and decide on their nominations for the three Vice-Presidents and for the Selection Committee and the Credentials Committee. The Conference then meets again in plenary sitting to elect the three Vice-Presidents and to appoint the Selection Committee.

The Selection Committee makes proposals for the number of committees and their composition. After these proposals have been approved by the Conference in plenary sitting, the Government, Employers' and Workers' groups meet again separately and make their nominations for the membership of the committees. Information upon the method of appointment of the various committees is given by the Officers at the group meetings. The nominations so made are submitted to the Selection Committee, which reports to the Conference in plenary sitting. When these preliminary arrangements have been completed, the Conference is in a position to proceed with the discussion of its agenda.

The times of the plenary sittings and the times and places of the group meetings and of the Selection Committee are shown on the notice board and in the *Daily Bulletin*.

The Committees of the Conference usually begin their work immediately after their appointment, but there may be a general discussion in plenary sitting before a particular subject is referred to a Committee for consideration. Plenary sittings are also held for the discussion of the Director's Report. Delegates (or advisers authorised to do so by their delegates) who wish to take part in the discussion at plenary sittings should give their names to the Clerk of the Conference by message sent to his room before the sitting, or by note handed to him on the platform during the sitting.

[1] International Labour Conference, *Provisional Record, Twenty-sixth Session*, Philadelphia, 1944, No. 1, pp. II–III.

The places and times of meeting of the various Committees are announced on the notice board and in the *Daily Bulletin*. It may be pointed out that all delegates and advisers are entitled to attend meetings of Committees even if they are not themselves members, and may also speak in those Committees (in the case of advisers, only if they have been authorised by their delegates); but only those delegates and advisers who sit on the Committee, either as regular members or as substitutes for regular members, are entitled to vote.

The procedure of Committees is governed by special Standing Orders, which will be found in the booklet *Constitution and Rules of the International Labour Organisation*.

In Committees dealing with the items on the agenda, it is the practice of the Conference to give equal representation to the three groups in the Conference — Governments, Employers and Workers. As it not infrequently happens that Governments desire representation on a Committee in numbers which it is impossible for one or both of the other groups to equal, the principle of equality between the three groups on the Committee can be maintained only by the adoption of special systems of voting. Two systems are employed, known as the "Riddell" and "Riddell-Tzaut."

Under the "Riddell" system, the Committee is constituted in the same proportions as the Conference, with twice as many Government members as there are Employers' or Workers' members, but each Government member casts one vote and each member of the other two groups casts two votes.

Under the "Riddell-Tzaut" system, the Government members are one and a half time as numerous as the Employers' or Workers' members, but each Government member casts two votes and each member of the other two groups casts three votes.

The Composition of each Committee is the subject of a proposal to the Conference by the Selection Committee, and the normal, the "Riddell" or the "Riddell-Tzaut" system of voting is applied as the case may require.

At its first meeting each Committee appoints its Chairman, a Vice-Chairman for the Employers' group, and a Vice-Chairman for the Workers' group. A Reporter and a Drafting Committee are also appointed, either at the beginning or at a later stage of the Committee's work. Separate meetings of the Government, Employers' and Workers' members of the Committee may be held for the purpose of nominating Officers and similar meetings may also be held from time to time for the discussion of the Committee's work. So far as possible, these meetings are announced in the *Daily Bulletin* and on the notice board, but members of Committees should keep in close touch with the Officers of their group.

Members of delegations wishing to speak at Committee meetings should send their names up to the Chairman or Secretary of the Committee (especially at the early meetings it is desirable to send up names in writing instead of merely "catching the eye" of the Chairman). Speakers are called on in the order in which their names are received. All speeches made in French are interpreted into English and *vice versa*, and, subject to the provisions of the Standing Orders, interpretations into other languages may also be given.

The work of Committee secretariats is facilitated if members always sit in the same places.

Amendments to proposals before a Committee must be handed to the secretariat of the Committee in writing.

The proceedings of Committees are not reported in full, but minutes in English and French giving a very brief record of the discussions and decisions are prepared by the secretaries, mimeographed and circulated to members of the Committee one or two sittings later than that to which they relate. A list of the Officers, members and secretariat of each Committee is given in an early number of these minutes and is reproduced in a revised edition of the *List of Delegates*.

In the interests of smooth and speedy working, members of Committees are requested to make their speeches as succinct as possible.

Members of Committees who are not already in possession of the reports under discussion by their Committee can obtain a copy on application to the Distribution Service. Other documents (minutes, amendments) are supplied by the Committee secretariat.

Members of the public are admitted, so far as accommodation is available, to meetings of Committees dealing with items on the agenda, unless the Committee decides otherwise.

The report of the Committee is prepared by the Reporter and submitted in draft to the Committee as a mimeographed document. With the approval of the report, the Committee's work comes to an end. The report is then published in the *Provisional Record* and is considered by the Conference in plenary sitting; the time is announced on the notice board and in the *Daily Bulletin*. Amendments to the Committee's proposals for consideration by the Conference must be given in writing to the Clerk of the Conference. In the case of a proposed draft Convention or Recommendation, after the Committee's proposals and any amendments thereto have been discussed and voted on by the plenary sitting, the text is referred to the Drafting Committee of the Conference to be put into final form. The text prepared by the Drafting Committee is then published in the *Provisional Record* and the final vote is taken in plenary sitting at a time which is announced on the notice board and in the *Daily Bulletin*.

XII

ADOPTION OF DECISIONS BY A MAJORITY IN COMMITTEES OF THE ASSEMBLY: MINORITY REPORTS [1]

EXTRACT FROM THE REPORT OF A SUB-COMMITTEE OF THE FIRST COMMITTEE ADOPTED BY THE ASSEMBLY ON SEPTEMBER 20TH, 1924

I. The Sub-Committee has carefully examined the Netherlands proposal, which was in the following terms:

There shall be added to Rule 27 of the Rules of Procedure of the Assembly a second paragraph worded as follows:
Provided that decisions of the Committees shall be taken by the vote of the majority of the Members of the League represented at the meeting.

The Netherlands delegate informed the Sub-Committee that his Government's intention was that the amendment should be purely explanatory, and should merely legalise the existing practice of the Committees.

Your Sub-Committee quite realised that the proposed interpretation was correct. Unanimity at plenary meetings of the Assembly is only necessary for the adoption of resolutions representing genuine decisions which are not connected with procedure and are binding on the States. Committee reports do not fall within this category, since they are merely a preliminary and provisional stage of the resolutions finally adopted by the Assembly.

Although the ultimate vote of the Assembly must be unanimous, it does not follow that majority votes in Committees can be of no effect. Indeed, experience shows that minorities on Committees, while endeavouring to secure the acceptance of their own resolutions, do not, as a rule, attempt to prevent the adoption of other resolutions if the majority are in favour of these.

It has occurred to your Sub-Committee, however, that in some cases the opposition of a minority in a Committee to a resolution, which cannot be adopted at a plenary meeting of the Assembly except by a unanimous vote, may render it useless to submit the resolution actually voted by the Committee to the Assembly without amendment. It would be inexpedient in such cases not to allow Committees to reconsider their decisions and, if the majority thinks it desirable, to amend the resolutions already voted with a view to meeting to some extent the objections raised.

For this reason, your Sub-Committee is of opinion that it would be preferable, not to bind the Committees by a rigid rule, as proposed by the Netherlands dele-

[1] Annex V of League of Nations, *Rules of Procedure of the Assembly* (Revised Edition — April, 1937), pp. 26–28.

gation, but to allow them to continue to use the elastic procedure which has hitherto been followed.

The Netherlands delegate has accepted this view.

II. The Sub-Committee then considered a proposal put forward by the Spanish delegation to amend Rule 27.

This proposal was to the effect that, if the amendment put forward by the Netherlands delegation was adopted, the new second paragraph of Rule 27 of the Rules should be completed by the addition of the following further paragraph:

At the request of one or more members of the Committee who have not voted in favour of a report adopted by a majority, the dissentient opinion, with a statement of the reasons for it, shall be communicated to the Assembly at the same time as the report.

As the Netherlands delegate had withdrawn his amendment, the Spanish additional amendment was also withdrawn.

The Sub-Committee was of opinion that the Rapporteur might be relied upon to give a fair statement of the dissentient opinions of one or more members, if asked by them to do so; moreover, the minority would have a check on this statement when the report came to be adopted.

III. The Chinese delegate on the Sub-Committee proposed, as an amendment to the Netherlands proposal, that the consent of any country mentioned in the resolution, or whose interests are principally or mainly affected by such a resolution, must first be obtained to the system of majority voting.

In view of the withdrawal of the Netherlands proposal, the Chinese delegate also withdrew his proposal.

The Sub-Committee was of opinion that the Committees might be relied upon, before deciding whether a majority resolution should be submitted to the Assembly as voted, to give special attention to the nature of any objections raised by States in the position described in the Chinese delegate's proposal.

XIII

CONVENTIONS AND AGREEMENTS ADOPTED UNDER THE AUSPICES OF THE LEAGUE OF NATIONS [1]

(*Status as of January 1, 1939*)

1. Disarmament and Security

Number of instruments: 6, of which 4 were not yet in force on December 31, 1938.

2. International Law

Number of instruments: 17, of which 10 were not yet in force on December 31, 1938.

3. Economic and Financial Activity

Number of instruments: 23, of which 3 were not yet in force on December 31, 1938.

4. Communications and Transit

Number of instruments: 19, of which 5 were not yet in force on December 31, 1938.

5. Social and Humanitarian Activity

Number of instruments: 16, of which 3 were not yet in force on December 31, 1938.

6. Intellectual Coöperation

Number of instruments: 3, of which 1 was not yet in force on December 31, 1938.

[1] Condensed from *Essential Facts about the League of Nations*, 10th edition, revised (Geneva: Information Section, 1939), pp. 339–44.

XIV

GENERAL PROVISIONS

INTERNATIONAL CONVENTION CONCERNING THE USE OF BROADCASTING IN THE CAUSE OF PEACE [1]

(Geneva, September 23, 1936)

. . . . .

ARTICLE 7. Should a dispute arise between the High Contracting Parties regarding the interpretation or application of the present Convention for which it has been found impossible to arrive at a satisfactory settlement through the diplomatic channel, it shall be settled in conformity with the provisions in force between the Parties concerning the settlement of international disputes.

In the absence of any such provisions between the Parties to the dispute, the said Parties shall submit it to arbitration or to judicial settlement. Failing agreement concerning the choice of another tribunal, they shall submit the dispute, at the request of one of them, to the Permanent Court of International Justice, provided they are all Parties to the Protocol of December 16th, 1920, regarding the Statute of the Court; or, if they are not all Parties to the above Protocol, they shall submit the dispute to an arbitral tribunal, constituted in conformity with the Hague Convention of October 18th, 1907, for the Pacific Settlement of International Disputes.

Before having recourse to the procedures specified in paragraphs 1 and 2 above, the High Contracting Parties may, by common consent, appeal to the good offices of the International Committee on Intellectual Cooperation, which would be in a position to constitute a special committee for this purpose.

ARTICLE 8. The present Convention, of which the French and English texts are both authentic, shall bear this day's date, and shall be open for signature until May 1st, 1937, on behalf of any Member of the League of Nations, or any non-member State represented at the Conference which drew up the present Convention, or any non-member State to which the Council of the League of Nations shall have communicated a copy of the said Convention for that purpose.

ARTICLE 9. The present Convention shall be ratified. The instruments of ratification shall be sent to the Secretary-General of the League of Nations, who shall notify the deposit thereof to all the Members of the League and to the non-member States referred to in the preceding Article.

ARTICLE 10. After May 1st, 1937, any Member of the League of Nations and any non-member State referred to in Article 8 may accede to the present Convention.

The notifications of accession shall be sent to the Secretary-General of the

---

[1] L.N. Document C.399.M.252.1936.XII., in *Official Journal*, 1936, pp. 1438–41.

League of Nations, who shall notify the deposit thereof to all the Members of the League and to all the non-member States referred to in the aforesaid Article.

ARTICLE 11. The present Convention shall be registered by the Secretary-General of the League of Nations, in conformity with the provisions of Article 18 of the Covenant, sixty days after the receipt by him of the sixth ratification or accession.

The Convention shall enter into force on the day of such registration.

ARTICLE 12. Every ratification or accession effected after the entry into force of the Convention shall take effect sixty days after the receipt thereof by the Secretary-General of the League of Nations.

ARTICLE 13. The present Convention may be denounced by a notification addressed to the Secretary-General of the League of Nations. Such notification shall take effect one year after its receipt.

The Secretary-General shall notify the receipt of any such denunciation to all Members of the League and to the non-member States referred to in Article 8.

If, as the result of denunciations, the number of High Contracting Parties should fall below six, the present Convention shall cease to apply.

ARTICLE 14. Any High Contracting Party may, on signing, ratifying or acceding to the present Convention, or at any subsequent date, by a written document addressed to the Secretary-General of the League of Nations, declare that the present Convention shall apply to all or any of his colonies, protectorates, overseas territories, or territories placed under his suzerainty or mandate. The present Convention shall apply to the territory or territories specified in the declaration sixty days after its receipt. Failing such a declaration, the Convention shall not apply to any such territory.

Any High Contracting Party may at any subsequent date, by a notification to the Secretary-General of the League of Nations, declare that the present Convention shall cease to apply to any or all of his colonies, protectorates, overseas territories, or territories placed under his suzerainty or mandate. The Convention shall cease to apply to the territory or territories specified in the notification one year after its receipt.

The Secretary-General shall communicate to all Members of the League and to the non-member States referred to in Article 8 all declarations received under the present Article.

ARTICLE 15. A request for the revision of the present Convention may be made at any time by any High Contracting Party in the form of a notification addressed to the Secretary-General of the League of Nations. Such notification shall be communicated by the Secretary-General to the other High Contracting Parties. Should not less than one-third of them associate themselves with such request, the High Contracting Parties agree to meet with a view to the revision of the Convention.

In that event, it shall be for the Secretary-General of the League of Nations to propose to the Council or Assembly of the League of Nations the convening of a revision conference.

XV

PROTOCOL OF SIGNATURE [1]

EXTRACTS FROM CONFERENCE FOR THE SUPPRESSION OF THE ILLICIT TRAFFIC IN DANGEROUS DRUGS

(Geneva, June 26, 1936)

When signing the Convention of 1936 for the Suppression of the Illicit Traffic in Dangerous Drugs dated this day, the undersigned Plenipotentiaries, in the name of their Governments, declare to have agreed:

1. To China making acceptance of the Convention subject to the following reservation as to Article 9:

"So long as the consular jurisdiction still enjoyed by the nationals of certain Powers in China is not abolished, the Chinese Government is unable to assume the obligations resulting from Article 9, involving a general undertaking by the Contracting Parties to grant the extradition of foreigners guilty of the offences referred to in that Article."

2. That the Netherlands make their acceptance of the Convention subject to the reservation that, according to the basic principles of penal law in the Netherlands, they are able to comply with sub-paragraph (c) of Article 2 only in circumstances where there is a commencement of execution.

3. That India makes its acceptance of the Convention subject to the reservation that the said Convention does not apply to the Indian States or to the Shan States (which are part of British India).

EN FOI DE QUOI les soussignés ont apposé leur signature au bas du présent Protocole.

FAIT à Genève, le vingt-six juin mil neuf cent trente-six, en un seul exemplaire, qui sera déposé dans les archives du Secrétariat de la Société des Nations et dont les copies certifiées conformes seront remises à tous les Membres de la Société des Nations et aux Etats non membres mentionnés à l'article 19 de la Convention.

IN FAITH WHEREOF the undersigned have affixed their signatures to the present Protocol.

DONE at Geneva, the twenty-sixth day of June, one thousand nine hundred and thirty-six, in a single copy, which shall remain deposited in the archives of the Secretariat of the League of Nations and certified true copies of which shall be delivered to all the Members of the League of Nations and to the non-member States referred to in Article 19 of the Convention.

[1] L.N. Document C.286(a).M.174(a).1936.XI. in *Records of the Conference for the Suppression of the Illicit Traffic in Dangerous Drugs, Text of the Debates* (Geneva, 1936), p. 222.

AUTRICHE   AUSTRIA

E. Pflügl
Dr Bruno Schultz

ETATS-UNIS DU BRÉSIL   UNITED STATES OF BRAZIL

Jorge Latour
ad referendum

GRANDE-BRETAGNE   GREAT BRITAIN
ET IRELANDE DU NORD   AND NORTHERN IRELAND

ainsi que toutes parties de l'Empire   and all parts of the British Empire
britannique non membres séparés de la   which are not separate Members of
Société des Nations.   the League of Nations.

Oscar F. Dowson
Wm. H. Coles

CANADA   CANADA

C. H. L. Sharman

[Here follow the names of the states and of the plenipotentiaries of the other signatories of the Protocol of Signature.]

XVI

FINAL ACT [1]

EXTRACTS FROM CONFERENCE FOR THE SUPPRESSION OF THE ILLICIT TRAFFIC IN DANGEROUS DRUGS

(Geneva, June 26, 1936)

The Governments of Afghanistan, the United States of America, Austria, the United States of Brazil, the United Kingdom of Great Britain and Northern Ireland, Bulgaria, Canada, Chile, China, Cuba, Denmark, Egypt, Ecuador, Spain, France, Greece, Honduras, Hungary, India, Iraq, the Irish Free State, Japan, Liechtenstein, the United States of Mexico, Nicaragua, Norway, Panama, the Netherlands, Peru, Poland, Portugal, Roumania, Siam, Switzerland, Czechoslovakia, Turkey, the Union of Soviet Socialist Republics, Uruguay, the United States of Venezuela, and Yugoslavia,

Having accepted the invitation extended to them in execution of a resolution adopted by the Council of the League of Nations on January 20th, 1936, for the purpose of concluding a Convention for the Suppression of the Illicit Traffic in Dangerous Drugs,

Have appointed the following delegates:

AFGHANISTAN

Delegate:

His Excellency General MOHAMED OMER KHAN, Delegate to the Assembly of the League of Nations, Deputy Permanent Delegate to the League of Nations.

UNITED STATES OF AMERICA

Delegates:

Mr. Stuart J. FULLER, Assistant Chief of the Division of Far Eastern Affairs, Department of State, Representative of the United States of America on the Advisory Committee on Traffic in Opium and Other Dangerous Drugs.

Mr. Harry J. ANSLINGER, Commissioner of Narcotics of the Treasury Department.

Legal Adviser:

Mr. Frank X. WARD, Assistant Legal Adviser of the Department of State.

---

[1] L.N. Document C.286(*b*).M.174(*b*).1936.XI. in *Records of the Conference for the Suppression of the Illicit Traffic in Dangerous Drugs. Text of the Debates* (Geneva, 1936), p. 225.

AUSTRIA

Delegates:

His Excellency M. Emerich PFLÜGL, Permanent Representative to the League of Nations, Envoy Extraordinary and Minister Plenipotentiary.

Dr. Bruno SCHULTZ, former Vice-President of the Vienna Police, Representative of Austria on the Advisory Committee on Traffic in Opium and Other Dangerous Drugs.

[Here follow the names of the other delegates appointed by the participating states.]

Participating at the Conference as Observers:

FINLAND

M. Helge VON KNORRING, First Secretary of Legation.

LATVIA

M. Kārlis KALNIŇS, First Secretary of Legation.

Participating at the Conference in an Advisory Capacity and as Experts:

International Criminal Police Commission:

Mr. Norman KENDAL, C.B.E., Assistant Commissioner of the Metropolitan Police, London.

Dr. Bruno SCHULTZ, former Vice-President of the Vienna Police, Representative of Austria on the Advisory Committee on Traffic in Opium and Other Dangerous Drugs.

who accordingly assembled at Geneva.

The Council of the League of Nations appointed as President of the Conference:

Mr. Joseph LIMBURG, Member of the Council of States of the Netherlands.

The Conference has appointed as Vice-President:

M. DE REFFYE, Minister Plenipotentiary, "Sous-Directeur du contentieux et des chancelleries" at the Ministry of Foreign Affairs of the French Republic.

The functions of Secretary-General to the Conference were assumed by:

M. Eric Einar EKSTRAND, Director of the Opium Traffic and Social Questions Sections, representing the Secretary-General of the League of Nations.

In the course of a series of meetings between June 8th and June 26th, 1936, the instruments hereinafter enumerated were drawn up:

I. CONVENTION OF 1936 FOR THE SUPPRESSION OF THE ILLICIT TRAFFIC IN DANGEROUS DRUGS

II. PROTOCOL OF SIGNATURE OF THE CONVENTION

The Conference also adopted the following:

I. INTERPRETATIONS

1. It is understood that the provisions of the Convention, and in particular the provisions of Articles 2 and 5, do not apply to offences committed unintentionally.

2. Article 15 is to be interpreted in the sense that the Convention does not in particular affect the liberty of the High Contracting Parties to regulate the principles under which mitigating circumstances may be taken into account.

II. RECOMMENDATIONS

1. The Conference.

Recalling that the International Opium Conference of 1912, determined to bring about the gradual suppression of the abuse of opium, inserted in the International Opium Convention of 1912 the following Article 6: "The contracting Powers shall take measures for the gradual and effective suppression of the manufacture of, internal trade in and use of prepared opium, with due regard to the varying circumstances of each country concerned, unless regulations on the subject are already in existence";

Recalling that the Parties to the Geneva Opium Agreement of 1925, in the Preamble, declared that they were fully determined to bring about the gradual and effective suppression of the manufacture of, internal trade in and use of prepared opium, as provided for in Chapter II of the International Opium Convention of 1912, in their Far Eastern possessions and territories, including leased or protected territories, in which the use of prepared opium is temporarily authorised; and that they were desirous, on the grounds of humanity and for the purpose of promoting the social and moral welfare of their peoples, of taking all possible steps for achieving the suppression of the use of opium for smoking with the least possible delay;

Desiring to take the opportunity afforded by the present Conference of urging the countries concerned to continue their efforts in this matter:

Recommends that Governments which still permit use of opium for other than medical or scientific purposes should without undue delay take effective action with a view to the abolition of such use of opium.

2. The Conference recommends that countries which recognise the principle of extradition of their nationals should grant the extradition of such of their nationals as, being in their territory, are guilty of the commission abroad of the offences dealt with in Article 2, even if the extradition treaty applicable contains a reservation on the subject of the extradition of nationals.

3. The Conference recommends the High Contracting Parties to create, where necessary, a specialised police service for the purposes of the present Convention.

4. The Conference recommends that the Advisory Committee on Traffic in Opium and Other Dangerous Drugs should consider the question whether it is desirable that meetings of the representatives of the central offices of the High Contracting Parties should take place in order to ensure, improve and develop international co-operation as provided for in the present Convention, and, should occasion arise, to give an opinion to the Council of the League of Nations on the subject.

EN FOI DE QUOI les Délégués ont signé le présent Acte.

IN FAITH WHEREOF the Delegates have signed the present Act.

FAIT à Genève, le vingt-six juin mil neuf cent trente-six, en simple expédition, qui sera déposée dans les archives du Secrétariat de la Société des Nations; copie certifiée conforme en sera remise à tous les Etats représentés à la Conférence.

DONE at Geneva, the twenty-sixth day of June, one thousand nine hundred and thirty-six, in a single copy, which shall be deposited in the archives of the Secretariat of the League of Nations and of which authenticated copies shall be delivered to all States represented at the Conference.

Le Président de la Conférence: *The President of the Conference:*
LIMBURG

Le Vice-Président de la Conférence: *The Vice-President of the Conference:*
P. DE REFFYE

Le Secrétaire général de la Conférence: *The Secretary-General of the Conference:*
Eric Einar EKSTRAND

AUTRICHE AUSTRIA
E. PFLÜGL
Dr Bruno SCHULTZ

[Here follow the names of the states and of the plenipotentiaries of the other signatories of the Final Act.]

Commission internationale de Police Criminelle *International Criminal Police Commission*
Dr Bruno SCHULTZ

XVII

DRAFT PROTOCOLS OF SIGNATURE FOR EXPEDITING THE ENTRY INTO FORCE OF CONVENTIONS CONCLUDED UNDER THE AUSPICES OF THE LEAGUE OF NATIONS

(Annexed to the Assembly Resolution of October 3, 1930) [1]

ANNEX I

PROTOCOL OF SIGNATURE

In signing the Convention of this day's date relating to .... the under-signed plenipotentiaries, being duly authorized to this effect and in the name of their respective Governments, declare that they have agreed as follows:

I. That the Government of every Member of the League of Nations or non-Member State on whose behalf the said convention has been signed undertakes, not later than ..... (date), either to submit the said Convention for parliamentary approval, or to inform the Secretary-General of the League of Nations of its attitude with regard to the Convention.

II. If on ..... (date) the said Convention is not in force with regard to ..... Members of the League of Nations and non-Member States, the Secretary-General of the League shall bring the situation to the attention of the Council of the League of Nations, which may either convene a new conference of all the Members of the League and non-Member States on whose behalf the Convention has been signed or accessions thereto deposited, to consider the situation, or take such other measures as it considers necessary. The Government of every signatory or acceding state undertakes to be represented at any conference so convened. The Governments of Members of the League and non-Member States which have not signed the Convention or acceded thereto may also be invited to be represented at any conference so convened by the Council of the League.

Note. — The procedure provided for in this Annex is generally suitable for most general conventions. In cases in which it is applied, the final article of the convention should be drafted in the usual form and should not fix any named or final date for the entry into force of the convention, but should permit its entry into force on receipt of a relatively small number of ratifications or accessions.

---

[1] *Records of the Eleventh Ordinary Session of the Assembly, Plenary Meetings, Text of the Debates* (Geneva, 1930); L.N., *Official Journal*, Special Supplement No. 84, p. 216.

ANNEX II

FINAL ARTICLE OF THE CONVENTION

ARTICLE X

The present Convention shall enter into force on . . . . . (date), provided that, on this date, ratifications or accessions have been deposited with or notified to the Secretary-General of the League of Nations on behalf of . . . . .[2] Members of the League of Nations or non-Member States.

PROTOCOL OF SIGNATURE

In signing the Convention of today's date relating to . . . . . the undersigned plenipotentiaries, being duly authorized to this effect and in the name of their respective Governments, declare that they have agreed as follows:

If on . . . .[3] the said Convention has not come into force in accordance with the provisions of Article X, the Secretary-General of the League of Nations shall bring the situation to the attention of the Council of the League of Nations, which may either convene a new conference of all the Members of the League and non-Member States on whose behalf the Convention has been signed or accessions thereto deposited, to consider the situation, or take such other measures as it considers necessary. The Government of every signatory or acceding State undertakes to be represented at any conference so convened.

Note. — The procedure provided for in Annex II is suitable for certain types of convention whose practical utility depends on their immediate entry into force for a considerable number of States.

[2] The figure indicated here should be a relatively large one.
[3] Same date as that indicated in Article X.

XVIII

SELECT BIBLIOGRAPHY OF SECONDARY MATERIALS

I. GENERAL TREATISES ON INTERNATIONAL LAW AND DIPLOMATIC LAW

Académie Diplomatique Internationale. Dictionnaire diplomatique. Paris [1933]. 2 vols.

ANTOKOLETZ, DANIEL. Tratado de derecho internacional público en tiempo de paz, 2ª edición. Buenos Aires: La Facultad, 1928. 3 vols.

BUSTAMANTE Y SIRVÉN, ANTONIO SÁNCHEZ DE. Droit international public. Traduction par Paul Goulé. Paris: Recueil Sirey, 1934-1939. 5 vols.

FAUCHILLE, PAUL. Traité de droit international public. 8e édition, entièrement refondue. Paris: Rousseau et Cie, 1921-1926. 2 vols.

GENET, RAOUL. Traité de diplomatie et de droit diplomatique. Paris: A. Pedone, 1931-1932. 3 vols. (Publications de la Revue générale de droit international public, Nos. 3, 5, 6.)

HERSHEY, AMOS S. The Essentials of International Public Law and Organization. Revised edition. New York: The Macmillan Company, 1930. 784 pp.

MARTENS, BARON CHARLES DE. Le guide diplomatique; Précis des droits et des fonctions des agents diplomatiques et consulaires. 5e édition, refondue par M.F.H. Geffcken. Leipzig: F. A. Brockhaus, 1866. 2 vols.

MARTENS, FEDOR FEDOROVICH DE. Traité de droit international: traduit du russe par Alfred Léo. Paris: Chevalier-Maresq et Cie, 1883-87. 3 vols.

MÖLLER, AXEL. International Law in Peace and War. Translated by H. M. Pratt. London: Stevens and Sons, Limited, 1931-35. 2 vols.

OPPENHEIM, LASSA FRANCIS LAWRENCE. International Law; A Treatise. 6th edition, edited by H. Lauterpacht. London etc.: Longmans, Green and Co., 1940. 2 vols.

PLANAS SUÁREZ, SIMÓN. Tratado de derecho internacional público. Madrid: Hijos de Reus, 1916. 2 vols.

PRADIER-FODÉRÉ, PAUL. Cours de droit diplomatique; A l'usage des agents politiques du ministère des affaires étrangères des états européens et américains. 2e edition. Paris: A. Pedone, 1899. 2 vols.

SATOW, SIR ERNEST. A Guide to Diplomatic Practice. 2d and revised edition. London, etc.: Longmans, Green and Co., 1922. 2 vols.

————— ————— 3d edition, revised by H. Ritchie. London, etc.: Longmans, Green and Co., 1932. 519 pp.

SCHIFFER, WALTER, comp. Répertoire des questions de droit international général posées devant la Société des Nations, 1920-1940. Genève: Geneva Research Centre, 1942. Publié sous la direction de A. C. de Breycha-Vauthier. 390 pp. (Preliminaries and index in French and English.)

VIDAL Y SAURA, GINÉS. Tratado de derecho diplomático; Contribución al estudio sobre los principios y usos de la diplomacia moderna. Madrid: Editorial Reus (S.A.), 1925. 576 pp.

II. WORKS ON THE GENERAL SUBJECT OF INTERNATIONAL COOPERATION AND ORGANIZATION

BUELL, RAYMOND LESLIE. International Relations. Revised edition. New York: Henry Holt and Company [1932]. 838 pp.

CONWELL-EVANS, T. P. The League Council in Action; A Study of the Methods Employed by the Council of the League of Nations to Prevent War and to Settle International Disputes. London: Oxford University Press, Humphrey Milford, 1929. 291 pp.

DICKINSON, EDWIN DEWITT. The Equality of States in International Law. Cambridge: Harvard University Press; London: Humphrey Milford, Oxford University Press, 1920. 424 pp.

HICKS, FREDERICK CHARLES. The New World Order; International Organization, International Law, International Coöperation. Garden City, New York: Doubleday, Page & Company, 1920. 496 pp.

HUDSON, MANLEY O. Current International Co-operation. Calcutta: Calcutta University, 1927. 149 pp.

POTTER, PITMAN B. An Introduction to the Study of International Organization. 4th edition. New York, London: D. Appleton-Century Company, Incorporated, 1935. 645 pp.

———— ———— "The Classification of International Organizations," American Political Science Review, Vol. XXIX (1935), pp. 212-24, 403-17.

SAYRE, FRANCIS BOWES. Experiments in International Administration. New York and London: Harper & Brothers [1919]. 200 pp.

WALTERS, F. P. Administrative Problems of International Organization. London: Oxford University Press, 1941. 20 pp. (Barnett House Papers No. 24.)

WOOLF, LEONARD S. International Government; Two Reports. New York: Brentano's, 1916. 412 pp.

III. SPECIAL WORKS ON INTERNATIONAL CONFERENCES AND RELATED QUESTIONS

ARNOLD, RALPH, comp. Treaty-Making Procedure; A Comparative Study of the Methods Obtaining in Different States. London: H. Milford, Oxford University Press, 1933. 69 pp.

AVRAMOFF, DAVID. Le président du Conseil de la Société des Nations (Essai d'étude sur les pouvoirs du président du Conseil de la S.D.N. en comparaison avec les présidents d'autres organismes internationaux à tendances universelles). Bordeaux, Librairie Delmas, 1932. 164 pp.

BAKER, RAY STANNARD. Woodrow Wilson and World Settlement. Garden City, New York: Doubleday, Page & Company, 1922. 3 vols.

BITTNER, LUDWIG. Die Lehre von den völkerrechtlichen Vertragsurkunden. Stuttgart: Deutsche Verlags-Anstalt, 1924. 314 pp.

BURTON, MARGARET E. The Assembly of the League of Nations. Chicago: The University of Chicago Press, 1941. 441 pp.

CALDERWOOD, HAROLD B. "The General Committee and Other Auxiliary Committees of the League Assembly," American Journal of International Law, Vol. 38 (1944), pp. 74-94.

CAMBON, JULES M. Le diplomate. Paris: Hachette [1926]. 120 pp.

DORÉ, ROBERT. Essai d'une bibliographie des congrès internationaux. Paris: E. Champion, 1923. 56 pp.

DUNN, FREDERICK SHERWOOD. The Practice and Procedure of International Conferences. Baltimore: The Johns Hopkins Press; London: H. Milford, Oxford University Press, 1929. 299 pp.

FRANGULIS, ANTOINE F. Théorie et pratique des traités internationaux. Paris [1934]. 208 pp. Académie Diplomatique Internationale: Séances et travaux, 8e année, Nos. 2, 3 et 4.

GASELEE, STEPHEN. The Language of Diplomacy. Cambridge: Bowes & Bowes, 1939. 75 pp.

GIL BORGES, ESTEBAN. Notas sobre la estructura técnica de los tratados multilaterales interamericanos. Caracas: Tipografía Americana, 1936. 64 pp.

GRUBER, RICHARD GILÁDY. Internationale Staatenkongresse und Konferenzen; Ihre Vorbereitung und Organisation, eine völkerrechts-diplomatische Untersuchung auf Grund der Staatenpraxis vom Wiener Kongress 1814 bis zur Gegenwart. Berlin: Puttkammer & Mühlbrecht, 1919. 348 pp.

HANKEY, SIR MAURICE. Diplomacy by Conference. [London: Printed by W. H. Smith & Son, 1920]. 27 pp.

HILL, NORMAN L. The Public International Conference; Its Function, Organization and Procedure. Stanford University, California: Stanford University Press; London: H. Milford, Oxford University Press, 1929. 267 pp.

HUDSON, MANLEY O. "Languages Used in Treaties," American Journal of International Law, Vol. 26 (1932), pp. 368–72.

————— "Procedure of International Conferences and Procedure for the Conclusion and Drafting of Treaties," American Journal of International Law, Vol. 20 (1926), pp. 747–50.

HUNT, EDWARD EYRE. Conferences, Committees, Conventions; And How to Run Them. New York and London: Harper & Brothers, 1925. 218 pp.

JENKS, C. WILFRED. "The Need for an International Legislative Drafting Bureau," American Journal of International Law, Vol. 39 (1945), pp. 163–79.

MARSTON, F. The Peace Conference of 1919; Organization and Procedure. London, etc.: Oxford University Press, 1944. 276 pp.

McNAIR, ARNOLD DUNCAN. The Law of Treaties; British Practice and Opinions. New York: Columbia University Press; Oxford: At The Clarendon Press, 1938. 578 pp.

MILIĆ, MILENKO. Les attributions communes et les rapports du Conseil et de l'Assemblée; Une étude de la Société des Nations. Paris: A. Pedone [1929]. 316 pp.

MOULTON, MILDRED. A Structural View of the Conference as an Organ of International Cooperation (An Examination Emphasizing Post-War Practice as Shown in the Organization of Some Typical Conferences). [Highland Park, New Jersey, 1930.] 118 pp.

NICOLSON, HAROLD. Peacemaking, 1919; Being Reminiscences of the Paris Peace Conference. Boston and New York: Houghton, Mifflin Co., 1933. 378 pp.

O'DAVOREN, WILLIAM. Post-War Reconstruction Conferences. Geneva: Alexandre Julien, 1942. 166 pp.

PRÉVOST, MARCEL HENRI. Les commissions de l'Assemblée de la Société des Nations; Commentaire du règlement intérieur, d'après la jurisprudence de l'Assemblée. Paris: A. Pedone, 1936. 278 pp.

RICHES, CROMWELL ADAMS. Majority Rule in International Organization; A Study of the Trend from Unanimity to Majority Decision. Baltimore: The Johns Hopkins Press, 1940. 322 pp.

—— The Unanimity Rule and the League of Nations. Baltimore: The Johns Hopkins Press, 1933. 224 pp.

ROUMIGUIÈRE, HENRIETTE. Le français dans les relations diplomatiques. Berkeley, California: University of California Press, 1926. 340 pp.

SALTER, SIR J. ARTHUR. Allied Shipping Control; An Experiment in International Administration. Oxford: At the Clarendon Press, 1921. 372 pp.

SATOW, SIR ERNEST. International Congresses. London: Published by H. M. Stationery Office, 1920. 168 pp.

SCOTT, JAMES BROWN. Le français, langue diplomatique moderne; Etude critique de conciliation internationale. Paris: A. Pedone, 1924. 330 pp.

SHENTON, HERBERT NEWHARD. Cosmopolitan Conversation; The Language Problems of International Conferences. New York: Columbia University Press, 1933. 803 pp.

SIBERT, MARCEL. "Quelques aspects de l'organisation et de la technique des conférences internationales," in Académie de Droit International, Recueil des Cours, Vol. 48 (1943.II), pp. 391-454.

TARDIEU, ANDRÉ. La paix. Paris: Payot et Cie, 1921. 520 pp.

TOBIN, HAROLD J. The Termination of Multipartite Treaties. New York: Columbia University Press, 1933. 321 pp. (Columbia University Studies in History, Economics and Public Law, No. 388.)

WILCOX, FRANCIS O. The Ratification of International Conventions; A Study of the Relationship of the Ratification Process to the Development of International Legislation. London: George Allen & Unwin, Ltd. [1935]. 349 pp.

INDEX

AUKS

Rooks o LS